The Satisfied Introvert

How I Broke Free from the False Self I Created
and Started Living Authentically
(You Can Too)

Benjamin Plumb

RIVER GROVE
BOOKS

Published by River Grove Books
Austin, TX
www.rivergrovebooks.com

Distributed by River Grove Books

Design and composition by Greenleaf Book Group and Chase Quarterman
Cover design by Greenleaf Book Group and Chase Quarterman

Publisher's Cataloging-in-Publication data is available.

Print ISBN: 978-1-966629-50-4

eBook ISBN: 978-1-966629-51-1

Second Edition

What Readers Love About
The Satisfied Introvert

BOOK AWARDS

Winner, 2025 Nonfiction Book Award Silver Medal

BOOK AWARDS (FIRST EDITION)

Winner, 2025 Nonfiction Book Award Silver Medal

First Place, 2022 Chanticleer International Book Awards,
Instructional & Insightful Non-Fiction

Winner, 2022 Global Book Awards Silver Medal,
Motivational Self-Help

Winner, 2022 Reader's Favorite Silver Medal,
Non-Fiction—Inspirational

SELECTED EDITORIAL REVIEWS
(FIRST EDITION)

" . . . an undeniably remarkable life . . ."
—Kirkus Reviews

" . . . revealing, and refreshing read . . . RECOMMENDED"
—US Review of Books

" . . . a page-turner which one moment would have me

smiling and the next brushing away a tear . . ."

"A liberating book . . . a useful tool for both introverts and extroverts alike."

" . . . an immense resource for helping professionals, teachers, and parents . . ."

" . . . a revelation . . . wildly honest . . . humorous, heartfelt, and deeply human . . ."

"Great for fans of: Holley Gerth's *The Powerful Purpose of Introverts*, and Jenn Granneman's *The Secret Lives of Introverts*."

" . . . read like a novel at times . . ."

"People who identify as introverts will find this an excellent read . . . a clear insight to a personality trait that is often misunderstood and little discussed."

SELECTED CUSTOMER REVIEWS
5 Star Ratings from
Amazon Verified Purchasers (First Edition)

" . . . a heartfelt and genuine memoir that is impossible to put down . . ."

—Alex

" . . . this book speaks to me from the first page."

—Jessica Evans

" . . . profound and beautifully written book
full of feeling and full of insights."

—Marina Lujan

" . . . an exciting read . . . Anyone who is an
introvert will gain insight into themselves . . ."

—Coffee Drinker in Florida

"Inspirational . . . extremely captivating . . ."

—Tatiana

" . . . a wildly exciting life . . . stunningly written and deeply engaging . . ."

—Sai Chauhan

"A must read!! . . . I highly recommend this book to introverts . . ."

—Ray Rowan

"I could not put this down! . . . reads fluidly with amazing stories."

—J. Cosentino

4 Star Ratings from Goodreads and Amazon Verified Purchasers (First Edition)

For my wife, Sandy

Contents

Introduction My Quiet Beginnings.............................. 1

Your Own Recipe: Its Identity, Origins, Structure, and Costs........ 13

PART 1—Six Early Costs of My Recipe

   1. Submission: Anabela......................... 31

   2. Inauthenticity: Two Girls in Rio......................... 45

   3. Recklessness: Blood on Ice............................ 59

   4. Confusion: Tropical Legacies 71

   5. Overconfidence: A Bipolar Connection 85

   6. Self-Deception: The Love of a Fellow Introvert 99

PART 2—Four Foundational Tools for Detaching

   7. Observing the Mind: Evasion and Escape 113

   8. Unified Awareness: Welcome to Vietnam, GI 131

   9. Emotional Context: Pleiku............................ 145

  10. The Little Voice: The Snake Pit........................ 163

PART 3—Three Deeper Costs of the Recipe

  11. Insensitivity: A Testicular Engineer 179

  12. Obsession: Chaos in Chile............................ 199

  13. Blindness: The Noriega Incident 215

PART 4—Four Breakthrough Tools for Detaching

14. Living Life Forward: Upside Down in Miami 235

15. Intention: On the Brink 249

16. Accepting Acute Loss: Good-Bye, My Sweet Children 263

17. Nonresistance: The Girl from Saga Bay 275

PART 5—Four Transformational Tools for Detaching

18. Completion and Possibility: The End of the Line......... 295

19. The Peak Recipe: The King of All Processes.............. 303

20. Choosing a Relationship: The Recipe Strikes Back 315

21. You Have No Defect to Fix: Baronial Splendor........... 323

Conclusion
The Satisfied Introvert.. 333

To the Reader 339

Appendix
The Road to Freedom: A Guide to the Twelve Tools of Detachment .. 341

Acknowledgments 347

About the Author 349

"Once you have mastered a technique, you hardly need to look at a recipe again and can take off on your own."

JULIA CHILD

Introduction

My Quiet Beginnings

When I was four years old, I ran away from home. I had to get away from my mother, who I knew loved me dearly but was so vivacious and talkative that I felt overwhelmed by the unbearable noise of being around her.

My destination was the house next door, where an elderly couple who always doted on me lived. Not only was their house much quieter than ours, but also they had a plywood scale model of a building complex under their bed. It was beautifully crafted, although unpainted, and I never tired of them bringing it out for me to see. The man was an architect and for years that was what I wanted to be too.

I had some serious parent exchanging to do, so I planned well for the journey. I found a large brown bag from Von's grocery store and threw in all the essentials: a pair of underwear, a T-shirt, two bright copper pennies that I had been saving for an emergency such as this, a stuffed dog named Woofie, and some canned goods (although I could not read the labels and had no clue how to get them open—that was what new parents were for).

Thus prepared, I left the house. Dad was out and Mom was cleaning, so my daring escape was fairly easy. The bag, however, was too heavy to carry, so I dragged it across the rough pavement of the driveway. By the time I got to the curb, a hole had appeared; halfway to the neighbors' house, the bottom fell out and everything spilled into the street. Devastated that I was never going to make it, I sat down on the curb to figure out what to do. I can still see the sun glinting off the shiny pennies, their image becoming blurred and then washed away by the tears in my eyes.

I sat there and cried, feeling discouraged—by running away I had distanced myself from my mother's love, and now felt unappreciated by both sets of parents. I was sliding deeply into the despair of having no one to love me when I felt my mother's arms picking me up and holding me to her breast, soothing me and telling me she loved me more than anything in the world. Ever alert, she had noticed my absence within sixty seconds and, with her warmth and sweet words, made all the hurt and fear go away.

She carried me back into the house and sat with me for the longest time, stroking my back and holding my head against her chest, making me feel like the most special and wanted little boy who ever lived. Dad soon came home carrying my precious belongings from the street and joined us where we sat. He put his arms around me and said beautiful things too.

Never again did I entertain the thought of leaving them for a quiet space and pieces of plywood.

Even today, I look back on that moment as the time when I learned what love was, and commitment, and the willingness to drop everything to make a difference in the life of a child.

~

During my escape, I discovered that I am an introvert. I did not know the word then, but I did know that I did not like being around other people all that much. The noise was too emotionally stimulating, filling me with painful anxiety. I much preferred to live inside my head, looking at books and thinking.

As I grew older, this personality trait became a problem as I came to realize society had designed the world for extroverts. I noticed that in school, teachers emphasized quick participation over slow reflection. Outside of class, small talk was a social obligation, and almost everyone celebrated loud, charismatic people. Overall, I sensed that the ideal personality was seen as outgoing. Writer Susan Cain points out in her best-selling book *Quiet: The Power of Introverts in a World That Can't Stop Talking*, "Many of the most important institutions of contemporary life are designed for those who enjoy group projects and high levels of stimulation."[1] In contrast, most introverts prefer *less* external stimulation and more silence.

> **As I grew older, this personality trait became a problem as I came to realize society had designed the world for extroverts.**

In reading her book, I saw other traits that described me with uncanny accuracy:

- Listening more than talking, and thinking before speaking

- Expressing myself better in writing than in discussions

- Detesting conflict

- Hating small talk, preferring deep conversations

- Concentrating on one thing at a time, working slowly, and being able to focus deeply on the task at hand[2]

Introvert children are encouraged from a young age to be more extroverted. Relatives admonish shyness. "Ben, why don't you go play with the kids down the street?" Strangers bend over backward to coax a smile or a giggle. "You're so serious, Ben, can you give me a smile?" Educators urge

1   Susan Cain, *Quiet: The Power of Introverts in a World That Can't Stop Talking* (Random House, 2013), 6.

2   Cain, *Quiet*, 11.

quiet children to be more expressive. "Speak up, Ben, so the whole class can hear you."

My first recollection of developing and implementing a plan to overcome what I perceived to be a weakness and appear more extroverted happened one Friday afternoon in 1953 when I was ten. My teacher told our Los Angeles public school class that each of us would have to pick a current event and report on it—without notes, standing in front of the room—that coming Monday.

I was terrified. But that afternoon, I calmed down. I realized that to get through this I needed to have some kind of a plan. I looked in the newspaper and found an article about our new president that interested me. I cut it out along with Eisenhower's picture and underlined the main points. I then walked into our garage and—amid the scent of engine oil—rehearsed the points out loud twenty-five times. Over the three chilly fall evenings that remained before Monday, I memorized my script.

The results astounded me. On Monday, I stood at the front of my classroom, panning my vision from the floor to the walls to the ceiling—anywhere but at the faces of my audience. The knowledge that I had memorized everything I needed to say diluted my fear, and helped me to engage the class. By the end of my presentation, I'd put a beaming smile on my teacher's face. This strategy—defining a sequence of steps (finding an article, memorizing the material in it ahead of my performance, and not looking into the eyes of anyone in the audience) shifted my focus from the external world, where I was nervous, to the internal one, where I was confident.

In junior high, a similar process helped me to do particularly well in Spanish. Grammar and pronunciation had rules, and sometimes even the exceptions had rules. For two years, I listed and rehearsed the rules, and soon I found myself speaking the language. My teachers—Ms. Romero and Mr. Mendoza—shook their heads at what this gringo kid was able to do.

Skinny and bespectacled, I became a process fanatic. In high school, I created one for every class—to learn the valences of chemical atoms, reconstruct the history of the United States, and solve quadratic equations. I broke each task down, put it back together as a series of steps, and then completed them in order.

This allowed me to interact with the world and get predictable outcomes without having to focus too much on people. I only had to complete the steps I had identified, and results would appear at the end. People came to me with praise, which was not as emotionally disruptive as having to interact with them to get outcomes.

All this compensated nicely for something that, at age four, I had decided was *wrong* with me—that as an introvert I did not have what it took to "win" in life on my own. Without a process in hand, I had had to improvise, failing often, and that was scary. But with a procedure of some kind, I could get results, and that made me feel safe.

The more processes I created, the more my grades soared. I became co-valedictorian of my high school class, went on to graduate magna cum laude from Stanford, and was accepted to the Harvard Business School.

I concluded that using processes was a terrific way for me to "win." Never mind that I had almost no friends, was socially inept, and got nowhere with girls. I had my lists of steps and believed those were all I needed to navigate the minefields of a world that constantly pushed me to be more extroverted. I was convinced that my lists would bring me security and ultimate success in life.

~

My theory is that as a quiet child you, too, decided early on to cover up what you believed was wrong with you—that you were not outgoing enough to succeed in an extroverted world.

To survive its intrusive noise and to ensure you did not experience it again, you likely created a "winning recipe" or mask of some kind, as I did, that allowed you to feel secure by projecting more sociability than you really felt. It allowed you to act in a more acceptable way than if you allowed your authentic self to come out.

My theory is that as a quiet child you, too, decided early on to cover up what you believed was wrong with you—that you were not outgoing enough to succeed in an extroverted world.

Throughout this book, I'll use the term "recipe" to describe the survival strategy I built as an introvert to survive in an extroverted world. What I built didn't present the real me, but instead a façade that allowed me to navigate relationships and situations while protecting myself.

A winning recipe is not a separate personality, but a socially adapted version of your true self, consciously or habitually shaped to meet external expectations or handle specific situations. Unlike multiple personalities, which involve distinct identities, a recipe exists within a single, unified self and does not involve a loss of memory, awareness, or control.

Thousands of winning recipes exist. We embrace things like be diplomatic, be thorough, be likable, be relentless, be dependable. The list is as extensive and varied as the entire introvert population. That Friday afternoon in 1953 as I faced needing to report on a news story in front of a live audience, I discovered my own winning recipe: be methodical.

I believe that all people, not just introverts, have created a recipe of some sort—being formal, being cute, being helpful, being precise, or any of the thousands of possible recipes that introverts tend to create. Extroverts tend to use theirs to compensate for *any* defect detected in childhood that they believed would prevent them from "winning" in life. Introverts, on the other hand, tend to compensate for something much narrower: simply not being outgoing enough to succeed in the world.

An introvert's recipe is ultimately about safety. It parades as a safe way for you to be more successful in the world. That is a large part of the hold it has over you. In situations where the recipe is inappropriate, or otherwise does not work, you will likely feel defenseless. As you will see in the story, my recipe led me into failed relationships, the wrong career, and limited self-awareness. It could not cope with solitude, fear, danger, or vulnerability. Yet it always insisted that I follow its advice. When you are in that state, despite how often the recipe has failed you in the past, it will still make a loud claim to be your safest strategy for success. In the pages of this book, you'll see how this has played out many times throughout my life.

An introvert's recipe is ultimately about safety. It parades as a safe way for you to be more successful in the world.

A recipe may work for a while when used in a narrow domain, as mine did in school. But when used as a general guide to living, a recipe eventually causes self-harm. It creates distant relationships, generates drama from unintended social missteps, and prevents you from feeling fulfilled. It is an attempt to cover up who you really are, so it ultimately does not make you feel any safer. Because of this, *the recipe itself is a major barrier to attaining a feeling of safety in your life.*

And the whole reason you sought a recipe in the first place was so you *would* feel safe.

If you are a dissatisfied introvert, your recipe may be the main reason why. In order to recognize this, it helps to expose a contradiction:

- **You built the recipe** to help you create a safe path through a scary, extroverted world.

- **Yet, the recipe is a tool for hiding your introversion** so you can appear to be something you are not.

- **As a result**, engaging in the recipe is unnatural, uncomfortable, and locks in the very anxiety you have designed it to overcome, leaving you feeling dissatisfied. *To become a satisfied introvert, you must first feel secure as an introvert.*

~

The purpose of this book is to help you find safety as an introvert in an extroverted world and gain more satisfaction in life. The best way to do that is to detach from your recipe as much as possible.

The recipe you've created for yourself is a coping mechanism that works in some—although most likely not even in the majority of situations. But you can't stay dependent on it. To feel truly safe, you must move beyond the recipe you created and take off on your own.

In the following pages, I will share my own life story and how I tried to rely on my recipe to help me become a satisfied introvert, and failed. By accompanying me on this journey, you will see how engaging in the false security of a winning recipe distorted my life. It can twist yours, too—especially if you apply it too closely for too long. But as you'll see from the story, it is never too late to put yourself back on track by detaching from it.

That is a challenge, because every recipe has three striking features:

- **Your recipe is static.** It never changes, always operating with whatever key element you designed into it as a child.

- **Your recipe is relentless.** It brings early successes, becomes entrenched, and despite repeated failures later in life, it keeps insisting that it is your best bet for dealing with any situation.

- **Your recipe is indelible.** It is so deeply rooted that you can never fully get rid of it. That does not automatically make you its victim; you always have the choice not to listen to it. But the overwhelming temptation is to do as I did: listen so closely that you end up hurting yourself.

Fortunately, my story shows that the recipe is also **escapable**. Escape starts with exposure, since most introverts are asleep to the nature and toxicity of their recipes. For coaching on how to identify your own recipe, please see the next chapter.

Once your recipe is out in the open, you will become more aware of the kinds of safety-related problems that it fails to solve. In this story, I illustrate four categories of events—solitude, fear, danger, and vulnerability—in which the recipe consistently kept safety out of my reach.

Seeing my recipe in action may help you to avoid blindly applying your own. In the end, your recipe will still be there. But the more you recognize it and detach from it, the more you will be able to render it harmless.

~

My working definition of an introvert is someone who prefers settings that are calm and have minimal external stimulation.

An introvert is someone who prefers settings that are calm and have minimal external stimulation.

This preference is probably caused by a genetic disposition to be highly sensitive to dopamine—a neurotransmitter in the brain. We introverts get satisfaction from very small amounts of it. In large groups and other loud situations, our brains generate greater amounts of it than we can handle, and we feel overwhelmed. We then withdraw into ourselves, seeking quiet.

Extroverts, in contrast, prefer just the opposite: stimulating environments that usually involve being physically present with lots of other people. This appears to result from a genetic inclination to be relatively insensitive to dopamine. To feel satisfied, extroverts need a lot of it. And to produce it, they tend to seek the company of others in loud environments.

It is widely believed that about 40 percent of the population have introvert tendencies. If a group that large exists, it stands to reason that introversion must have had some kind of an evolutionary advantage. In fact, we can point to many different benefits that quiet people likely brought to early human societies:

- By avoiding social gatherings, introverts may have **conserved mental and physical energy**, a critical skill during times of food scarcity. By avoiding high-risk hunts, introverts may have **steered clear of situations leading to injury or death**.

- Introverts may have been adept at **noticing subtle signs** such as brewing conflict in the group or the approach of predators. Introverts tend to avoid confrontation, which could have **prevented dangerous disputes** within early human groups.

- Further, in spending time alone, introverts likely could have produced **effective strategic thinking**, long-term planning, or problem-solving. Overall, introverts might have been the steady, thoughtful members who **shared wisdom, caution, and long-term perspectives** to guide the clan.

Thus, far from being a "defect," introversion likely has long been a major source of positive contributions to human societies.

Because both introversion and extroversion occur along a spectrum, there is no clear point at which one tendency switches to the other. And since both tendencies are genetic, it does not matter whether your parents are introverts or extroverts—if you are an introvert, that personality trait is hard-wired into you. The whole purpose of a winning recipe for an introvert is to make you seem to be more outgoing. But eventually, it bumps up against your genetics, so it cannot deliver sustained results over a lifetime.

Introversion is a significant piece of several theories of personality that you may have heard of:

- **Enneagram.** Three of the nine Enneagram types (4, 5, 6) are most likely to be introverts, while two others have partial introvert tendencies (1, 9).

- **Myers-Briggs Type Indicator (MBTI).** Eight of the sixteen personality types involve introversion in some way.

- **Highly Sensitive Persons (HSPs).** About 70 percent of HSPs are thought to be introverts.

The prevalence of introversion in these prominent theories of personality confirms once again that there are many introverts out there. It also indicates that introvert tendencies can have many forms, ranging from the expressive, creative Enneagram type 4—often called the Romantic—to the logical, knowledge-hungry INTPs and the sociable, dutiful ISFJs of the Myers-Briggs. As you will soon discover, the many manifestations of introversion means that there are myriad recipes that introverts concoct to exaggerate their outgoingness or mask their shyness.

~

When I first succeeded with my recipe at age ten, I chose to become dependent and even fixated on it. This brought triumphs that helped me avoid some of the pain of being an introvert, so I used the recipe to overcome every major challenge I faced in my life—first in academics, then in love and war, and finally in business.

The cost of doing so was high. The recipe did not make me feel protected when I faced almost every one of the events I describe in this book. In fact, it often made things worse. My obsession with it impaired what had been a promising life until it was almost too late to turn things around. Only by accident did I discover the tools that finally defused the recipe and allowed me to feel secure in my authentic, introvert self.

My story spans sixty years, takes place in more than a dozen locations across Europe, Asia, Latin America, and the United States, and plays out in the extrovert-dominated, high-performance environments of Stanford University, the Harvard Business School, the US Army, and the competitive world of international business.

This book chronicles one particular winning recipe: being methodical. But it is a case study in what can happen when *any* introvert's recipe is carried too far. And it shows the extent to which the hunger for the safety promised by a recipe can warp a life. Only after I distanced myself from the passion to live by it, did I find the security, satisfaction, and peace I always wanted.

This book chronicles one particular winning recipe: being methodical. But it is a case study in what can happen when any introvert's recipe is carried too far.

To help you apply the many lessons I have learned, this work is part memoir and part self-help book. I end the story in each chapter with four sections: What I Could Have Done Differently, Key Takeaways, Reflective Questions, and Practical Exercises. As you work through these elements, the book will help you to mitigate nine costs of the recipe (Chapters 1–6 and 11–13), and detach from it using twelve tools (Chapters 7–10 and 14–21).

For introverts and those who love them, this story is both a warning and a ray of hope.

Your Own Recipe: Its Identity, Origins, Structure, and Costs

IDENTIFYING YOUR RECIPE

In reading about my own quiet beginnings in the Introduction, you may have already identified your winning recipe. If not, here are some questions to ask yourself:

- What way of being do you often rely on **to gain success in life?**

- What way of being do you **tell other people to use to be successful in life?**

- If you asked **your boss, what would they say you are really good at?**

- If you asked your **spouse, coworkers, or friends, what would they say?**

- If you have **a resume, what recipe stands out on it?**

- Failing all that, **look at the key wins in your past**—what way of being did you use to achieve them?

If you are still having trouble, I present some lists of examples in the following pages so you can see if one or something close to one of them resonates. The lists are by no means comprehensive—there are thousands of ways to compensate for being an introvert.

To simplify the process, it helps to start with identifying which of four different widely recognized behavioral styles you tend to use, and then check the list of winning recipes that often are associated with that style.[3]

- **Dominant:** You focus on overcoming challenges and exerting control. You are decisive, determined, and results-oriented, but at times can also be insensitive, impatient, or autocratic.

- **Influential:** You seek to influence or persuade others. You are enthusiastic, innovative and stimulating, and you tend to seek inspiration. However, sometimes you can be undisciplined, egotistical, and poor at planning or follow-up.

- **Steady:** You prioritize consistency, reliability and cooperation, and you tend to seek intimacy. You are relationship-oriented, conscientious, and friendly, but can also be too tolerant, unassertive, or driven to please.

- **Conscientious:** You strive for accuracy, quality, and structure, tending to seek certainty. You are analytical, thorough, and organized, but sometimes can be too detailed, aloof, indecisive, or risk-averse. This is the behavioral style under which my own recipe falls, "being methodical."

---

3   This approach is based on the widely accepted DISC model—dominance, influence, steadiness, and conscientiousness (DISC). It began with the exploration of emotions and behavior in Dr. William Marston's *Emotions of Normal People* (Kegan Paul, Trench, Trübner, and Co., 1928). Others, like industrial psychologist Walter Clarke, popularized DISC as a way to categorize the various behavioral styles of individuals. Over time, DISC evolved into a widely used tool for assessing personality and behavior in organizations, education, and personal development. Today, DISC is often used in team building, leadership development, and communications training. https://www.discprofile.com/what-is-disc#history.

Please choose the style that most closely reflects your general behavior, and check the winning recipes under it to see if any specific one seems right for you. Note that all behavioral styles are valuable—there are no "right" and "wrong" ones.

Winning Recipes Often Associated with Dominant and Influential Behavioral Styles

DOMINANT Winning Recipes	INFLUENTIAL Winning Recipes
Being accountable	Being casual
Being aggressive	Being charming
Being cagey	Being childish
Being committed	Being clever
Being competitive	Being colorful
Being controlling	Being cosmopolitan
Being dominant	Being curious
Being extreme	Being cute
Being formal	Being effective
Being honest	Being energetic
Being independent	Being fearless
Being open	Being flagrant
Being persevering	Being flighty
Being powerful	Being flippant
Being relatable	Being focused

continued

DOMINANT Winning Recipes	INFLUENTIAL Winning Recipes
Being righteous	Being funny
Being self-sufficient	Being generous
Being significant	Being good
Being strong	Being gregarious
Being unflappable	Being inspirational
Being unforgiving	Being intense
Being withdrawn	Being irreverent
Being results-oriented	Being laid-back
	Being loud
	Being neat
	Being outgoing
	Being outrageous
	Being pretty
	Being proud
	Being quick
	Being relentless
	Being risky
	Being sexy
	Being silly
	Being superficial

Winning Recipes Often Associated with
Steady or Conscientious Behavioral Styles

STEADY Winning Recipes	CONSCIENTIOUS Winning Recipes
Being approachable	Being agitated
Being calm	Being aloof
Being caring	Being analytical
Being coachable	Being balanced
Being comforting	Being bland
Being concerned	Being careful
Being different	Being certain
Being diplomatic	Being clueless
Being emotional	Being depressed
Being fatherly	Being detail-oriented
Being forgiving	Being distant
Being grounded	Being doubtful
Being happy	Being fearful
Being helpful	Being frugal
Being humble	Being intelligent
Being intimate	Being knowledgeable
Being kind	Being methodical
Being mature	Being mysterious

continued

STEADY Winning Recipes	CONSCIENTIOUS Winning Recipes
Being moderate	Being non-committal
Being motherly	Being organized
Being nice	Being particular
Being philosophical	Being precise
Being polite	Being process-driven
Being quiet	Being prudent
Being reliable	Being serious
Being responsible	Being slow
Being stoic	Being smart
Being supportive	Being stupid
Being thoughtful	Being subdued
Being truthful	Being thorough
Being understanding	Being thrifty
Being welcoming	

If you're still having trouble determining which style you fall under, try one of these options:

- **Check all the lists.** Any recipe can work with any behavioral style, so if you don't see a recipe that describes you under the list you selected, take a look at all the lists.

- **Find something close and modify it.** There are well over one hundred recipes on the four lists. Find the one that's the closest, and change it to reflect your recipe more accurately.

- **Pick something and go with it for now.** As you work through the book, you may get more clarity and find that the recipe snaps into place. Feel free to change your choice anytime you become more sure of an accurate description.

FIND THE ORIGINATING INCIDENT

Knowing what triggered your winning recipe is not essential for detaching from it. However, finding the originating incident will help you confirm that you in fact do have a recipe, which *is* essential if you are ever going to escape from it.

My guess is that as a child, you likely endured an event that was too emotionally stimulating to the point where you realized three things, probably unconsciously:

1. The world is full of painful noise and stimulation.

2. I crave quiet.

3. Therefore I must *do* or *be* something that will lessen the noise.

These events could be anything from relatives or playmates talking too loudly, the TV or radio volume turned way up, the whine of a vacuum cleaner or other appliance in the home, or any other source of noise that you could not control and felt desperate to get away from.

When I was four, as described in the Introduction, all I was capable of was to *do* a runaway attempt to get away from my noisy home. At age ten, I was old enough to craft a more sophisticated response—to strive to *be* some way other than as an introvert (to be methodical by devising a step-by-step process as a coping mechanism).

But even at four, the outlines of my winning recipe were present. I had carefully prepared to run away, going through a step-by-step process to pack a grocery bag from Von's Market. Later that would blossom into my full winning recipe—to create sequential processes in every area of life to ensure favorable results without having to deal too much with people.

You may already remember the first traumatic event that led you to realize the three previous insights. But if not, make a short list of the two or three earliest memories that you have of times when you felt overstimulated.

- Who was there?

- What happened?

- As a result, what action did you take? Did you *do* something, or did you decide to *be* a certain way to deal with the world from then on?

- Then do the same for the next one or two memories.

If nothing comes up, try a meditation approach. Go into a quiet room with your phone, turn off incoming calls, and set it to record audio. Sit with your feet flat on the floor, your hands on your thighs, and your eyes closed. Breathe in deeply. Recall one of your earliest memories of suffering from too much emotional stimulation. With your eyes still closed, describe out loud who was there, what happened, and what action you took. Then repeat for one or two more memories.

With that done, review your responses. If you were old enough to go beyond doing and to start *being* some way that allowed you to deal with a noisy world, the incident is likely the origin of your winning recipe. If, like me, your earliest incident produced just *doing* something, see if in that doing you were exhibiting the skeleton of the recipe you identified earlier. Maybe you hit somebody. Maybe you cried and screamed. Maybe you wet your pants. Whatever it was, it was probably the crude beginnings of your winning recipe.

UNPACKING THE RECIPE'S STRUCTURE

Every recipe has three moving parts. Regardless of whether it calls you to be organized, energetic, clever, responsible, or any other of the thousands of possible ways of being human, it gives you a payoff when you translate it into action:

Being → Doing → Having (the Payoff)

Here is my recipe:

Being: Methodical

→ Doing: Breaking things down into steps

→ Having: Getting results without needing to deal with people

It is critical for you to expose the moving pieces of your winning recipe so you can gain access to its controls.

- To detach from the recipe, you later will need to alter the **Having** piece (the Payoff) so it no longer compensates for your being an introvert, but rather becomes pure enjoyment for something that you do for itself.

- But right now the things you are **Doing** drive the Payoff, so you first have to address those actions.

- Unfortunately, you cannot do so yet—because how you are **Being** drives the engine of the recipe, and that way of Being is inauthentic; it is not who you are as an introvert. You can only detach from the recipe by targeting Being in such a way that it becomes an authentic expression of yourself as an introvert. When you do, it will change what you are Doing, and thereby alter the nature of the Payoff. In my case, I changed "Being methodical" to "Being an authentic introvert." This allowed me to openly Do the things that "out" introverts do (avoid phone calls, avoid parties, make no excuses for having very few friends, tell others that I'm an introvert when they ask me to make a video). I can then **Have** the things that authentic introverts have—a very quiet, subdued life free of emotional stimulation and noise.

It is fairly easy to uncover the inner controls of your winning recipe. All you have to do is look at its three elements and ask what Being, Doing, and the Payoff look like in your situation.

For example, let's say the winning recipe is to be thoughtful. That is the **Being** piece. In being that way, what are you **Doing** to compensate for your introversion?

- Perhaps you look at every project at work or school, and every request from your partner or family, to determine exactly what they want, and then try to provide it.

- Or maybe you put yourself in others' shoes to see how you can best support them.

- Whatever you do, you do things to be thoughtful. To a certain extent that makes you feel good—my processes usually did that for me. But the fundamental reason you do them is to cut down the noise level in your life. Over decades that becomes quite unsatisfying since you are not being thoughtful because it's satisfying to be thoughtful, but as a way to compensate for being an introvert.

Your **Having** is likely to be similar to mine—to find a Payoff that distances you from people so that you can have more quiet in your life.

Before moving on to the next section, please name the content of each of the three pieces of your recipe, and write them down. As examples I indicate my own choices in brackets:

Being: My default, recipe-driven trait is being _____
_____ [methodical].

Doing: In being _____ [methodical], I
engage in doing _____ [step-by-step processes
for almost everything].

Having: In doing _____ [step-by-step
processes for almost everything], I have _____
[results without needing to deal with people very much].

ASSESSING THE COSTS OF THE RECIPE

Recall the three biggest wins you have ever had in using your recipe—one
each in **school**, in **relationships**, or in your **career**.

In each case, ask yourself how it was **ultimately unsatisfying**, and
what **unintended consequences** flowed from that. As you'll see in
more detail in the stories in the following chapters, the following are just a
fraction of the many costs my recipe levied on me over the years:

- **Win in school:** I used my recipe to get admitted to the Harvard
  Business School, which seemed to offer a clear stepwise path to
  financial success. The win was ultimately unsatisfying because I am
  not temperamentally suited to be an entrepreneur or a top executive. The unintended consequences were years of unhappiness, job
  firings, and a bankruptcy.

- **Win in a relationship:** I used my recipe to convince myself that
  my first wife, a fellow introvert, was right for me. The relationship
  ended up not being satisfying because we were incompatible in ways
  the recipe had hidden from me. The unintended consequence was a
  divorce after being married for twelve years and having two children.

- **Win in my career:** I used my recipe to land a leadership role
  at a major health insurance company in my sixties. It ultimately
  was not satisfying because the recipe had prevented me from seeing

that the job would require me to be extroverted. The unintended consequence was getting fired within two months of joining the company.

Keep looking at the costs of those wins, and any others you can recall, until you wake up to the damage that your winning recipe has caused. Once you look at those failures, you will likely, as I did, become passionate about detaching yourself from it.

Takeaways from Understanding Your Recipe

1. You almost certainly created an introvert winning recipe as a child. It probably allowed you to appear more outgoing than you actually were and get results without dealing too closely with people.

2. It comes at a high cost. It may have produced short-term results in a narrow domain, but eventually it hardened into a behavior pattern that held back your personal development, your relationships, and your workplace performance.

3. The first step in detaching from your recipe is to identify its identity, origin, structure, and costs, either in this chapter or by working through the rest of the book.

Reflective Questions

1. What was the most recent time you saw your recipe appear in a personal relationship? In your job? Were the two experiences similar, or different?

2. What action does your recipe drive you to take across many different situations? Does it have you being persistent, in turning most

situations into a test of endurance? Being generous, in often feeling incomplete unless you have given something away? Being humble, in refusing to accept praise? Being frugal, in disliking to spend or waste anything? This will help you to confirm that you have put your finger on the right one.

3. What type of negative judgment does your recipe encourage you to make about a person or a situation? These "negatives" help to point toward an accurate description of your recipe.

Practical Exercises

1. **The Direct Opposite Test:** Identify the behavioral style that is the opposite of the one you have chosen. Opposites tend to be the following: Dominant—Steady, Influential—Conscientious

   a. Within the opposite DISC list (to see all the lists, you can flip back a few pages), pick at least five winning recipes that irritate you. If you can do so, it's a good reverse confirmation that your DISC choice is accurate. Within your own DISC choice, then look again through the recipes to see if any of them strikes home.

   b. Otherwise, go back to the opposite DISC list, pick five that hit you as undesirable, and look at your own DISC style to find recipes that seem to offset those five. For example, if your DISC style is Conscientious, you might be turned off by "Being flagrant" and "Being flippant" in the opposing Influential list. If so, find recipes that seem to counteract "flagrant" and "flippant" in your own Conscientious list.

2. **The Disaster Test:** Imagine that your house was destroyed in a hurricane. The structure is still there, but it is severely damaged and is a complete mess inside. Now imagine that you have arrived

at the door to clean up. What is the first thing that you think to do? That is likely the default response of your winning recipe. For example, in the story you will see that this scenario happened to me. The default response of my "being methodical" recipe was to make a list of the step-by-step tasks we should perform before doing anything. (Fortunately, my wife talked me out of that and caused us both just to jump into action.)

3. **The High School Test:** What approach did you use to get through high school, both academically and socially? You probably formed your recipe long before high school, so it was in full flower by your early teens.

~

We are now ready to begin the story of how my own winning recipe unfolded over the span of sixty years, and how over a decade ago I successfully detached from it. Each chapter is designed to provide insights you can use to get clear about the nature of your own recipe, and—when you are ready—to detach from it.

In what follows, parts 1 and 3 dive into the costs that my recipe imposed on me. In contrast, parts 2, 4, and 5 focus on becoming more conscious—expanding your mental landscape with ideas to absorb and implement so you can escape from your recipe. The hold of an introvert recipe is so tenacious that it takes a good deal of growth in awareness to loosen its grip. The insights, Reflective Questions, and Practical Exercises in each chapter will help you do that.

For convenience, throughout the book I refer to the recipe as if it were an independent actor. Of course the persona or mask you have created is not a separate personality. Sometimes, however, it seems to have its own agenda and urgings, so I refer to them that way to make the story more relatable.

As the story unfolds, I discuss Twelve Tools of Detachment in the order they emerged in my life. However, the sequence in which you learn them in your own life doesn't matter, so long as all of them are part of your journey toward detachment. For a concise summary of the twelve tools, please see the Appendix.

Part 1

Six Early Costs of My Recipe

1

Submission: Anabela

OCTOBER 1960. LOS ANGELES, CALIFORNIA. To attract a girl in a suburban LA high school in 1960, a guy needed one of three things: a hulk of a body honed through years of athletic competition, a group of cool and good-looking friends—rich, if possible—or a hot car, preferably a 1932 Ford Little Deuce Coupe.

Fig. 1. High school picture, age 17. Van Nuys, CA, 1960.

The correct look was mandatory. Even on the hottest days, if you were an athlete, you wore a heavy cardigan sweater with a big school letter on the side and walked around so serenely that you never broke a sweat. If you were a cool guy, you wore an oversized black leather jacket with a menacing name like "The Retaliators" arched across the back above a drawing that in some way featured dripping blood. And if you had a car that looked even remotely like a Deuce Coupe convertible, you roared up to school with a grin on your face and the skin peeling off your nose.

As for myself, I had flat feet and was in a remedial gym class. My few friends were the ugliest, most socially inept guys in the school—people who carried tiny plastic chess sets in their shirt pockets and blew their noses on handkerchiefs that they stuffed back into their jeans. My car was the family sedan, a 1946 Plymouth four-door that looked like a blue balloon turned on its side.

Thus, it was with great hopelessness that in October I observed the arrival of a mysterious olive-skinned sixteen-year-old girl at our school. She had short hair, wore no makeup, and dressed in a plain white blouse and black skirt. Stunningly beautiful, she carried herself with the assurance and piercing gaze of a runway model.

Nobody could talk to her. It was not that the surfers and jocks didn't try. It was that she spoke no English, and nobody could figure out what language she did speak.

At seventeen, I was desperate for a girlfriend, but all girls intimidated me. Approaching one required being bold, confident, and entertaining. This girl's silence, her bearing, and my lack of the attributes needed to approach any girl—let alone one as gorgeous as this—kept me away.

Several weeks passed. Word circulated that her name was Anabela, and that she had just arrived from Portugal. That tidbit sent my mind racing. One attribute I did have was that after three years of Spanish, I was a whiz and knew it to be a close cousin of Portuguese. Spanish was excessively uncool, and much too hard for the athletes, the social climbers, and the hot-rodders on campus to bother with. Those who spoke Spanish as a first language did not approach Anabela because they had a nearly impervious social clique.

I was too scared to seek the new girl out. But one crisp fall day, I bumped into her in the outdoor lunch pavilion and before I knew it, amid the aroma of hamburgers and grilled cheese sandwiches, I found the courage to introduce myself to her in Spanish. Her eyes narrowed because—I assumed—she thought that language was crap, and at once began correcting me on the right words to use if I was going to speak to her. She particularly detested *usted* (oo-STED), the Spanish word for "you," and insisted that I use the more mellifluous Portuguese *você* (voh-SAY) from that instant forward.

I complied and we were soon talking in a jumble of all three languages while I struggled to understand the Portuguese words she was using. We both thrashed around at a two-year-old level until we ended up laughing at the whole mess. I was the first person she had said much of anything to at school, and she was the first beautiful girl I had ever approached in my life.

It is impossible to overstate the thrilling effect that Anabela had on me. I had never had a girlfriend, never kissed a girl, and here I was gradually getting closer to this lovely, exotic young lady. She had full lips, a bust that challenged every blouse, a tiny waist, and a soft voice that spoke a tropical language. The great irony was that a consummate dork such as me should be the one hanging out with her, sharing laughs over things that nobody else could understand.

~

One cool afternoon several weeks later, I found myself walking up the front steps of Anabela's house. It was a three-bedroom bungalow in Northridge near our high school in the San Fernando Valley. I had offered to teach her English and help her with her other courses, but doing so during school hours had been difficult to arrange. One day she stunned me with an invitation to meet her parents and study at her house.

I rang the bell. My heart was pounding. I had no idea what I would find. Luana, a slender, attractive woman in her mid-thirties, with black hair, a kind face, and the same olive skin as Anabela, appeared and thanked me in Spanish for coming to help her daughter. Before she could finish, however, a giant German shepherd raced from inside to the doorway and buried her nose in my crotch.

Embarrassed, Luana yelled a tumble of Portuguese back into the house, after which I heard, "GERTA, *HOP YER PLOTZ!*" The dog understood whatever language *that* was and skulked around the corner.

We walked into the living room, where I saw Anabela's stepfather, Lars, sitting in a recliner, the big dog settling down at his feet. Lars was quite young—only about thirty—a lanky, affable Dutchman with curly blond hair on top and a close shave on the sides. In good English, he apologized for the dog and gave me a grin that revealed a set of blackened, crooked teeth; I later learned his teeth were a legacy of the Nazi occupation of Holland during his childhood when no dental care was available.

Anabela came in all giggly and gay, showing none of the regal stance she kept at school, and shook my hand. We sat on the couch with Luana and began to talk as best we could. Lars translated, since the women spoke no English, my Portuguese was a joke, and he did well in both languages. It was an odd group, but they were warm and kind.

That was the first of many such visits to Anabela's house. I was there to help her learn, but I quickly discovered that she had little interest in studying. She was bright, picking up English from TV and the girls at school, and refused all lessons. The rest of the subjects were nonsense to her, and she declined even to discuss them.

Our visits became purely social. The three family members accepted me as one of their own, each for their own reason. Luana saw me as a Lars-in-training, a person who might take care of Anabela one day in the way she herself had found a man to rescue her from a dead-end life in Algarve Province, Portugal—the poorest part of one of the poorest countries in Europe at the time. In me, she saw none of the rapaciousness of the stereotypical Latin male, a type from whom she had probably fled in her past.

Lars saw me as a safe bet. He would not have to police me to keep my hands off his stepdaughter; I was doing just fine in that department and, if anything, I needed to be encouraged to get a little closer to her. He often tried to get the two of us to pose for a photo, only to find me turning red with embarrassment and Anabela saying, in broken English, "Oh, Pa, you so *silly!*" and prancing away.

For Anabela, I was a toy. No doubt she saw how besotted I was with her and enjoyed driving me crazy with flirtations in front of her parents. One of her favorite tricks was to climb into the easy chair beside Lars, all tits and arms and legs, put her hand behind his head, and mess up his hair while looking at me as if to say, "See, if you weren't such a wimp you could be getting some of this too." Lars was a stand-up guy who had massive quantities of ice in his veins. As soon as he had had enough, he told her to get off him and she did so without a peep, but always with a sideways glance at me.

If English lessons for Anabela were off the table, Portuguese lessons for me were a passion. I had gone into overtime building a process for learning the language, thinking it could help me win her over as her boyfriend and not just an object to play with. And I thought it might help to handle Anabela's controlling behavior. She told me where to sit on the couch, slapped my shoulder when I tried to offer a different opinion on just about any idea she held, and angrily corrected me on any of my accidental lapses into Spanish. She was sometimes downright unfriendly, and I was constantly anxious around her. But I persevered.

Luana was thrilled that I was trying so hard to learn their language. She showed me her two-volume Portuguese-English dictionary set and helped me order my own copy from Lisbon. Anabela was annoyed that I was not learning faster, curtly correcting me when I did not get a verb ending right, especially if I had used the Spanish version.

She gave me three or four teenage romance novels to read in Portuguese, which I took home and devoured, looking up anything I could not understand in my wonderful new dictionary. I got up early before school every day and read about cardboard characters acting out puerile plots as if it were the grandest literature ever written.

As part of my plan, I devised a set of rules for translating Spanish to Portuguese and wrote them on 3x5 index cards for easy review—a sign that I was using my recipe for being methodical to achieve what I wanted. I got better and better at the language but only once got a compliment from Anabela for my progress. I received scorn and laughter from her when I inevitably misspoke, which left me feeling like an idiot. Nevertheless, I kept plugging away with a slow and steady approach, convinced that if I could learn her language, I could attract her to me. When I spoke it, even haltingly, it somehow made me more outgoing. For the first time, I was extending my step-by-step approach from academics to getting a girl, and I was sure it would work.

~

As the months rolled by, the visits degenerated into watching *Make Room for Daddy* and *Leave It to Beaver* on the couch with Anabela and Luana. Lars was working part-time and studying engineering at California State University at Northridge, so I saw less and less of him.

The shows bored me, but I kept busy by translating the fragments they did not understand into Portuguese. This provoked great howls of laughter from Anabela when I did not quite get the words right, and admonitions from her mother to treat me a little better, which Anabela ignored.

~

After Christmas, I was on two tracks. The first was shining and exhilarating: my assembly-line processes had made me co-valedictorian of my high school class.

I wrote a speech and rehearsed it in the chill of the garage with one hand on the fender of the blue balloon Plymouth for security. During that time, I got the joyous news that I had been accepted to Stanford for the class entering in September 1961 and had been awarded some financial aid from the state of California. It was only an $800 stipend, but it felt like a million dollars.

The second track was dismal. I continued to go over to Anabela's house, even though it was always the same. Anabela would only flirt with me when Luana or Lars was in the room, and then she'd abruptly flip a switch when we were alone, reverting to the lofty indifference that she adopted at school. I was constantly off-balance.

I felt powerless, hypnotized. Her every movement, word, facial expression, and playful shoulder slap bound me more tightly to her in a submissive way I could not explain. Maybe I was so drawn to her because she was my near opposite. While I was reserved, stiff, and stuck in my head, she was free, sensual, and dominant. She knew what she wanted, and I found that to be irresistible—and a little frightening.

It did not produce a sense of security, and that was what I longed for in a relationship. Despite that, I futilely continued looking for safety in Anabela. I now understand she was just a sixteen-year-old girl trying to make sense of an entirely new world in America, exercising control in the only way she knew how.

At times I thought, "Do I really want this?" I did not know what I wanted in a girl but was coming to think that maybe this was not it. Beauty alone was not turning out to be enough for me to build love on.

Then I would say to myself, "She is gorgeous. I just have to figure out how to attract her." I did not have muscles, cool friends, or a nifty car and had no idea what would appeal to a girl like her. Despite my wanting us to get close emotionally, she always kept her distance. I kept persevering with the language, but clearly the process was not working.

I graduated from high school in February 1961 because LA County had split its huge number of students into winter and summer cohorts. Six months remained before I would leave for Stanford, and I was so alienated from Anabela that I could not bear the thought of keeping up the mindless routine with her for that long. But neither could I face letting go of her.

I wanted to get away for a while and fill the coming months with something interesting to do. So, I came up with a plan that solved everything.

It involved getting on a plane and going to Mexico City.

~

When it came time for the flight, I was overjoyed to head to the LA airport with my father.

He had made the trip possible. He was an immensely loving man with a broad face and wavy black hair whose own father had died when he was three. He wanted to be the father he himself never had. A source of deep kindness and wisdom, he was a role model, a good man who was humble, proud, and thankful for the happiness he possessed and was able to pass on.

Fig. 2. Neely Plumb producing a live recording session at the top of the Mark Hopkins Hotel, San Francisco, CA, 1961.

A talented saxophone and clarinet player with the unforgettable name of Neely Plumb, my father had perfect pitch and often wrote the score for an entire orchestra on huge pages of yellow sheet music, automatically transposing the notes in his head for whatever key a given instrument was played in. He honed that skill on the road in the 1930s with Ray Noble, Artie Shaw, Tommy Dorsey, and other big bands of the era, as well as in the pit orchestra of RKO Pictures in the 1940s, recording the musical scores for motion pictures. By the late 1950s, after largely recovering from Bell's palsy, he had parlayed himself into a job as director of artists and repertoire with RCA Victor Records in Hollywood. A dapper dresser, Dad often walked around town sporting a skinny white tie, a red vest, and a blue sport coat.

One of his recording artists was Juan Garcia Esquivel, a hugely popular Mexican bandleader who also had a following in the US and was quite close to Dad. I hatched a plan for Dad to ask Esquivel to help me find a job in Mexico that would keep me busy until I started at Stanford. Esquivel was enthusiastic, and shortly afterward, at age eighteen and with an arm sore from inoculations, I was on a Western Airlines flight to Mexico City.

~

The trip gave me seven weeks of relief from Anabela, but despite Esquivel's best intentions, I was not able to get a job. I needed a work permit, and for *norteamericanos*, they were almost impossible to get.

While there I did meet Eduardo, the dark, thin, and intimidating attendant at the Angel of Independence, one of the biggest monuments in the city. We talked and my initial fear of him quickly passed. I found him to be warm and compassionate. He was twenty-two, had a wife and a baby girl, lived in a two-room apartment, worked two jobs to earn fourteen dollars a week, and read Tolstoy.

It may seem unusual that I, as a young introvert, was so comfortable in reaching out to a stranger, particularly one who initially intimidated me. The difference was, all the encounters occurred in Spanish. Speaking the second language somehow took me out of myself, and put me into the personality of someone more outgoing.

As unhealthy as Anabela had been for me, I ended up missing her and returned to LA.

~

The day after my arrival I visited her family. She, Luana, and Lars were happy to see me and restored the old routine in every detail. Gerta went into my crotch, was told to go to her plotz, and Anabela and I sat on the couch with Luana to the unfolding of sitcoms and shoulder slaps.

Quickly disillusioned, I saw Anabela less frequently, and when one of my few friends invited me to go with him to his grandmother's house on Balboa Island, south of LA, I went. After two weeks there, I received word that a car had struck Anabela and broken her pelvis. She was in a hospital in the Valley and was asking for me.

It took me three days to get to her. That was the soonest I could arrange transport off the island and back to LA, but the delay allowed me time to ask my father to get something for me that I knew Anabela would want.

Through business dealings at RCA, Dad knew Colonel Tom Parker, the talent agent who had masterminded the career of Elvis Presley. Dad relayed the story of Anabela's accident to the colonel with a request for an autographed photo of the King, and it arrived just in time for me to take it to the hospital.

When I got there, I saw Anabela sitting up in bed, looking shaken but beautiful as always. A vase of bright yellow flowers was on the table next to her. Luana was there and gave me a hug; I leaned over and gave Anabela an awkward embrace over the bed, careful to avoid the vase. I could not get a straight answer from either of them about what had happened. It sounded like Anabela had stepped off the curb into the street in front of her house without looking, but neither she nor Luana wanted to get into it, seemingly embarrassed by the story.

I handed Anabela the large manila envelope I had brought with me, and she slowly withdrew the picture, letting out a shriek as soon as she saw what it was. I had never seen her so ecstatic. The inscription was not personalized, but it looked like Elvis had signed it with something like

"To a big fan—Elvis." The glossy black-and-white photo showed him in a classic pose, legs apart and a sneer on his face as he held a guitar and looked seductively into the camera.

"Ma, look at his *peesha*," Anabela said in Portuguese. Luana instantly doubled over, her face turning red as she tried to stifle a scream of laughter.

Peesha? What was a peesha? In all my vast studies of the language, I had never run across that word and had no idea what it meant. Surely it referred to a part of the body I was not familiar with, such as the elbow. Alternatively, perhaps it referred to some aspect of his demeanor, such as the smirk on his face, or the flow of his hair, which of course was provocatively out of place.

I should have known something more consequential was involved from the snorts, the hoots, and the tears coming from them both every time in my best Portuguese I said, "Peesha? What is a peesha?" I grabbed the photo, looked at the bulge in it, then looked at Anabela and Luana with the dawning realization that, yes, this peesha (spelled p-i-x-a, I later learned after much coaxing) was indeed worth commenting on.

Armed with her photo of Elvis, Anabela was joyous. From all the noise we continued to make, I was surprised the hospital staff did not throw the three of us out.

~

The peesha incident in the summer of 1961 was the high point of my relationship with Anabela. My hopes after that grand gesture were quickly dashed, however, when Anabela returned home and promptly forgot about my Elvis offering.

A few weeks after the hospital visit, I got so dissatisfied with the boredom and the insecurity of the on-again, off-again flirtations at her house that I stopped seeing her altogether. One night during *Gilligan's Island*, I could not take it anymore. I simply got up, said nothing, and walked out the door, riding my bike home in the smoggy LA air with tears streaming down my cheeks at the futility of it all. Today, I am embarrassed at how rude and childish that was but also appreciate how desperately I wanted to avoid any potential conflict with her.

Two years passed. During that time, I moved three hundred fifty miles north to Stanford University without making any effort to explain myself to Anabela or otherwise contact her. My studies captivated me, and after a rocky start to adapt my high school study process to college-level courses, my winning recipe—being methodical by using step-by-step processes—once again began producing one success after another.

The only course I did not enjoy was ROTC, which I had signed up for on registration day to avoid getting drafted right after graduation. Given the ructions in Southeast Asia, the future did not look bright for any con-script. Anti-war sentiment at Stanford would grow steadily during my years in the program, but I figured being an officer might someday save my life, so I held my nose and stuck with military studies.

At the end of my sophomore year, I spent six months at Stanford's campus in Tours, France. A few months after my return to California, Anabela called me. She was now a professional model, spoke fluent English, and, to my great surprise, was pursuing me. Against my better judgment I began seeing her again, but in the end we had too little in common for the relationship to work.

One day during the holidays we were alone in the back seat of a car when she came on to me strongly, and I pushed her away, saying I could not do this anymore. She let loose with a string of words that impressed me with her command of English obscenities. Masking tears, she exploded in indignation and wrath. She got out of the car, slammed the door, and I never saw or heard from her again.

WHAT I COULD HAVE DONE DIFFERENTLY

I could have been more alert to the double surrender that I was engaged in—to Anabela's aggressive behavior, and to the urgings of the recipe to study Portuguese—and left the relationship much sooner than I did.

Takeaways from Chapter 1

1. All recipes involve a degree of hidden submission. They become so ingrained that you do not even realize that you are living out their insistence on a specific way to be.

2. Sometimes they can also involve a degree of overt submission. This is less likely if you have a *dominant* winning recipe. But if your recipe is *influential*, or *conscientious* like mine, or especially a *steady* one, the risk of overtly surrendering to the behavior of another person is probably higher.

3. No form of submission is healthy long-term. Denying your individuality is never in your best interest. But the obedience to your recipe will probably continue for decades until you wake up and detach from it.

Reflective Questions

1. The first time you submitted to your recipe in a relationship, did it cause you to submit to that person's behavior as well?

2. In what way did your recipe make you blind to key aspects of that relationship?

3. What unintended outcome did your recipe generate in that relationship?

Practical Exercises

1. In your current primary relationship, write down how submitting to the urgings of your recipe shows up, and whether you are also submitting to an undesirable behavior by your partner. Then note the cost of each.

2. Perform the Exercise 1 tasks for your current role at work, substituting "your supervisor" for "your partner."

3. Perform the Exercise 1 tasks for your current state of personal growth, substituting "a precept" such as Stoicism, or "What you think you become," or "Outwork everyone," or "Less is more" for "your partner."

~

By the time I left Anabela, I had achieved near fluency in another tongue beyond Spanish. Now that the tactic had sort of worked with one girl, I was eager to overcome my solitude by trying it once more.

I did not know it, but an opportunity to meet two Portuguese-speaking belles was about to come my way.

2

Inauthenticity:
Two Girls in Rio

AUGUST 1964. RIO DE JANEIRO, BRAZIL. As our plane descended into Rio, I relaxed in the morning sunshine, panning my sleepy eyes along the sweeping arc of Copacabana beach below us.

My head was shaved and I was exhausted. I had just come from ROTC summer camp in Fort Lewis, Washington, about forty miles south of Seattle. The purpose of the camp was to help prepare us cadets for commissioning as second lieutenants when we graduated from college in a year's time. I was sore, recovering from the nonstop fear and harassment that the US Army had put us through. It was all I could do to stay awake.

The white sand below the plane reminded me of Zuma Beach, the prosaic little LA County beach where I had swum many times since childhood. I slipped into a daydream about California. *Mary Poppins* had had its world premiere two days earlier in Los Angeles, catapulting Julie Andrews into the international spotlight. My dad was a big fan of hers.

We could not have imagined it, but the following year he would sign her with RCA Victor Records and go on to produce *The Sound of Music*, one of the best-selling soundtrack albums of all time, selling twenty million copies. Despite all that success, we would continue to live in the same small three-bedroom, stucco-clad bungalow in a classic 1950s-style middle-class neighborhood in the San Fernando Valley. Except for a second-hand Cadillac that he bought, we had none of the trappings of the artists and executives he worked with.

The growl of the engines brought me back. I was on this plane because, at the end of my junior year at Stanford, my near-fluency in Portuguese had gotten me selected to be part of a State Department seven-week cultural exchange program with a university in Brazil, along with five other young men. The country was huge—bigger than the lower forty-eight states. The six of us had spent weeks touring from north to south, meeting with college students along the way. Our last stop was in Rio.

Over the roar of the jet, I kept hearing our student sponsors using a Portuguese phrase: *a filha do reitor*, meaning "the rector's daughter." In Rio, we were to be the guests of a university, and our hosts kept talking among themselves about the girl whose father was the president of the institution.

I could understand them well because while they were visiting Stanford, I had used their help to shed the European Portuguese accent I had acquired from Anabela and Luana, and had adopted the Brazilian one.

"Who are we going to put in with the rector's daughter?" said one.

"I don't know. Why do you keep asking me?" replied the other.

"Because we're about to land in Rio, and we need to get this right or we're screwed."

I was not sure why the topic kept coming up, figuring she must be eight years old and a real brat or they would not keep referring to her as someone to be reckoned with. Yet they were debating a serious question: Which one of us would they place in the rector's home? Just before we arrived, they announced that her name was Ana Maria, and that the person they had selected to move in next to her bedroom was me.

After we landed, Rio overwhelmed me with its dreamlike atmosphere. Egg-shaped mountains jutted high into the clouds, brightly colored shops lined the streets, and the smell of sweet coffee wafted out from curbside stalls. Being in Brazil was so wholesome and enjoyable that it was hard to believe it was happening to me.

The fantasy doubled every time I returned to my room in the Botafogo section of town, where the university president and his family lived, because on top of the unbelievable world outside, I had an astonishing situation going for me in the home. Not only had they accepted me as one of the family, but they had also introduced me to their beautiful daughter—Ana Maria—who had dark blond hair and was not eight years old but almost eighteen, and played bossa nova on the guitar and sang as if she had invented that style of music—and the instrument as well.

~

One day, shortly after I moved into Ana Maria's house, we six Americans stood on the lawn in the backyard of a luxurious private home where our student hosts had arranged a party.

Looming above our heads—close enough to touch, it seemed—were rounded mountain peaks, lush with vegetation.

When invited, we all turned and went inside, glad to get out of the late-afternoon heat. In a large recreation room, we found six chic Brazilian girls waiting to dance with us. To approach one of them, I would need to be more outgoing than I was comfortable with. But I knew my Portuguese was good and quickly found my confidence. I approached a petite, pretty girl, who smiled up at me and accepted my invitation to dance.

As we moved to the rhythm of the hit song *"Chega de Saudade"* ["I've Had Enough Sadness"], I learned that the girl's name was Sofia. Refined in manner and appearance, she was the daughter of a German-Brazilian family in Rio.

I loved her smile and her laugh and asked her to dinner. Her older sister Aliza was there, so we double-dated with her and Jake, my friend and fellow exchange member. We were amazed that the girls would even go with us, a sign of their highly un-Brazilian behavior.

Quiet and judicious, Sofia was fascinated with people and spent long moments watching them. Her mother was a practicing psychologist, so it was no doubt an inherited trait. Sofia kept a journal—an outgrowth of her analytical approach to life—and had frighteningly adult opinions of herself and of the people she saw. In her maturity, she seemed more outward-focused than Ana Maria, who had her eye more on herself.

"I have a troupe of *bandeirantes*," she said, referring to the Portuguese word for "pioneers."

"Do they have machetes?" I asked, half-serious.

Sofia laughed. "No, silly. They are little girls. Seven to ten. We go on hikes, visit museums, and talk about life." I later learned that they were the Brazilian counterparts of the Girl Scouts in the US.

We had dinner and strolled along the magnificence of Copacabana beach for two hours. Beautifully lit apartment towers paralleled the shoreline as far as we could see in either direction.

Afterward, we went back to the girls' apartment in Ipanema. Their parents were gone for the night, so we came inside to dance. Sofia impressed me far more than I wanted to admit; she was so gentle that I wanted to hold her in thanks for such a rewarding evening. An animalistic desire for her came over me.

Jake began to hustle Sofia's sister Aliza with great success, in spite of the bright lights in the room, but I felt paralyzed. I wanted to touch Sofia, yet made no move toward or away from her, staying on an awkward neutral ground amid the parlor love scene to the right. Jake spoke Portuguese, was good-looking, rich, and smooth; except for the language, I was none of that and feared this high-status young Brazilian woman might be out of my league. I could easily blow it if I touched her, so I didn't—even though the way she looked at me made me fairly certain she was hoping I would. Because I could not bring myself to embrace her, the night that had been so beautiful began to go sour. I was lucky to leave before it became completely ruined. As we left, Sofia was sweet and polite, seeming not to judge me for my lack of initiative with her.

Afterward, I was glad of my good sense. I would rather have her see me for the introvert I was than for her to be disgusted at a typically Latino advance on her body. Time remained to pursue her, and my conscience was clear that I had done the right thing.

Apparently, I had. The next night we sat in the back seat of a taxi that was taking us from her parents' apartment to Copacabana beach for another walk. It was dark and we snuggled close, holding hands. Her touch was so incredibly soft.

~

More days passed and all the logic in the world could tell me that Ana Maria had a personality that was simply incompatible with mine, but I could not help myself from slipping into a warm, comfortable attraction to her. The distance between us got smaller every time we looked at each other.

I was interested in Sofia, but I could not help being drawn to Ana Maria. Oddly, my daily contact with these two fascinating girls produced little conflict within me. I considered Ana Maria to be forbidden, and that was that. But like a kid in front of a candy store, I couldn't stop looking.

I sought signs that Ana Maria knew I was alive and that she, too, felt the tickling of something about to begin. She looked at me and smiled on a crowded bus, and I was happy for an hour; she leaned over to whisper a secret to me on the couch at home, and I was weak with excitement; she shook my hand to say good-night, and I had enough to dream about until morning. It was crazy. It was unreal. But it produced a special kind of happiness that had me on a warm emotional cloud. The Portuguese language-learning process I had built four years earlier was paying off handsomely.

Because a relationship with her was so forbidden, my desire for her was likely far sharper than it would have been otherwise. Her father was the president of the university that had received the six of us, she had a reasonably steady boyfriend, and I was in a foreign country where I could unwittingly blow everything up at any moment. Being around her was risky. Yet I could not stop the feelings that were growing inside me.

~

After several lengthier walks and intimate talks along Copacabana beach, I came to know Sofia, the German-Brazilian woman, better. But more contact was dampening my desire and enthusiasm for her.

I felt like I had nothing in reserve. In no time, she found me out intellectually and emotionally. When her beautiful eyes set upon me and looked gently from top to bottom, I knew she saw straight through. She detected that my confidence with women was shaky, that I was sensitive to every word or glance that came from her, that I was confused and evolving politically and religiously, and that I had seen more than half of the world but remained a kid looking for warmth and security. I had revealed so much of myself to Sofia she could almost read my mind, giving me pause about making advances toward her and making me feel insecure in her presence.

"We must only remain *colegas* [friends]," she said, reinforcing my hesitation.

In Sofia, as in Ana Maria, I had met my mental match. Sofia could run circles around me in psychology or philosophy—not because of her extensive education, but rather out of her acute common sense and reasoning powers. Critical and clear-sighted, Sofia analyzed people and ideas with ease and precision. Everything she said was simple and unpretentious, and I often wondered if my mind could stand all the exercise that she put it through.

"Remember that we must only remain friends," she said again.

I agreed. I loved every minute of contact with her, but I knew inside she deserved a lot more than I could offer.

I should have felt content after Sofia suggested we remain friends. But the next day, despite interlaced fingers and encircled waists, our talks as we walked along Copacabana beach turned into moments of frustration and resentment for me. A little conversation with her was enough to make me furious. I wanted closeness; she wanted distance.

The endless expanse of sand and sea before us was a painful contrast to Sofia's reserve.

I took her frankness to be an open attack on my ego. I was not yet big enough to keep from feeling chagrined when a girl gave me a handshake rather than a kiss. With her oft repeated line about friendship, Sofia had given me a handshake.

Oddly, once I realized all that, I was able to go back to enjoying being with her. Now that I could see *why* I was upset at all the talk about just being "friends," I let it pass before I ruined our time together. We told each other that we regretted none of our pleasure. The proof later was petting in the stairwell of her apartment building, thoroughly enjoying one another with no questions asked.

~

After spending more time with Sofia, I did not know what I thought of her. She was mature and conscientious, tender and affectionate. She was a beautiful companion for many happy and instructive hours, and I was willing for her to get a grip on my heart. But the intellectual bantering had been too relentless and emotionally draining for me. I took comfort in thinking that because it had not taken place in English, I still had a tiny corner of myself that she had not analyzed. But if all she wanted was friendship, then she could not be the intimate life partner I longed for.

The process I was following with Sofia was not about learning Portuguese, as it had been with Anabela. It was about *using* the language, seemingly to stimulate my brain into new neural pathways that would allow me to be outgoing enough to engage in mental games with her. I was much like the character Colin Firth would play almost half a century later in *The King's Speech*. When the king sang, his stutter disappeared. In an extroverted world, what I considered to be my equivalent "stutter" at the time (introversion) temporarily disappeared when I spoke Portuguese, just as it had in Mexico when I spoke Spanish with Eduardo. Like the music that King George sang to, the beauty and passion of those tropical languages took me out of myself whenever I spoke them.

Consequently, I had not been authentic with Sofia. I responded to her wordplay by acting as if I loved it when I truly did not. She was so perceptive that I do think she saw through my talkative façade to the quiet person inside. But amid so much give-and-take, all in a foreign language no less, I was not able to project that person. I came off as much less of an introvert than I really was, attracting her as if I were an eager debater. It was inauthentic.

~

The more I watched Ana Maria, the more I concluded that probably every young woman occasionally displayed a condescending side to her parents, which Ana Maria certainly did. But the kindness she extended to me far outweighed any of the negative such behavior I saw. The most thoughtful thing she did was offer to teach me how to play bossa nova, the quintessential Brazilian music that in the mid-1960s was sweeping the world.

Suddenly, I was thankful both of us would be focusing on music. My Portuguese ability and introversion back in LA had made Anabela nuts with desire, and I most certainly did not want to have the same thing happen here. Music would be an outlet for Ana Maria's extroversion and reorient my growing desire for her, hopefully preventing both of us from getting too involved. I had been exploring music on the piano since childhood and on the guitar for the past two years. I saw it could be another formula for transmuting whatever might be going on between us into something harmless and beautiful to listen to. It would be safe.

I was drawn to music as a system with its own processes for chord fingering, rhythm, melody, and lyrics. But I foolishly hoped it could work to *avoid* attraction rather than encourage it and ignored whether I could even keep at it, since playing guitar and singing in front of an attractive girl were exercises in extroversion. I simply leaned into music as a way to lessen the risk I felt being in such close physical proximity to Ana Maria every day.

The living room couch, which began as the site of our sharing many mutual secrets, was now the classroom. The first lesson took place one day in the late afternoon when she got back from school. Outside it was hot and humid, but inside—thanks to the thick stone walls of the house—it was cool despite the lack of air-conditioning. We sat together, guitars in hand—I had brought mine from home—as the sounds and smells of dinner preparations floated in from the kitchen.

Ana Maria had a deep, resonant singing voice that matched the sonorous sounds that came from her guitar. Brazil was famous for its hardwoods, and they gave the guitar (in Portuguese called the *violão*) a rich sound, the likes of which I had never heard. I imagined hers had been made from wood harvested deep in the Amazon, and that the dark mysteries of that jungle had somehow been ported to this instrument to give it the unparalleled bass notes and crystal clear high notes I heard every time she played.

My guitar, hauled all the way from California and probably made from a pine tree in New Jersey, simply did not cut it and we both knew it. After our first lesson, she kindly offered to help me buy a locally made instrument, and I jumped at the chance. She took me on the bus to several shops and tested instruments until the word *ótimo* (AHH-chi-mo), meaning "top-notch," came easily out of her smiling mouth.

During that first lesson, we had done some playing together with my American guitar, but she had also brought out a Brazilian one for me to try. It felt like a completely different instrument. As I held it, I could feel the deep bass notes surge from the box of the guitar into my chest, filling me with even more sound than was emitted into the atmosphere when I plucked the strings. It was intoxicating, even more so when I looked over at Ana Maria with her head tilted, her long blond hair hanging to one side, her husky voice complemented by the chords from her own instrument. Seeing and hearing her like that was incredibly alluring.

We had agreed to teach each other some songs we knew, but in the ensuing days, the instruction was lopsided in her favor. My repertoire was very '60s, with folk songs such as "Where Have All the Flowers Gone?" that had mindlessly simple chord progressions and sweet, haunting melodies. They were so utterly different from the music Ana Maria played that often she would sit open-mouthed and sometimes have tears in her eyes when I played and sang. For someone as skillful in music as she was, this was not a sign of awe at my talent, but at hearing beautiful sounds that seemed to come from another planet.

Her music, in contrast, was complex in the extreme. She played the songs of João Gilberto, whom audiences in the US were just coming to know. "The Girl from Ipanema," sung by his wife, Astrud, was a huge hit and demanded great skill from a performer. The melody had an enormous range and was anything but simple. The guitar accompaniment required changing musical keys, had dissonant chords—nothing like the simple Cs and Gs of American folk music—and progressed to a complicated rhythm that was very hard for a gringo like me to even pat my foot to. She saw that.

"Okay, now we need to work on the bossa nova beat," she said in Portuguese. "Here, use your thumb, forefinger, and middle finger to tap it out on the box of the guitar."

"I hear you do it, Ana Maria, but my brain doesn't get it," I confessed.

"Nonsense. You will get it." She tapped it and watched while I tried and failed a dozen times. Not once did she make fun of me.

"That's close—but here—put in an extra beat . . . YES! You got it!"

Once the syncopated rhythm snapped into place in my mind, I could then focus on the next step in the process: the finger positions of the strange-sounding chords on the fret of the guitar. Again, she patiently walked me through it until the positioning became second nature. She was a fabulous teacher, and my only regret was that I did not have more to offer her in return.

She took enormous pride in my progress, singing in Portuguese with me by the hour, correcting a little here, showing me a little flourish there, and beaming when, after struggling for a bit, I was able to replicate her sounds. Moreover, I took pride in her work, especially when she sang an American song in English. Her exotic Portuguese accent made the songs sound truly remarkable, sung in a deep and mellow voice that injected the sound of the tropics into the Anglo folk songs she was gradually mastering. The American music was rural, born of the plains and mountains of the West; the Brazilian sounds were urban, born in the small apartments that lined Copacabana, and never before or since have I heard the two executed so well as when Ana Maria sang and played them.

~

Ana Maria was only the fourth girl I had ever gotten close to. Her social position as the only daughter of the president of a major university made her far too dangerous for me to approach, so I channeled my desire for her into music. The strategy of not pursuing Ana Maria was a compromise and turned out well. The musical results were exquisite and extremely satisfying, reducing the risk of something awful happening due to my being near her. And by not getting involved with her, I avoided blowing up the foreign exchange experience for us both.

But I paid such close attention to the music that I did not see how acutely lonely she was. The night before I left Rio, I was in my room packing when she came in. She touched me for the first time, bringing me close to her in a tight embrace. She said she feared we would never see each other again, then put her head on my shoulder and wept.

Shortly afterward, I left the house and took a cab to Ipanema to the apartment tower where Sofia lived. She led me into the stairwell, sat us down at the top of the flight, and embraced me with such fervent kissing and touching that it left my head spinning when I went back to Ana Maria's house for my final night in Rio.

I could not explain why she wanted to do that after she had pushed the concept of friendship so often. I guessed she was starved for affection, or she wanted me to have a good last night in Rio, or she wanted some experience now that she had it at hand.

The next morning, when my plane pulled away from the gate at Rio's Galeão airport, I saw Sofia waving to me. When we took off, I cried, and did not stop until I could no longer see Copacabana beach below me.

WHAT I COULD HAVE DONE DIFFERENTLY

Had I been more mature, I could have realized that I was inauthentic not only with Sofia but also with Ana Maria. I could have been more open with both girls, telling Sofia gently that I would like to find a way for us to get beyond all the banter, and telling Ana Maria that I found her exceptional but knew that, given her social position, we could never be together. Such honesty would have enriched the two relationships.

Takeaways from Chapter 2

1. Every recipe is soaked in inauthenticity. As a child you concluded that being an introvert was the same as being a loser, so you found it much easier to be your recipe than to be yourself.

2. There is no satisfaction in that. If you were living by your instincts as a rat, you would constantly be on the lookout for cheese at the end of any tunnel you were in. Likewise, the recipe calls you down tunnel after tunnel chasing the reward of satisfaction, but you rarely find any of it because you are not looking to satisfy your authentic self.

3. For introverts, authenticity is the key to fulfillment in life, but you cannot be authentic until you detach from your recipe. You may feel genuine as you act out the recipe, but at some level you know it's a sham, and you spend your life hoping you won't be found out.

Reflective Questions

1. In what peak situation does your recipe make you feel the most inauthentic?

2. How do you handle it? For example, do you simply double down on the recipe? Or are you embarrassed by it because it shows you something negative about yourself?

3. What have been the long-term costs for you of bearing that feeling of inauthenticity? Emotional or physical exhaustion? Increased anxiety or depression? Career or life dissatisfaction? Accumulated regret over time?

Practical Exercises

1. The Authenticity Audit: Write down three recent incidents in which you acted in the way your recipe called you to be, one each in a relationship, in your career, and in your personal growth. On a scale of 1 to 5, with 5 as the highest, rate each one in terms of how strongly they made you feel inauthentic.

2. The Mask Reveal: When you are with other people and are acting out your recipe, what sort of a "mask" do you wear? Write down how you imagine you look. How is that picture different from how you actually look when you see yourself in the mirror? Note how inauthentic your real physical image makes your mask look.

3. The Values Scorecard: Write down three core values that are extremely important to you. Then score each value from 1 to 5, with 5 as the highest, according to how true to it you are when you run your recipe. Finally, write down what you would have to do to score a 5 for each value.

~

On my way home from Brazil, my recipe caught me up in a misguided, reckless escapade. It involved a thermos of blood and a mission I couldn't resist. Eventually it would cost me dearly, because I took away precisely the wrong lesson from the exploit.

3

Recklessness:
Blood on Ice

SEPTEMBER 1964. BELÉM, BRAZIL. On my way back to LA via New York, I first stopped for a few days in Belém, a Brazilian metropolis near the equator where the massive Amazon empties into the Atlantic. The river and the surrounding jungle had fascinated me since childhood, and I figured this might be my last chance to see either one of them up close. Thoughts of my good-byes with Ana Maria and Sofia were with me the whole way.

Every time I walked out of my hotel to sightsee, the heat and jungle of Belém hit me in the face, making me wish I were still in Rio. Exotic plants invaded every square foot that was not occupied by concrete. Lizards and huge spiders turned up everywhere, themselves terrified at this bustling settlement on a river that many creatures had found inhospitable even before the arrival of humanity. Sweaty clothes stuck to my armpits. I fervently wanted to be back with those two stunning girls.

On my last day in Belém, I returned to the hotel looking forward to a cold shower and a quiet meal. At the reception desk, my glasses began to steam, and I hardly noticed the note a messenger handed to me; only upstairs did I look at it. It was in English—a curious request from a British medical student to be downstairs in a few minutes to discuss something of great importance. I laughed, expecting to be hit up for some money, but decided to cut my shower short to go see what he wanted.

Downstairs I ordered dinner, and shortly two young English gentlemen joined me. Both were ruddy and brisk. One was a chubby and bearded fellow who looked like a young Sebastian Cabot, the actor who played Santa in the 1974 version of *The Miracle on 34th Street*. The other was a hollow-eyed and lanky imitation of a young Peter O'Toole in *Lawrence of Arabia*. Wearing shirtsleeves and boots, they had just come in from the jungle, where they were working at a Brazilian government outpost doing research on a drug-resistant form of malaria. They were going to leave Brazil themselves, but could not do so for a few days and consequently came to me with an urgent request.

After weeks of searching the Amazon forest, they had finally found a native Brazilian who would not only admit to having the disease but would also let them take a blood sample for research. As yet, no cure existed for this particular strain of malaria. Although the sickness was becoming serious among Brazil's Indigenous people, it was hard for the researchers to locate and gain cooperation from enough of them to run a viable study.

Their success in finding a willing participant was only partial. The obstinate refusal of the Brazilian authorities to let the blood out of the country without the proper papers meant the valuable malaria sample would soon be worthless. The red tape would have taken days.

"Only London has the facilities for proper analysis," said the thin one.

"And it has to be done within seventy-two hours or the blood won't be useful," said the stocky one. "Either the blood has to get out right away, or five weeks of effort will be lost."

I looked from one to the other across the table. "So why are you telling me this?"

To make their lengthy, tactful, and well-constructed reply short, they wanted me to take the sample in a thermos bottle to New York, and, during my layover there, get it on a London-bound plane as soon as possible. We talked for a solid hour, and in the end, despite my hesitation because of my introvert-driven risk aversion, I agreed to do it.

~

To act in a way that was so thoroughly against my nature, and do so without reservation, was unprecedented for a cautious introvert like me.

These were two strangers, asking me to add another item to my huge hand-carried load, a large thermos bottle with a handle. I had two guitars and a stack of records to carry on the plane as it was.

More important was the consideration of risk. Who the hell were they, and how could I be sure I wasn't carrying narcotics, jewels, or a bomb aboard? And how did they know I was leaving for New York in the morning anyway? In retrospect, given the almost total lack of airline security in those days, it was not hard to imagine them tipping somebody to find out who would be on a given flight. But when I look back now, it seems I should have shied away from agreeing to become their mule.

Yet I know why I was willing to do it.

After only an hour's conversation, I respected and trusted these two. They answered my every question humbly and frankly, no matter how suspicious and pointed it may have seemed. I could see they understood my desire to know everything. Their story was internally consistent and after a while quite believable, enabling a wave of idealistic trust to come over me.

I accepted also because I identified with them. Their story was so forthright and straightforward that I could put myself in their place. I felt as if I had experienced their frustrating trip into the jungle and the infuriating encounter with the civil functionaries who were destroying all their work. I loved hearing about the meticulous process they had followed to obtain the sample, and totally understood their desire to bring everything to completion and save the world from malaria.

I stepped back and looked at what was happening here. Two English scientists were appealing to another English-speaker in a faraway jungle city where such contact was rare, and were asking him to take an action that could benefit humanity. How cool was that?

But there was more. After I left Rio, I had thought a great deal about my relationships with the three Portuguese-speaking girls I had met. What stood out was my reluctance to take initiative with any of them, even though I was sure I wanted a relationship one day. In a sense it was positive, because in time it had provoked all three of them, even Ana Maria, to reach out to me. That felt good. But it was a terribly lengthy and passive way to seek a lifetime partner. If I was serious about finding one, I needed to change my approach.

In the back of my mind, just below the level of consciousness, the blood project attracted me because, of all things, it would get me more comfortable with risk. That would make it easier for me to hazard approaches to more women than in the past, which in turn would increase the chances that I would meet someone who was right for me. I never articulated that stupidly naive sequence in so many words. But it operated subconsciously and helped to explain why I did not run the other way when the Englishmen came to see me.

To me, the risk involved seemed small. I was an experienced international traveler and prided myself on thoroughly understanding the step-by-step process of bringing goods into one country from another. On the plane, I would fill out a form declaring the nature and value of the things I was bringing in, usually limiting them to the categories shown. Incredible as it seems today, back then I could not remember ever seeing medical specimens as an item to declare. Once I landed, I would arrange all my stuff on a table for the customs inspector to see. In an age before terrorism, these staffers were overworked and underpaid and gave only the most cursory look at the items before them. I would then collect my things and walk out the door. That was it. I had done it so many times that the risk seemed to be trivial.

As I climbed the stairs back up to my room, I realized the British scientists had called my cargo not a "thermos bottle" but a "vacuum flask." The exotic name portended that this could indeed be a memorable adventure.

~

The next morning, the two earnest Englishmen met me at the Belém airport and stood by in case I could not take the blood on board. The sky was clear except for the beginnings of a few puffy clouds that would surely billow into blackness by noon. But for now, the weather was perfect for flying.

As I walked to the boarding gate with the handle in my fist, I could feel the weight of the vacuum flask. A letter of explanation was in my pocket in case of trouble, along with an important-looking label to put on it if, in New York, I felt that would help me get it to London. With typical British calm and thoroughness, they even gave me a roll of Scotch tape for affixing the label. In an era when the authorities inspected nothing before a passenger went on board, I was on the jet before I even had time to reflect on the success of the first step.

I had checked the inside of the thermos bottle before attempting to board and checked it again before we took off: It contained a small test tube with ten cc's of dark red liquid wrapped in moist cotton, surrounded by ice cubes. Satisfied that I could at least get it safely to New York, I put the flask on the empty seat next to me and started to plan what I would do when I got there. New York customs might be a challenge, but I knew the real issue was finding a way to transfer the goods to a London-bound plane.

Between Belém and New York, the plane was to make four stops. My hope was that more Americans would board and that they could give me a hand. Reaching out to them would not be something an introvert would normally do. But neither was reaching out to women, and I needed the practice.

At Paramaribo, Dutch Guiana, only a handful of people got on, all of them speaking Dutch. But at Georgetown, British Guiana, a flood of English-speakers joined the flight and I started to look for likely help.

Just after we took off for Trinidad, our next stop, I heard a young man behind me speaking to a girl in English. I looked between the seats and was floored to see that he had a ticket for London laid out on his lap. I could not believe such luck, and inside of five minutes I was explaining my problem to him. Stylish and debonair with a goatee and tinted glasses, he was a British Guiana resident in his early twenties like me, on his way to study art in London. After only the scantiest bit of picture painting, he agreed to take the flask to England; I would hand it over to him later. Jubilant, I went back to my seat and began to relax, aware of the great concern I had developed for the welfare of that thermos bottle. I thought of the two Englishmen and was glad I was going to be able to deliver on my promise.

I slept through the stops in Trinidad and Barbados and tried to think of other things on the way to New York. But about an hour before landing, it occurred to me that Howard, my cooperative friend, would likewise have to pass through US customs even though he was merely in transit to a London plane two hours later. I decided to take the thing through customs myself, since I could explain more than he could about the blood sample, and we agreed that after we touched down at JFK airport and the flask was safely through, we would meet and I would hand it over to him.

Despite my bravado the night before, I began to get worried as I put my suitcase, duffel bag, and two guitars on the display table for customs inspection. I placed the thermos bottle innocently in the middle of the whole pile, knowing well that my best hope for success was in keeping the contents unknown to the inspecting officer. I was going to have enough trouble with the collection of curious biological souvenirs in my duffel bag—a coiled, stuffed rattlesnake and the hairy skin of a wild Amazonian boar—and began to fear the discovery of a test tube of blood containing virulent malaria parasites would be enough to try the officer's patience.

Unexpectedly, the inspector became the least of my problems. Howard was in line directly behind me, and just as I was opening my suitcase, he was informed that as a transient he did not have to go through inspection after all. So much for my expertise about the procedures at a point of entry! Quickly, silently, Howard was gone before I could turn my head to agree on a meeting place.

That was strike one.

The officer gently pawed through some of my belongings. I was nervous, searching for Howard in the crowd across the vast room, then watching the officer's hands glide back and forth past the thermos bottle between my suitcase and duffel bag. My forehead was cool with sweat.

Evidently the duffel bag served as a decoy, for the officer never touched my precious flask. He ended the search suddenly and cheerfully, moving on to another passenger before I was fully aware that I was free to go. Hastily, I pulled my things together and called a redcap. I ran into the main lobby of the Pan Am arrival terminal and searched frantically for Howard.

My heart pounded in my ears. All I had to do was find him, but he was nowhere. Pan Am told me his flight was to leave in one hour, and that it was the last flight to London until the following morning. I had him paged, and then when nothing came of it, I put my baggage on a pushcart and searched the lobby for fifteen minutes.

Another talk with Pan Am had me struggling with the pushcart outside, in the dark, making my way to the departure terminal two blocks away; he had to be there. Nervous and frustrated, I entered a new crush of people after a slapstick trip of falling guitars and suitcases and was in no mood for face-searching. I parked the cart in a corner, and recklessly abandoned it to run to the departure gate with the flask. After a minute, I spotted a woman I recognized as Howard's mother. Surprisingly young-looking despite a dowdy flower-pattern dress, she seemed intelligent and capable of reason.

My nerves were so frayed by this time that I changed from depression to over-exuberance. I nearly trampled the woman in asking for Howard.

I had done it. I had succeeded after so many heart-pulling worries, and I began to feel weak throughout my body.

"Howard is about," she said with a clipped British accent. She looked at me from top to bottom. "What do you want with him?"

Distraught, looking over her shoulder and around the room, I mumbled something unfortunate about "blood" and "malaria" and "your son," not even seeing the look of horror that came over her face. I stopped myself for a moment and fixed my eyes on hers, then closed mine tight as I gritted my teeth at my own stupidity.

That was strike two.

I spent half an hour with her, pleading, explaining, even begging, but it did no good. Pan Am told her it was legal, even though an employee could be fired for taking the flask. I told her it was legal, recounting my own trip four times and showing her the letter twice. Howard reappeared just then and told her it was legal, reminding her that he had been through London customs many times with many strange things. She reminded him that she was a worrier and had never been happy with that behavior of his. Time came for their departure, and they left without the blood.

In subdued fury—more at myself than at Howard and his mother—I turned my back and returned to my luggage cart to pout. I sat down in a corner and cradled the flask in one arm. Sweat dribbled down my face. I felt protective of the little bottle nobody wanted. Tenderly, I opened it to see how it was doing, and found the test tube surrounded by a pitiful slush of melted ice.

Not even considering that I had absolutely no way to get the thing to London, I slowly picked myself up and with my cart took an elevator up to a coffee shop on the second floor to get some fresh ice. The waitress looked at me with frightened curiosity, but I hardly noticed, gently packing individual cubes around the red test tube.

On my way back downstairs, I had a flash of an idea. I ran outside with my luggage cart to hail a cab. There was a chance, just a chance, that another airline, British Overseas Airways Corporation (BOAC), would have a flight that evening. Already twenty-six hours were gone, and unless the thermos bottle got out that night, the doctor in London would have very little time to examine the sample. I was sick of explaining and wheedling, and decided to try the air freight office of the airline for help. My thought processes were so clouded that this had not even occurred to me before. If they could ship the thing out right away, I would gladly pay for it. If they could not, that would be strike three and my foray into risk would be a failure.

Typical of the day's ups and downs, as soon as I arrived at BOAC, I hit the jackpot. Not only did the airline have a flight in three hours, but they could also reverse the charges to the hospital and have the flask shipped as life-and-death cargo. It would arrive in London the next morning, and word would be rushed to the hospital immediately with the same British thoroughness and calm that had gotten me into this mess in the first place. It also ended up saving the day.

Tremendously relieved that the blood would get there in time, I patted my little thermos bottle good-bye, hailed a cab out in the street, slapped the driver on the back, and collapsed in his taxi for a ride out to my cousin Angie's brownstone in Brooklyn.

I never learned whether the flask got there in time, or if it helped the doctors come up with a cure for the drug-resistant mutation of malaria that the blood contained. But I had done my part and had overcome all the odds. I took subconscious comfort in knowing that if I ever needed to take a big risk again, I was qualified to do so.

At the same time, I had the uncomfortable feeling that next time my risk-taking might not have such a happy ending. I had succeeded here only because somebody else's process—the BOAC's—had taken over when I floundered.

WHAT I COULD HAVE DONE DIFFERENTLY

Because I had triumphed by being methodical in getting the blood to London, my reliance on the recipe had now increased to the point of overconfidence. It would have served me better to refuse the researchers' request. I would have avoided reinforcing a behavior pattern, one driven by my winning recipe, which later would cause me untold pain.

Takeaways from Chapter 3

1. When the recipe succeeds in doing something it was not designed for, such as neutralizing your natural risk aversion and achieving a difficult end, it can make you feel invincible. That is a highly dangerous illusion.

2. Recklessness is a dangerous drug, especially for introverts. When I agreed to take the blood sample to New York, I saw myself as an actor in a movie: an exotic city in the Amazon, jungle-stained Brits seeking a cure for a new strain of malaria, a cautious young American seeking to live more fully by taking a risk. The emotional high set me up later for a risk that I'd wish I had never taken.

3. In our society, risk aversion is a gift. One of the core advantages of being an introvert is that you naturally are able to see through specious arguments about how everything will work out. Stay risk averse, and you help to restore a bit of balance to society.

Reflective Questions

1. Recall a time when your winning recipe led you to take a reckless action. How did your recipe cause you to suppress your normal risk aversion?

2. What unintended consequences flowed from your taking that risk? Did they encourage or discourage you from doing it again?

3. What conclusion did you draw from the experience after it was all over?

Practical Exercises

1. **The Recipe Override:** Write down a risky action that you are considering. Then write down how you would approach it if you were overriding your recipe instead of disregarding your natural risk aversion.

2. **The Risk Timeline:** Write down three significant decisions in the past where you ignored the risks (for example, a financial gamble, an impulsive career change, a dangerous relationship). What was the outcome in each case?

3. **The Gut Check:** Recall a time when your gut told you not to take a risk, and you went ahead anyway. Was your recipe the reason? What was the result?

~

More than fifty years after my return to the US from Brazil, I had the stunning realization that I had been deeply confused about my whole relationship with Sofia, and my recipe was the cause. It prevented me from focusing on whether she was the right girl for me, and instead caused me to put my attention on the process of speaking Portuguese with her. I got hung up on her choice of words, leading me to a complete misunderstanding of what she was really saying.

Soon after I left Brazil, Sofia gave me the opportunity to discover my mistake. But I would not take advantage of it until many decades had passed.

4

Confusion:
Tropical Legacies

SEPTEMBER 1964. LOS ANGELES, CALIFORNIA. A few days after my return to the States, I flew from New York to LA. Dad was there to greet me at the airport as he always was, without fail, whenever I returned from a trip.

Dressed in a cashmere sport jacket and fruit boots—which in the mid-sixties did not refer to rollerblades but to soft leather shoes that came up around the ankle—he looked casual and elegant. We took my luggage to the curb, and I waited for him while he went to get the car.

Fig. 3. Experiencing saudade—*longing Los Angeles International Airport, 1964.*

It was late afternoon. Even though the terminal was less than a mile from the Pacific, I could smell the city smog. I looked along the vast expanse of curb in front of me and saw a parade of people being picked up and dropped off.

As I stood there, it occurred to me that for someone who lived in his head so much of the time, prone to analyzing everything down to the last detail, I also had a deeply emotional side. It drove me to seek love and affection from girls in hopes of finding a lasting relationship. But too often it also drove me to think of the past with pangs of sadness.

That was happening now. I plunged into sorrow that would last for weeks. The Brazilians had a poignant word for it: *saudade* (sow-DA-gee), a melancholy longing for what had been in the past and now was no more. The song that Sofia and I first danced to was about *saudade*, and now it had me in its grip.

I spent the first five days at home in the Van Nuys suburb where my parents lived. What little I had to do, namely unpacking, was precisely the thing that brought my mind to Sofia's doorstep time after time. I kept finding little things that she had given me: a rock we kicked along Copacabana beach for half a mile late one night, a toothpick she broke in half to make peace with me after an unkind remark.

I talked to my parents about the trip. Doing so caused the difficulties I had with Sofia to move into the background and the good times to stand out much more than they had at the time. Sofia started to appear in my dreams at night. When she was right at hand in Rio, I did not once have those dreams.

In longing for her, I gathered all the beauty and warmth that I found in Rio and put it into her face. She was now the incarnation of the seven happiest weeks of my life, and my feelings for her grew stronger every time I thought about her.

That September, I returned to Stanford to begin my senior year. I had hoped to break free of my melancholy, but once I smelled the eucalyptus and asphalt that filled the air with a distinctively Stanford aroma, I felt even more remorse at what I had left behind.

~

Sofia's first letter reached me a few days later on October 1, 1964. Hoping for some joy to lift my spirits, I instead found five pages of heart-break. Her words were quiet, so quiet that I could barely hear her voice as I read the Portuguese, but so touching that they exposed the depth of my feeling for her.

To her I was not cold and aloof, or mentally and emotionally stunted, or a bungling and inexperienced foreigner who failed to communicate, but the man she now realized she was in love with. This made me put aside my previous hesitations and brought me great happiness, but also a sense of devastation that she recognized her feelings only now. She could well have been an intimate partner. And maybe after she got to know me better, she would not be so intrusive in her intellectual probing and thereby allow me to feel more secure around her.

Sofia's letter drove me out of my mind. Each time I read it I was in Rio, seeing her close to me and hearing her voice. Then I would look up and find my dorm room staring at me. This could be the kind of relation-ship I had always wanted, but now I would never be able to experience it. I wondered if there was a Portuguese word that described the top of the scale of *saudade*, because that was where I was.

Why did I rush off from Rio when even one more day with Sofia might have allowed the love she expressed now to blossom between us? It could have changed everything. But that universe had closed itself to us now. Given my commitment to graduating from Stanford with honors—driven by my obsession with a whole suite of study processes—reopening my relationship with Sofia was unthinkable.

Or so I thought. When I was the saddest, I went up to San Francisco to have dinner with Mom and Dad, who were in town for one of Dad's recording sessions. Both wore their city-by-the-bay finest, Dad in a coat and tie and Mom in a dark dress with a sparkling pin on the front. I expected to hear them say they were proud of me for enduring this as well as I was and give me advice on how to hold on until things passed.

"You know," Dad said, "years ago before Mom and I met, we both went through the same kind of thing you are going through now."

Mom nodded. "It was excruciating. It's so hard for us to see you like this."

"What we want to say is to stop thinking that the situation is hopeless," Dad said. "Rio is only twelve hours away, and you could be there any time you wanted."

If I truly chose her, then she and I would end up together, they said. If she was the girl for me, then they would make sacrifices to help eliminate the distance between us.

My head spun. Over the years, they had given me valuable advice about my girl problems but nothing as specific or as well-timed as this. In retrospect, I marvel at how deeply and consistently they always supported me, given that they often did not understand me. I was utterly different, the only introvert and scholar in the family. The other four were or had been performers: Dad, a big band musician; Mom, a dancer; and my two sisters, actors. Yet whenever their loner son needed help, they were right there to provide it.

Their support, and especially their coaching to change the way I was thinking about the situation, gradually made life more tolerable for me. Sofia was still in the forefront of my mind and emotions. Now when I thought of her, I no longer shrouded myself in blackness.

Still, I took no action on their offer. I was committed to finishing Stanford, graduating from Reserve Officers' Training Corps, and accepting a commission as a second lieutenant in the army. Right after college, I was likely to be drafted as an enlisted man, and getting a commission was the safest option. I could be sent to Southeast Asia, and it would be far less risky to serve there as an officer.

~

In late October, I received a letter from Ana Maria, the university president's daughter.

She was alone in her parents' big house among people with whom she had little communication. I saw her missing the joy of having me as a trusted companion in word and song for so many days, picturing her passing by my vacant room with the knot in her throat and the tears in her eyes that she so vividly described in her letter. My heart went out to her as I read through each line of her sad and labored text.

I was overjoyed that she thought so highly of me, that I had made such a deeply positive impression on her, and that her daily routine had centered on me far more than I had known at the time. I was flattered that such an attractive and intelligent young woman would write such a touching letter so many days after I left Rio. She said she and her family planned to come to the US in six months and hoped to see me then.

~

I did not hear from Sofia again until December, more than two months after her previous letter. I was beginning to wonder if the present had captivated her, but when her next letter arrived, I learned that, if anything, her feelings for me had intensified.

She said she felt overwhelmed by the card and flowers I had sent for her birthday; until they reached her, she had been sad and alone, surrounded by unsatisfying and insipid people. In that, she was like Ana Maria, who had made a similar comment about her own life. In retrospect, this helps me to see why both girls might have been so interested in me. My impression of most men back then was that they rarely listened to women or showed them much respect, and here this gringo was, consistently doing both.

Sofia felt this year was particularly significant for her development and had accorded me a place in her pantheon that was at least as high as the one I accorded her in mine. She said she loved me sweetly and gently and was sorry for the terrible heartbreak I had gone through over our separation. Even though I could not hold her close to me, I was happy at the thought that such a girl even existed, and that I meant so much to her. Our full and open self-expression had drawn us closer than ever before.

One morning in January 1965, I bounded up the flights of stairs to my dorm room with another letter from Sofia in my hand, its familiar scent filling me with anticipation. The sun outside was bright and LBJ had just proclaimed the hugely optimistic Great Society in his State of the Union address. Something new called Medicare would be available for seniors. There would be money for a Teacher Corps, a Head Start program for children, new housing, mass transit, and a slew of other initiatives that made me proud to be an American.

I hoped Sofia's letter would bring good news about the upcoming trip to California that she mentioned in her last letter, but as I eagerly scanned, I realized she was not coming. She had planned to travel with Ana Maria and her family, whom she had met and did not know well, but they had postponed their trip from the spring to six months later in the fall. She knew that by that time I would be in the army and stationed at a base who knew where. Sofia's parents would not let her travel alone, so she could not come sooner. The blow hit me hard.

In the months afterward, life intruded on us both and we wrote less and less often.

~

Although Sofia never came, Ana Maria did arrive, but not in the six months she'd promised. For the next year we exchanged letters, cards, and little gifts. Each time I heard from her, she was warmer and more tender than the time before.

When Ana Maria finally did travel, it was September 1965 and I was already in army officer boot camp at Fort Benning, Georgia. She and her parents were in California and managed to get a call through to me at the base.

Over the phone, all three of them sent me an outpouring of emotion that I did not expect after the passing of a year since I left Rio. In came a flood of love and kindness that I hardly knew how to integrate into the Spartan military atmosphere I was living in.

The sincerity, the genuineness and wholeness of the emotions that the entire family expressed, moved me. All, and especially Ana Maria, were unequivocal in their praise and expressions of love, warm and approving of all that I was and had done. They gave of themselves in a way and at a time that meant more to me than they could have known. It was as if the cultural differences between us were a filter, a screen shutting out any impurities of feeling. Only the most constructive, the most joyful and warm emotions passed through in either direction.

"Ben, I miss you!" Ana Maria said over the phone. "I am so sorry we are near your home, and you are so far away!"

"I am too, Ana Maria. I'd give anything to be able to give you a hug right now!"

It was ironic that Ana Maria was now free of the constraints that had kept me away from her in Brazil. The cultural exchange program was long over, so there was no longer any risk of breaking program rules. Her parents were far more welcoming and accepting of me than they had been when I was staying in their home. I did not know if her boyfriend Bruno was still in the picture, but she herself was reaching out with emotions stronger than anything she had allowed herself to express in Rio except on that last night. All of this affected my heart, and in the quiet of the night at Fort Benning, I saw her smiling face and long, dark blond hair. I asked myself whether I should reconsider and seek to find with her the love I had been looking for with Sofia.

I did not realize it at the time, but the flaw in my winning recipe—its automatic shift in my focus from the character of the girl I was with to a step-by-step process that had me focusing on music—had appeared again in my pursuit of Ana Maria. My winning recipe had attracted another girl like Anabela back in LA—one with a controlling behavioral style who would not have been right for me. Ana Maria tried to dominate her parents. She was haughty with servants like the rector's driver, Wilson. She laced into our Brazilian student hosts when they played a prank on me at the Cabo Frio beach house where we all once stayed. Plus, due to her class position in Brazil, she was used to a lifestyle with servants, something I would never want.

The music-learning process with Ana Maria did work to redirect the energy toward music and away from a growing attraction between us, so in that sense, it was a success. But in the end, we were attracted to each other anyway. I was so caught up in learning the steps to play Brazilian music I naively missed seeing that spending so much time with her might lead to complications—such as her possibly becoming less interested in Bruno than in me.

With Ana Maria, I learned that no amount of distraction provided by a winning recipe—the music process in this case—could prevent an inappropriate attraction from developing. Back then, I was too young to see that this had happened because I was trying to use the recipe in the wrong area of life. More than ever, I was committed to finding someone I could experience satisfaction and safety with by sharing intimate feelings and thoughts. But I still had not learned that trying to use a process to do so would be a problem.

After the phone call, the emotional disruptions from fear that I faced in the army training became unprecedented, as I will discuss in Chapter 7. Those nighttime thoughts about Ana Maria quickly vanished, and I never had contact with her again.

～

In November 1965, two months after I got the phone call from Ana Maria and her family, I received another letter from Sofia. Her brief note exposed a misunderstanding that had characterized a good part of our relations. It was not until that letter that I fully understood what her choice of words meant when she had described our tie as one of "friendship."

"I wonder if perhaps the language got in the way when we were together in Rio," she wrote in Portuguese. "I used the word *colegas* to describe us."

She was right—she had studiously avoided the word *amigos*, the usual word for "friends," and instead used *colegas*.

"*Coleguismo*," she continued, "means camaraderie and spiritual rapport. That is what we have. I meant it to be used in opposition to simple friendship, but in Rio I think maybe you took me to mean the reverse, namely friendship in the normal sense."

She was right. Given my growing feelings for her, I had been upset at being just a "friend." But I now saw she had elevated my tie to her as *coleguismo*, a much higher place. In all those walks on Copacabana beach, I had totally misread her intent. Where she thought of me as a partner in spirit, I assumed she was thinking of me as an ordinary friend. Relying on my recipe—hiding my introversion behind my enthusiasm for communicating in a foreign language—ended up causing me to misunderstand what Sofia was really trying to say.

Writing this now, over half a century later, I'm stricken by two additional insights. First, for years I held *her* to be the one largely responsible for the relationship going nowhere at the start—I wanted it, but in Rio she held back by wanting to be just "friends." Now I see my responsibility was huge. At the time, I was too immature to just accept what she was saying. Instead I resisted, and it made things much worse than they would have been otherwise. I could have laughed off the "friendship" conversations and let them go away on their own.

Which brings up the second realization, an even deeper one: When she kept insisting on being *colegas*, she was probably directing those words not at me, but at *herself*. In her very first letter after I left Brazil, she said with great eloquence that she loved me. To me, that suggests in Rio she was fighting the growing love she felt by insisting on friendship, then caved in after I was gone when she first sat down to write.

By the time I got that latest letter, I had finished with the required infantry training for intelligence officers at Fort Benning and was now at the Army Intelligence School in Baltimore. Sofia simply was not an available choice. I had to complete my two years of military service and after that intended to go on to graduate business school. So, for reasons of mental and emotional health, I pushed her into the realm of fantasy. There was no happiness to gain by deeper feelings now. I could not have her, so I began to tell myself that I did not want her.

Like Ana Maria, Sofia was used to an upper-class lifestyle that I would never want to adopt. More importantly, my youthful infatuation with her after I left Rio made me forget how unsafe I had felt around her when I was there. Her scrutiny of me was so penetrating it made me uncomfortable. Being near that kind of energy for years would not have been particularly healthy or much fun.

However, Sofia was still delightful to contemplate, and I expected I would think about her whenever great periods of happiness were triggered in my memory. But until I could do something about her, she would have to stay where she was, floating in a pleasant daydream.

I had fallen harder for Sofia than for anyone before, but time had proven that a Portuguese-speaking woman—for me—did not work. This third time, the language had helped me to be less of an introvert and brought me love, far more than I had ever hoped for. But it had again produced only delayed success and now revealed a new flaw: a problem in the approach itself. The mechanics of the language had killed a promising relationship because I had misunderstood Sofia's meaning.

I have no record that after November 1965 she ever wrote me again.

~

Decades later, I was glad to learn that Ana Maria had become a published author and prizewinning professor of philosophy at a university in Brazil. By the time she was in her early seventies, she had three children and nine grandchildren.

Sofia became a clinical psychologist, married a civil engineer, and by her seventies had two sons and two grandchildren. Someday in the far, far distant future there would indeed be a slender, sweet, and insightful woman for me to share my life with. But her name would not be Sofia.

~

In retrospect, Portuguese had served me well. It compensated for my quiet nature and lack of boldness when approaching women.

But Portuguese as an approach was clunky. It could be used only with women who spoke little or no English. The results it produced were always delayed—two and a half years in the case of Anabela, thirteen months for Ana Maria, and eight weeks for Sofia. And it had the flaw of always creating unintended consequences that produced little safety or satisfaction. All three times it had attracted girls who were not right for me in some way, and in the last case it had killed off the most promising prospect of the three.

Processes are about achieving things, not about building relationships. Had I thought about it, I would have seen how obvious that was. As a ten-year-old, I had formulated my first series of steps precisely to get a result *without* having to focus on people too much.

WHAT I COULD HAVE DONE DIFFERENTLY

With Ana Maria I could probably have guessed that being in close daily contact with her through music was not the best way to put distance between us. And with Sofia I could have been more curious about the difference between *amigos* and *colegas*. But that would just have led me into a deeper relationship with Sofia while I was still in Brazil, and we were too different from each other to last. So it was good that I did not act on my parents' offer to fly me back to Brazil. In time I came to realize that both girls were inappropriate for me.

Takeaways from Chapter 4

1. Your recipe is not about facilitating relationships. It is about avoiding people so as not to become overstimulated. Because when you're overstimulated, you suffer mentally—from cognitive overload, decision fatigue, self-doubt, and a "shut-down"

mode that makes it hard to think. You also endure emotional symptoms such as irritability, anxiety, dread of more stimulation, and numbness. And there are physical issues such as fatigue, headaches, tense muscles, and extreme sensitivity to light and sound.

2. Recipes almost always sow confusion, especially in relationships. We tend to focus on the formula more than on how to relate to other people.

3. Even when the confusion is cleared up, be careful about jumping into action. It turned out that Sofia loved me after all, but she would not have worked for me as a life partner.

Reflective Questions

1. Does your recipe tend to put distance between you and other people? If it does, then it is working exactly as you designed it.

2. What confusion have you experienced recently in a personal or professional relationship? In what way did your recipe contribute to that?

3. If you had acted authentically as an introvert, instead of artificially through your recipe, how could you have avoided that confusion? Could it have simplified things so that you achieved more clarity than you did?

Practical Exercises

1. Think of a relationship or workplace issue that you frequently deal with. Write down three ways that your recipe tends to make the problem worse because it isolates you from others.

2. Imagine that you respond to the confusion in Reflective Question
2 in a way that does not involve your recipe. For example, if
"being powerful," "being laid-back," "being mature," or "being
serious" is your recipe, try to step outside of that pattern and do
something different when responding to the confusion. Write
down how that might help to clear things up.

3. Recall the last time something you were puzzled about got
resolved. Write down whether you were then tempted to jump
into action, or stepped back for a minute to see if that was really
the right solution. Note the result.

~

Two months after returning to California from Brazil, I was so lonely
that I could not think clearly. My long-distance contacts with Ana Maria
and Sofia were still alive, but when I saw the chance to be involved with
another girl, this time an American at Stanford, I jumped at it.

5

Overconfidence:
A Bipolar Connection

NOVEMBER 1964. STANFORD, CALIFORNIA. The wonderful summer days in Rio were receding into the background. One night as the cold rain tapped against my window, I sat in my room at Stern Hall and noticed my emotions for Sofia had settled into a dull ache.

I was lonely and still so inexperienced in love that as soon as a new girl appeared, I leapt into pursuing her. I had left Brazil just eight weeks before and felt strangely confident in taking the risk of approaching her.

Her name was Roberta Jones and she was a freshman from Ohio. Five feet five inches tall, she was a little withdrawn herself—sweet, kind, serious, and intense in conversation. I was attracted to her because I thought she might be a fellow introvert. She appeared to be mature, conscientious, and fun—everything I was looking for. Plus, she was luscious and affectionate, just the thing to assuage my loneliness, I thought. After several dates, her warm lips and engaging talk made me hope I had found another Sofia, especially now that I was not willing to upend my life to go back to Brazil for the real one.

Yet I could not have been more wrong. Roberta was a volcano of hidden emotions that quickly surfaced.

The first indication of trouble came ten days after I met her. She had disappeared, so I called her dorm.

"She went to San Rafael," said Wendy, her roommate. "She put herself on a bus."

"What? Why?" San Rafael was in Marin County, an affluent area across the Golden Gate Bridge just north of San Francisco.

"She has relatives up there. She was confused and couldn't stand being on campus for another second."

That did not sound good. Neither was the news that Roberta was not going home to her parents, but to her aunt and uncle. She had told me she had not seen her parents in five months, and that she was not close to her mother's Bay Area sister and husband either.

A few days later she was back, seemingly better. I took her to a party at the Lake Lagunita boathouse where my former roommate Jeff Henderson lived. He asked me to bring my guitar, so I did and sang "Meditation," a popular bossa nova tune by Antonio Carlos Jobim that Ana Maria had taught me. Roberta loved it. Afterward she rewarded me with lots of kisses and hugs, and a warm, subdued tenderness when I pressed her to me.

Later that week, I flew home to LA for Thanksgiving where I took long walks around the neighborhood in the warm evenings. As I watched the twinkling lights on the mountains above the San Fernando Valley, I took stock of what I knew about Roberta. She had been educated in England and traveled all over Europe and America with her aunt and uncle before arriving at Stanford. They gave her many material things, but during those years she had suffered from uncertainty and unhappiness. Starving for companionship and guidance, she turned to the Mormon Church, of which her relatives were members. She rejected most of the dogma but got some comfort from the sense of community it offered her.

When I got back to Stanford after Thanksgiving, I learned that Roberta had attempted suicide. After she failed and an ambulance had taken her to a hospital, she descended into a catatonic state, withdrawn so far into herself that she neither spoke, recognized speech, nor moved. I rushed to the hospital with her roommate, but because Roberta's condition was so critical, they would allow no one to see her for an indefinite time.

Attempted suicide and nervous collapse were blatant signs that she was dangerously ill. Still, I did not walk away—just the opposite. I took it upon myself to save her, to "fix" her with a recipe-induced, step-by-step process of loving her and giving her the support and care that she obviously needed. I had lost Sofia because I left Rio too soon. I was not going to lose Roberta by giving up now and making the same mistake.

However, I failed to understand just how severe Roberta's mental illness was. My hubris had me believing that I had the ability to use a process of loving attention to simply encourage her to be okay, when, in reality, Roberta needed professional help. Heavily influencing my passion to hang on to her was the powerful lesson I had learned just two months before with the Brazilian blood sample. It showed me that I could succeed at a difficult task if I was willing to take a risk and keep going no matter what.

On the fourth day of her catatonia, she woke up, but her mother arrived from Ohio and whisked her away to Toledo before I or anyone else could get into the hospital.

The sensible thing for me to do at that point would have been to let go of her, but I could not. Instead, I became angry that the very people who were probably the most responsible for Roberta's mental and emotional condition, namely her mother and stepfather, were now in charge of caring for her.

At age twenty-one, I had a dangerously inflated opinion of my own ability to help her. I had no idea that she was mentally ill, suffering from what today we would call bipolar disorder. That condition did not appear in the *Diagnostic and Statistical Manual of Mental Disorders* of the American Psychiatric Association until 1980, some sixteen years later. People with the disorder cycle through bouts of lows and highs, depression and mania of various intensities, with the cycles lasting anywhere from hours or days to weeks or even many months. Roberta tried to kill herself most likely during a prolonged period of severe depression and breakdown. It ended up lasting two months, from November through December 1964.

I knew none of this at the time, only that she was sweet and I thought all she needed was the kind of love I could provide. This made me forget everything I knew about how my recipe could cause problems in relationships. Instead, I was ready to launch a new one designed to rescue her. I would coach her, give her love and attention, and, through the example of my positive outlook, would help her to get well. This conveniently allowed me to avoid taking an honest look at her illness and thereby avoid realizing she needed the kind of help only a trained psychiatrist could provide.

The successful outcome of my risky adventure with the Brazilian blood sample had left me naive and overconfident, and through my recipe, I sought to help in the only way I knew how. It made me supremely certain that by caring for her in a patient, methodical way I could overcome any obstacle. I resolved that if she were only to reach out to me I would rush to save her.

She did so in January, saying in a call from Ohio that she had recovered. It would have been more accurate to say she had cycled from depression into the beginnings of a manic phase, but at the time I did not know such distinctions existed. She said I was the first person she thought of when she came to and was the first one she had written to.

Yet just as with Sofia, a girl was becoming attracted not to me but to the shell of a winning recipe I had presented to her. I took her call to mean that she saw me as being just who she needed—someone who could rescue her. But in that role, I was not authentic. Rescuing her required not only medical expertise that I did not have, but also a high degree of extroversion to cope with the manic phase she soon would be cycling into.

~

I went into overtime figuring out how I could get myself to Toledo to see her over the upcoming spring break. On the morning of my train departure, March 18, I went into the Student Union for some breakfast. The newspapers for sale at the door had headlines about a huge civil rights march from Selma to Montgomery, Alabama, but I was too excited about my trip to read about it.

When I arrived in Toledo, a bit dazed and depleted from the long trip, I found that Roberta was rebuilding her life in possibly one of the bleakest environments possible—a crowded apartment in a cold, industrial city. She had created her own world of happiness at the University of Toledo by using her persuasive talents to open doors.

Each day she took us through a full round of activities in the courses she was taking in math, literature, and music. The prestige of Stanford went a long way in Toledo, and she showed great skill at saying she had spent time there and at my being a senior there. Bright, optimistic, and analytical, Roberta had cheerful and animated expressions on her face that, by contrast, made the people around her seem colorless.

I had never seen her like this. Years later, I learned about type II bipolar disorder and realized that was likely what Roberta had been suffering from. Type II was more common in women than in men and did not consist of full-on mania. Instead, it entailed "hypomania"—a high energy level, impulsiveness, and an extremely excited state, exactly what I was observing without seeing it for what it was.

I did begin to get uncomfortable with the negative gestures, facial expressions, and words that sometimes tumbled out of her. In the heat of argument, her eyes blazed with hatred, but I rationalized that they only reflected her passion. When I mentioned this, she encouraged me to grow up and learn to deal with her intensity. She convinced me that I needed to become more of an adult.

~

The morning after I got back to Stanford, I stood in the lobby of my dorm house and used my mailbox key to raise the thin, squeaky plate that covered the slot under my name. The brilliant sun outside was such a contrast to Toledo that it filled me with joy, but that was nothing compared with my elation over what I found in the box.

Starting that day, Roberta sent me a steady barrage of letters, phone calls, cards, tapes, and pictures. She said she loved me and found so many ways to communicate it that she overwhelmed my heart. Rather than seeing her excessive behavior as a sign of instability, I used it to wipe away the memory of the petty conflicts and worries I had endured with her in Toledo.

In one of her letters, she reported that she planned to arrive in late June and needed a cheap place to stay, so I began working on it. I asked if she would be willing to come earlier in the month, since I would be going into the army in July. I was overjoyed when she said yes, she could come in early June.

I succeeded brilliantly in finding Roberta a place to stay—the same house where I would be living in the few weeks between graduation and my induction into the army. It was at the thirty-room mansion on Jackson Street in San Francisco that belonged to the family of Drew Faulkner, a former Stanford roommate of mine. Drew and I were still friends, and when he learned a few weeks earlier that I needed a place to live before going into the army, he kindly offered up the roomy basement apartment in the building. When Roberta's need for lodging came up, I went back to him to see if there could be a room for her as well, and—after talking to his mother—he said they would be happy to help.

Drew's father had made a fortune in the mining business in Peru. While he was rarely around, his wife was a leading community organizer in the city and kept a constant parade of fascinating people coming through the house for dinners and parties. I knew the stimulating environment would be to Roberta's liking, so I was happy to tell her about the arrangement.

However, so many unexpected twists occurred in our relationship between securing lodging for her and her arrival that by the time her train pulled into Oakland on June 5, 1965, I was tentative. Despite the initial torrent of letters, I saw that the time apart since Toledo had caused some backsliding in our rapport. But I was not prepared for what happened next.

Two days after her return, we met on campus and stood next to the dry bed of Lake Lagunita, not far from the boathouse where months earlier I had sung "Meditation" for her. I looked out to where there should have been water and saw only weeds.

"You know," she said, "in Toledo I had virtually no choice. You were the only desirable guy in my life at that point. Something very rapid occurred within both of us."

I did not like where this was going.

"But time has diluted the feelings on both sides, and I'm now in a wonderful world which offers me opportunities at every turn, even in love."

"So what are you saying?"

"Well," she said, "you can expect neither rapid developments nor single-minded attention from me."

In retrospect it is hard to believe that she spoke in such stilted language, but that was exactly what she said. She meant our relationship was not going to get any better, and the reason would be her focus on other things, presumably other men. In her voice there was no apology and quite a bit of condescension.

If I needed any further proof that I could not trust her judgment or stability, that was it. Once again, incredibly, I ignored it. I had invested in her for so many months that I could not turn and walk away. Instead, I regrouped and told myself part of the rescue process had to include her freedom. It made sense not to pollute the relationship with a sense of obligation. Even though I was dying inside, I felt magnanimous in dispelling her concerns.

~

On a brisk, sunny morning, predictably cool and breezy for early June in San Francisco, Roberta moved into a room on one of the upper floors of the mansion on Jackson Street. The house was perched on a hill, with some of its windows looking out on snippets of the blue waters of the bay.

For the moment, I was still at Stern Hall. "I Can't Get No Satisfaction" by the Rolling Stones had just been released and was in the air every-where. It was perhaps one of the greatest rock-and-roll songs of all time and perfectly encapsulated how I felt about my frustrating relationship with Roberta.

After her long convalescence and isolation in Ohio, Roberta seemed determined to embrace her life in California again with a frightening ven-geance. She talked about herself quite a bit, was supremely confident in her views or at least sounded like it, and proved herself to be a poor lis-tener. I knew and understood these traits in her, but others did not. People around her saw them as cover-ups for a case of anxious insecurity.

Communication between us became awkward and difficult. I wanted to talk things out with her but found myself inhibited for fear that I would forget something she had told me, and she would call me out on it.

I would ask, "Roberta, for Christ's sake, can we just sit down and talk?"

Her eyes would narrow as she shot me a stare of exasperation. "Don't ask me that. I already told you not to. Don't you remember that? Why do I have to keep reminding you?"

I was not used to having anyone talk to me like that, but I let it pass.

On June 15, ten days after Roberta's return, my Stanford graduation took place, and thanks to Reserve Officers' Training Corps, I was now a second lieutenant in the US Army. Soon after my family went back to LA, I stood in my dorm room, dazed. I looked through the window from tree to tree, realizing that for the first time in days, I was just a guy rather than a celebrated institution.

And I was not the vaunted rescuer I thought I would be by now, just someone coping with his own naivete. This whole situation was a sequel to the risk I had taken with the two Englishmen in Belém, and this time it was not ending well.

I soon moved into the basement at Jackson Street and was now sure of several things about Roberta. Her constant talking about herself was not something born of a desire to reestablish herself in California but was the sign of a desperately unsure self. What I took for a genuine expression of the fullness of life was simply a constant, feverish need for attention. My parents saw the red flags when they came to town for my graduation and refused to let Roberta and me babysit for my young sister, Nan.

I saw the deterioration of our relationship not as a result of her mental illness, but rather as a result of my exhaustion and failure to make it work. I had a deep, quiet confidence based on years of loving care from my parents and years of real achievement in the academic world. I wish I had seen sooner that there was no possibility of Roberta providing the sense of safety I wanted in a relationship.

~

By now, my friend Drew had moved into the house. He and Roberta soon became attracted to each other. I kept to myself, staying in the basement as much as possible.

It was oddly light and airy down there, since half windows peeked aboveground, and through them, I could see small parts of the bay below. The large room had the clutter of old furniture and a washer and dryer in it, but I had a comfortable twin bed in one corner and access to my own bathroom. I found a small space heater in a closet and used it to offset the cold that crept in even in June.

Late one night, soon after I moved in, I looked up from my bed through a half window and saw the stars. Ed White was up there. He had just made the first ever spacewalk, and his *Gemini IV* spacecraft was still circling the earth.

While I was trying to keep warm under the covers, I thought about how excruciating it was to watch the growing magnetism between Roberta and Drew at close range. I did not blame either of them; I just did not want to know anything about it. Yet soon it was obvious to me and everyone else in the house that the two of them were sleeping together, something Roberta and I had never done.

I thought of what might have been with Ana Maria, and especially with Sofia. They were so healthy, so stable, and, in comparison, had been so kind to me. In the end, I faced up to the tremendous extent of my self-delusion. I had created an entire world based on false premises and did not even know it until the whole structure collapsed.

Mrs. Faulkner, Drew's mother, brought me out of my gloom in an act of pure kindness and compassion. She had a solid grasp of the situation and cared about me enough to spend time talking through my problems. Her experience, warmth, and realistic approach helped me to get over Roberta.

A handsome and impeccably dressed woman in her late forties, Mrs. Faulkner was politically energetic, had a commanding presence, and spoke in a husky voice from years of smoking. She saw how much I had been hurt by Roberta's switch of affections from me to Drew, and she made not the slightest suggestion that I should be taking the whole thing more nobly. More importantly for my ego, she showed me the attraction between her son and Roberta would probably turn out to be one-sided. As soon as she said that, it helped me to remember that Drew, who was known around Stern Hall as "the Snake," was not satisfied with any one girl for long. He was just too busy. It was not about *if* but *when* Drew would dump her.

Mrs. Faulkner sat in an easy chair with a magnificent view of San Francisco Bay behind her and studied my face. "You're going to be fine, Ben. This will pass. I will help you."

I was wide open to more of Mrs. Faulkner's views. She pointed out that Roberta's mental illness was apparent. She was dangerously insecure and not being able to "handle" her or keep up with her mind were not shortcomings on my part. A quiet sense of contentment came over me as I realized how much I had respected my limits and maintained my integrity when I had refused to operate at Roberta's manic speed.

By mid-July, Roberta was deteriorating before everyone's eyes. At dinner with the family and the other residents, I looked across the table at her and saw a complexion blotched with dark areas of skin placed forebodingly at the corners of her mouth, under her eyes and below her nostrils. She said she had not been able to sleep well for days, so maybe that was the cause. She kept her face locked in a hard, cold stare—eyes wide open as if attacking an unseen object. She gobbled every meal as though she feared someone would steal it from her.

On July 16, I was ecstatic to leave Jackson Street for Fort Benning, Georgia, to begin active duty in the army. I was still corresponding with Ana Maria and Sofia, and after what I had just gone through with Roberta, I missed them both.

Six months later I learned from Jake Mayer, my good friend and traveling companion in Brazil, that Roberta had returned to Stanford in September but by December had dropped out again and was back in Toledo. That news was the last thing I ever heard about her. I hoped she was getting the psychiatric care that she needed.

Recently, I was sad to learn that thirty-two years later, in 1997, Mrs. Faulkner died a long and painful death in a Bay Area hospital due to emphysema. Only seventy-six years old when she passed away, she was one of the finest people I ever knew.

~

My winning recipe had now failed to bring me romantic success four times in a row.

Captivated by my early achievements with the recipe as a child, I kept coming back to the same strategy even when it stopped working. Twice I allowed it to seduce me into paying far more attention to processes—learning Portuguese with Anabela and learning Brazilian music with Ana Maria—than I did to the girl herself. And twice I fell into being inauthentic, projecting an outer shell that attracted Sofia as if I were a willing debater, and Roberta as a capable rescuer. Except when playing music with Ana Maria, I never felt safe with any of them. I was still alone.

At the time, I was not yet self-aware enough to realize it, but I must have felt that having someone else could help shield me from an extroverted world. If she were an intimate companion whom I trusted, we could face life's noise and commotion together. This might explain why I searched so devotedly in one relationship after another to have that person in my life.

As a child, I had created my winning recipe to help me feel safe in the world. My formula—being methodical by executing some kind of a process—had worked brilliantly in high school and college academics. But with women, it had ended up being a counterfeit and unsatisfying solution. Instead of bringing me the safety of a lasting relationship, it had turned out to be perhaps the greatest obstacle to finding one.

WHAT I COULD HAVE DONE DIFFERENTLY

In retrospect, it's obvious that I should have walked away from Roberta at the very beginning when she disappeared from school, and certainly when she slid into a catatonic trance. I would have avoided months of drama and pain.

Takeaways from Chapter 5

1. A recipe tends to succeed only in narrow domains. When it happens to do so elsewhere, it can make you tend to become overconfident—and in most cases, that is exactly the wrong lesson to draw.

2. Transferring the recipe's success from one area of life to another can be dangerous and ineffective. Success can swell your ego and cloud your judgment.

3. A successful recipe in a new domain can cause an introvert to become indiscriminately relentless—pursuing it to the point of exhaustion both where it works and where it does not.

Reflective Questions

1. In what ways has your recipe led you to become overconfident? Look for examples where it surprised you by succeeding beyond your expectations in a new area.

2. When you tried to transfer your recipe from one area of life to another, what was the long-term result?

3. In what way does your recipe make you relentless? Identify a behavior in which you are absolutely driven, and look underneath it to see if the recipe might be there.

Practical Exercises

1. Briefly note down an episode when your recipe succeeded in a new area, and you used the experience to become overconfident. What was the eventual cost?

2. Describe on paper an episode when your recipe failed in a new area, and what the failure ultimately cost you.

3. Write down a situation in which you were relentless in the execution of your recipe, even though it was not working. What happened, and what was the cost?

~

After four attempts, I was thoroughly disillusioned with my ability to find a life partner. I was ready to turn the page, and the US Army was the perfect place to do it.

Or so I thought. In reality, being in the service would bring me close to a woman who I believed was perfect for me. But in time events would prove otherwise.

6

Self-Deception: The Love of a Fellow Introvert

OCTOBER 1965. DUNDALK, MARYLAND. One cloudy afternoon, I moved into an apartment just outside of Baltimore with Les Gorman, a skinny and toothy second lieutenant I had met a few months earlier during officer basic training at Fort Benning, Georgia.

The crisp fall air brought a wonderful atmosphere of promise. Would it include meeting a girl? Possibly, because my cousin Angie in Brooklyn had done a lot to set the stage with one of her girlfriends at New York University. The girl, whose name was Ida Bergstrom, was so favorably disposed after a year of hearing about me that when I met her, I was relaxed despite having no process to lean on. I did not need to be extroverted to approach her. I could just be myself.

Ida had a pleasant, attractive face, a slim figure, and beautiful legs. She dressed in good taste and wore her hair long, so that while her femininity was not overpowering, it was unmistakable.

When I first saw her, I had no thunderbolt of chemical desire, but her gentle warmth soon grew on me. Ida was sure of herself, easygoing, and cheerful. She gave a picture of internal happiness that was contagious. She was warm and inviting, open to touch. It had been six months since I had anything physical to do with Roberta, so the slightest contact with Ida brought tremendous satisfaction.

Ida was as much of an introvert as I was. Neither of us was adept at playing games. We both had been hurt in the past and saw in each other a sympathetic companion who would not even know how to cause pain. I felt so wholesome in her presence.

~

I spent Thanksgiving 1965 with Ida at her parents' modest house on Lake Candlewood just outside Danbury, Connecticut. It was unfamiliar and marvelous; not since Brazil could I remember having been so careless of time.

In Ida, I had stumbled across just the kind of girl I now realized I valued. As a student of psychology, she had a deep and sincere concern for human life and a desire to discover her own answers about it. She was one of the most gentle and affectionate girls I had known, one highly sensitive to my moods and desires, one who could talk ethics or kiss and hold me at four in the morning, do something for me before I asked or get me to do something for her with a wordless request.

Despite all the positive signs that Ida was different, I felt myself pulling back. For days I tried to analyze my own feelings, to discover why such a girl did not have me in hand, but I drew a blank. The scars from Roberta ran deep—I would no longer let myself fall in love without an idea of what I was getting into.

Something gnawed at me, but I could not pinpoint it.

In the experiences with Anabela and Ana Maria, I was focused on the goal of getting or avoiding the girl—but my devotion to the process to achieve that end left me blind to whether the goal was worthy in the first place. That had prevented me from seeing how wrong either one would have been for me as a life partner.

I knew Ida had grown up in a world different from mine. Her family was steeped in reserved communications, conservative morals, and traditional religion. But now I am embarrassed to say it did not even occur to me that one day she might embrace all of that. I was so taken with the warm sense of shelter she provided that I did not filter out the possibility that she, like the others, might not be the person to spend my life with.

Instead, I believed that because we were young, we could overcome the way her parents had raised her.

A week after Thanksgiving, I lay in bed back in Baltimore scanning the dots of light on the ceiling that filtered through the curtains from the parking lot outside. I had written her and thought over her reply. Her letter, quiet and gentle, made me realize she was beginning to love me. She said she could sense how much I wanted to be near her, to hold her close to me. And she had asked herself, "What more can I give?"

Ever analytical, I read the letter many times and turned my concerns into a sequential process, ticking them off one by one. She was not the prettiest girl I had ever gotten close to, but Anabela taught me that external attractiveness counted for nothing. Internal beauty was what mattered, and Ida's was abundant. Ida was not the most talented girl I had ever met, but Ana Maria taught me that talent was no substitute for the kind of intimacy Ida repeatedly expressed. Neither was Ida the most analytical girl in my life, but Sofia taught me that analytics often just got in the way of love. Ida's thinking was clear and direct, and I respected her. Overall she was the anti-Roberta, someone of great stability and self-confidence who made me feel good about myself every time I was with her. She was the first girl I had ever been with who made me feel safe. I felt no need to protect myself from her in any way.

I saw my worries were phantoms. I started to sense there were no restraints, no faults, no shortcomings, no negative factors blocking the possibility of loving her. As soon as I let go of resistance, the love began to shine through. Lying in bed, I began to see all she had to give, and that she, too, was lonely and in search of a tender person to share life with. I cried tears of joy recognizing I had found someone so special that I no longer needed to keep looking for love.

Over the next few weeks, my devotion to Ida grew stronger each day, taking on new and deeper roots within me. A new Beatles song called "Michelle" ran endlessly through my head, with its poignant lyrics of repeatedly declared love.

~

After Christmas, I was back at Lake Candlewood. Looking down from the house, I could see that so far, there were no patches of ice around the shoreline that would signal the true arrival of winter.

Ida's parents, Leo and Kate, were good people. They worked hard and only wanted what was best for their four children, of whom Ida was the eldest. That said, a cultural divide separated us, one that was as wide as the gap between the beaches of California and the snows of Minnesota where they had been raised.

Of Swedish descent, Leo had a full head of white hair even though he was only in his forties. He was handsome, outwardly jovial, and inwardly aloof. Kate, perky and happy, looked very much like the future actor Meg Ryan in *When Harry Met Sally*. Kate had Finnish ancestors and often served fruit salad made with little marshmallows.

Immigrants from Scandinavia had heavily influenced the culture in the Minnesota where Leo and Kate grew up. People called it "Minnesota nice." On the plus side, it included reserved manners, gracious courtesy, and friendly politeness. On the minus side, it was truly—at its core— about keeping up appearances, and it could be exhausting pretending to be something no human actually was all the time.

When I walked in with Ida, I likely had three strikes against me. First, I grew up in liberal, anything-goes California, where people simply laughed at the somber attitudes of the Midwest. Second, I came from a family in show business, which went out of its way to ridicule the strictures of

Midwest thinking in a public and articulate way. And third, I was a soldier, potentially a love-'em-and-leave-'em Lothario who could ship out at any time. If Garrison Keillor of *A Prairie Home Companion* was to be believed years later, the conservative inhabitants of the Upper Midwest had a dark outlook on life: When things were going well, they knew that if they just waited a bit, surely things would get worse.

The Bergstroms' simple house on the hill overlooking Lake Candlewood was the only place Ida and I could be together, and that was a big deal. I lived in Baltimore, and she lived in New York City with a roommate in a women's dorm. It meant we could not have time alone together unless we were right under her parents' noses.

I wanted Ida to go back to Baltimore with me and brought it up at dinner.

"It will only be for two days, and I'll bring her right back," I explained.

Leo frowned. Kate grimaced. Looking down at the table, she said, "We don't think that is such a good idea, Ben. You hardly know each other."

With two short sentences she succeeded in keeping up appearances and putting me in my place. From their faces, I could see their position was firm.

We should not have been surprised at their refusal, but we were. Ida became wistful and sad. When I saw her sweet face with such a look of pain on it, my own sadness vanished. We retreated to the downstairs bedroom that belonged to her brother, who was away. I took her in my arms, talked softly to her, played the guitar, and sang to her for two hours. When I sang "The Twelfth of Never," a popular Johnny Mathis song, my eyes shone with tears.

~

The next morning, there was frost on the ground. In a quiet moment, Ida and I sat again in her brother's bedroom. It was carved out of the hill and always had a musty smell.

We talked deeply and decided we were so much in love that we wanted to get married. Not right away, but in the future when I had finished with the army and grad school. The date was three and a half years away, yet we now were committed to each other and felt wonderful about it.

Around Ida, my craving for process was fading into the background. I had found what I thought was my life partner, so I no longer needed to be methodical to try to find one. That made intimacy more possible with her than with any girl I had ever known. When we were near each other, we jumped up and down like little kids, hardly able to contain ourselves. The frigid reaction of Ida's parents—such a contrast to the physical warmth of their home—was only driving us closer together. They had not seen my worth, had not understood her love for me, and were doing their best to slow our pace. This caused Ida great suffering.

In February, my father made a surprise business trip to New York. He was as dapper as always, wearing an understated sport coat and slacks that had a California flair to them. Ida and I had dinner with him and could not help telling him about our still-secret decision to get married.

He had already guessed what was in the air just by hearing me on tape recordings that I had sent to him and Mom, and by seeing us together. It was wonderful for Ida and me to sit together and talk of our plans with someone who was so dear to me.

"She's exceptional, Ben," he said later when we were alone. "Mom and I hope it works out for you two to stay together."

"I guess after Roberta she's an improvement, no?"

He laughed. "They're not even on the same planet. Ida is wonderful, very solid. Strong emotionally. You couldn't ask for more."

As I drove back to Baltimore, I realized how important it was to have Dad's approval. He legalized us. He proved that the process I went through to dispel my doubts about Ida—going through a step-by-step examination of the concerns I had and methodically discharging them—had produced the right conclusion about her.

A few weeks after Dad's visit, we celebrated our February 1966 birthdays—Ida's twenty-first and my twenty-third—which fell just a few days apart. To commemorate that and make my commitment to her public, I gave her the Phi Beta Kappa honor society key I had earned at Stanford. It meant I had pinned her. She put it on a chain around her neck to have something to show to her friends. I looked across at her wearing it and felt doubly proud—not only that I had won it, but also that I had such a wonderful girl to give it to.

In an act of stunning bravery, Ida wore the key home and showed it to her parents. They surprised us by receiving it warmly, and we did not know why. Maybe they recognized the academic achievement it represented and realized this kid who was sniffing around their daughter might not be such a loser after all. Or maybe it finally penetrated that she and I were serious. Whatever the reason, we hoped this unexpected high point would be the beginning of a thaw between all of us.

It was not. During our weekend visits to Connecticut in March, Leo and Kate made little effort to reach out to me, make me feel wanted, or even comfortable. Nevertheless, by mid-April, we decided it was time to tell them our secret. I spoke to Leo in the family room downstairs while Ida talked to Kate on the upper level. He was cheerful and businesslike in his acceptance, as if agreeing to something he had seen coming from a long way off. But he never once said anything that led me to believe he thought I would make a good husband for his daughter.

With her mother, Ida ran into a brick wall. Kate refused to face the fact that Ida and I had chosen one another. She had none of the pleasantness and chilly grace that Leo had shown. Ida hardly knew what to say. Afterward, Kate said not one word to me about having just learned I was going to be her son-in-law.

~

I hoped I would be able to find contentment in my first army assignment to match the happiness I had in my relationship with Ida, but soon discovered otherwise.

At the Army Intelligence School, I had received twenty weeks of training in how to conduct background investigations on people so they could receive a security clearance.

Almost 190,000 American troops were now in Vietnam, and more were arriving every week, so there was a high demand for clearances. Yet after five months of teaching me a specific skill, the army assigned me to a job in Manhattan for which I had absolutely zero preparation. I was to be the adjutant—the chief administrative officer—of the Northeast region of the 77th Intelligence Corps Group. It fielded three hundred men from Pennsylvania to Maine who knocked on doors to do background interviews.

As adjutant, I was the first person to know when the army was ordering someone in the 77th to go to Vietnam. A lieutenant at the Pentagon in Washington would call with the list of names and serial numbers; I would then relay them to my superiors and to the hapless soldiers' commanding officers. It was not pleasant, since, for all I knew, I was communicating death sentences.

Oddly, I had been receiving such phone calls for months with only the vaguest notion my own name might be on that list.

One bright Tuesday in June, I headed into the office as usual. When the phone rang, I answered the lieutenant's call like every other time before, thinking about the poor guys whose lives were about to change. But this time, a name and serial number on the list were mine.

~

The alert quashed any further introspection I might have engaged in about Ida. During the next year, she was to be my lifeline to sanity, and I only had eyes for the love and tenderness she had to offer.

What I did not realize was that even after four relationship failures, I had again lost focus about who a girl might really be. In my room in Baltimore long before we got engaged, and was pondering why this sweet young lady had not captured my heart, I used the methodical process of my recipe to analyze each objection to her that I might hold.

One by one they fell away, and I ended up embracing her less for who she was than for having successfully made it through the labyrinth of my analysis.

Unfortunately, I had focused more on the process of evaluating Ida than on the vague sense of unrest I had detected within myself. The lack of any identifiable danger signs was a problem. It hid a mismatch between what my heart was saying and the conclusions from my logic. I was oblivious to any concern that a long-term relationship with her might have an unrewarding outcome. Instead, my winning recipe made it easy to put aside my doubts. It had me rejecting them simply because I had completed a methodical analysis.

Long after Vietnam was over, those doubts would resurface. But right now, I was going to war and even if such thoughts had occurred to me, I would have squashed them. She was a rock, and I desperately sought to anchor myself to her.

In this, I was looking for a relationship to make the world safe for me to live in. The intrusion of the war was crude and life-threatening. The next eight months until my two-year commitment was over would force me to be even more extroverted than during a terrible night being chased by dogs at army training in Georgia, which I will discuss in the next chapter. Now, just as then, no recipe could protect me. But this relationship might.

In Vietnam, thoughts of Ida would be a safe emotional space to retreat into when the relentless pressure on me to be extroverted got to be too much. That space would allow me to be more comfortable with my introversion, rather than try to flee from it through a recipe. It was only a short-term solution, but I welcomed it.

WHAT I COULD HAVE DONE DIFFERENTLY

It would have been better to look directly at Ida, rather than through the filter of my recipe. Had I done so, I would have discovered things about the two of us that made us incompatible.

Takeaways from Chapter 6

1. Using your recipe to evaluate another person as a business or romantic partner is a formula for disaster, because you did not create the recipe for that purpose. You built it to succeed in a world designed for extroverts without having to interact too much with people.

2. Beware of assuming that because another person seems to be an introvert they are right for you as a business or romantic partner. They could well not be.

3. Beware of using an external crisis to end your appraisal of another person as a business or romantic partner, as I did when the pressures of heading to Vietnam made me stop assessing whether Ida was right for me. Need is a poor basis for a long-term relationship.

Reflective Questions

1. Do you often use your recipe to evaluate people? How does that typically work out?

2. Do you assume that because someone is an introvert they are good material for a romantic or business partner? Has that ever been accurate?

3. Have you decided that you needed someone because you were facing an external crisis? How did that work out?

Practical Exercises

1. Recall a time when you used your recipe to evaluate someone. What was the cost of doing so?

2. Recall a time when you let your evaluation of another person slide because they were an introvert. In what way did that turn out to be a mistake?

3. Recall a time when an external event made you think you needed someone, so you suspended your evaluation of that person. How did that work out?

~

The thought of going into a war zone gave me a painful reminder of the terror I had experienced in my army officer basic training course just two months earlier. In the next chapter, I take a step back in time to relay those moments.

Part 2

Four Foundational Tools for Detaching

7

Observing the Mind: Evasion and Escape

AUGUST 1965. FORT BENNING, GEORGIA. At dusk on a steamy evening, I sat on a bench in the back of a two-and-a-half-ton truck with eleven other young men. We bumped along a dirt road in a convoy of eighteen trucks near a forest that harbored dozens of angry German shepherd dogs and their handlers.

The 216 of us—all newly commissioned second lieutenants in the US Army—were about to jump out of the backs of the trucks in groups of threes and fours as soon as the vehicles came to a stop. We were to scurry across an open field and into the forest beyond without getting caught.

Faces and hands darkened with shoe polish, shirts reversed to hide labels, all shines dulled and clinks muffled, we had only a compass as our guide across nearly five kilometers of treacherous, rattlesnake-infested terrain through the woods that night. The air was thick with humidity, and there was no moon. Hidden holes, briar patches, creek beds, sharp sticks, and, above all, more than sixty hardened soldiers with dogs, clubs, and flashlights were between us and a designated rendezvous point to the north. Eager to see how much a second lieutenant could endure, they would beat and harass us beyond the breaking point if they caught us.

This was the dreaded Evasion and Escape exercise, the high point of the Infantry Officer Basic Course at Fort Benning that I, as an intelligence officer, had to complete. This was half a decade before the army became involved with today's Survival, Evasion, Resistance and Escape (SERE) training, although the US Air Force, Navy, and Marines had been conducting it for years.

The exercise took place in a patch of wilderness among the Georgia pines. Just three months earlier, I, and every one of my classmates, had been celebrated at our college graduation ceremonies and had looked forward, some with excitement and some with fear, to the prospect of our army induction after completing four years of Reserve Officers' Training Corps (ROTC) classes. The Vietnam War was raging, and ROTC provided an honorable way to beat the draft; but now as the drop-off point approached, I would have bet not one man was convinced that joining the service voluntarily had been a good idea.

Sitting in the truck, I recalled that my normal response to the exercise would have been to think it through, nail down the alternatives and probabilities, and create a process to increase my safety. Despite my failure in relationships, I knew my recipe worked in academics, and I assumed it would not fail me in the army. As an introvert, I had achieved fabulous, repeated success by doing just that: becoming dependent on rigid, highly evolved plans and their sequential steps to manage the world for me.

But the army had designed the exercise in a way that rewarded the extroverts among us. To succeed, we had to be bold, take risks, and, more than anything, not *think* too much. As we bounced along, I realized I had spent my entire twenty-two years doing just the opposite: foreseeing problems, avoiding risks, and designing elaborate schemes to control my environment.

Fear had pried me loose from my normal world. Rather than examine the details of what was going to happen, I fell prey to unfounded rumors, fantastic dreams, and unlimited speculation on the horror of being alone in the woods at night, chased by savage German shepherds and enlisted men who thought nothing of beating a young officer senseless.

Fear overtook me because I did not have the comfortable safety net of a process. I now wanted one badly. As the truck moved deeper into the forest, I tried to build something on the fly by asking myself things I should have thought about days ago.

How did a person chased by dogs at night in a dark forest avoid detection? Of the five senses, touch and taste were not likely to give me away. The pursuers would touch me only if some other trigger had gotten them close enough to do so. And while taste might apply to a dog that sank its teeth into my leg, it would happen only if the animal found me by some other means.

The most obvious giveaway would be sight. I was well protected in that sense, having rubbed half a can of black Kiwi shoe polish on the back of my neck, forehead, nose, cheeks, and hands. I had turned my green army-fatigue shirt inside out so no insignia or labels would stand out in the dark; my soft baseball cap had nothing on it. Yet no matter how diligently I smeared black wax on my skin, there were still lily-white streaks showing through because of how much I was sweating. All it would take for the privates to see me would be the quick scan of a flashlight through the woods.

Another obvious betrayal would be by sound. As a guy who grew up in suburban Los Angeles, I knew a lot about how to maintain a swimming pool on a sunny day. But I knew absolutely nothing about how to pick my way through dense growth in silence on a slate-black night and uneven ground. It was best that I did not think this part through, because it was hopeless. Far from tiptoeing to avoid snapping twigs, I was going to be running full out, crashing through anything smaller than a tree that stood in my way, evoking all the night goblins in the forest.

If fear had not so overtaken me, I might have realized that mine would not be the only show on display for the eager young privates and their dogs. There would be over two hundred other guys running for their lives in a line stretching to my left and right. There would be two dozen dogs barking their brains out. There would be dog handlers shouting commands to the animals, and another forty privates swearing and calling to each other. It would be absolute bedlam, which meant my potential captors might not hear me if they were even a few meters away.

The way they would catch me, I was sure, was by smell. That was why the dogs were out. They were aggressive, carefully trained military animals that received prompts day after day to follow the scent of a human. As far as the designers of the exercise were concerned, the spectacle of dogs snarling and straining at their neck chains added a nice touch of horror. However, that was just a side benefit. The real advantage of the dozens of canines was that their brains could penetrate through the darkness and the cacophony of sound to sniff out a trembling man, especially since he would be sweating. Against those beasts there was simply no defense; they would lock on to me and bring a club-wielding soldier right into my face.

Yet, would they? In the depths of my anxiety, I neglected to recall two things that might confuse and disorient the dogs. First was the sheer number of bodies they would have to detect. For all I knew, the air would be thick with the smell of humans; there was little wind, and having so many of them clustered in confined spaces between bushes and trees might well have the dogs going in circles.

Then there was the mosquito repellent. The woods were teeming with hungry insects. The instructors cautioned us to slather the chemical on thickly, and even put it on our fatigues so the bugs would not bite us through the cloth. To apply the mosquito goo and shoe polish on a hot, fetid Georgia night was disgusting beyond words, but I did so diligently— perhaps too much so, since the repellent caused my light skin to show through the shoe polish. Here was an unexamined question: Were the dogs trained to home in on repellent, or in the infinite wisdom of army planning would the designers of the exercise have overlooked that detail?

In the days leading up to the exercise, none of this fact-finding entered my brain. Even if it had, I knew that analysis was necessary but not sufficient. I had to convert the thinking into a series of practical steps, and in this situation, that was impossible.

Terror dried my mouth and filled my bladder.

I went over it all again: The trucks would drop us off at the edge of an open field. Our would-be captors lurked just inside a tree line several hundred meters away. There seemed to be no possibility of escape—they would catch me, beat me for an hour, and toss me outside the prison compound to crawl my way through the rest of the night.

~

The convoy slowed and lurched to a stop. The drivers did not kill the headlights, so as men jumped out of the backsides of the trucks they were in full view of the captors in the woods, lit brilliantly as if to whet the appetite of the privates and their dogs. When I hit the ground, I made the mistake of looking directly into the lights of the truck behind me, causing my night vision to vanish as I stared blindly toward the distant forest.

At the prelaunch briefing an hour earlier, the trainers had impressed on us to honor Article V of the Armed Forces Code of Conduct: If captured, all we could reveal were our name, rank, service number, and date of birth, despite what the privates might do to get more out of us. But at this moment, when I strained to see anything at all in the darkness, the admonition seemed to be a perfect setup for some aggressive guy my age to whack the daylights out of me until I betrayed a friend or begged the kid to stop hitting me. In a world long before smartphones, there was no way to document what the captors might do to us.

There was no starting gun; the stopping of the convoy signaled the beginning of the exercise. With several others, I turned and ran out of the headlights and soon felt bumpy soil beneath my combat boots. I struggled to keep my balance and not twist an ankle as I ran as fast as I could across what felt like a plowed field. My night eyes gradually returned as I ran, allowing me to see the shadowy outlines of the long line of men to the right and left of me lurching toward the forest. Dogs were barking in the distance along our entire advancing front.

The more we ran toward the dark tree line in the distance, the more it seemed to recede. Then suddenly, it was upon us, just ahead but blocked by unexpected clumps of tall grass we had to part with our arms to get through. This slowed us down and confused us. Stupidly, four of us clustered together against all warnings not to do so, and now all we could think to do was hunker down to get our bearings.

As soon as we crouched down, a dog handler spotted us from the right, and two soldiers came at us from the left. They charged us with lit flashlights, screams, and snarls, the highly trained dog straining against its neck chain and pleading for freedom so it could tear into whatever was hiding in the grass.

We scattered. We could not go back; the only way was directly ahead. So we all broke into a run, driving straight into the forest. I was in the lead, with two of my classmates behind me to the left and one behind me to the right.

Our pursuers were now behind us. I was outrunning them, but, in the darkness, I slammed into a tree and busted my lips. The escapees to my left passed me by. Now at the rear of the others, I fell on the ground near the base of the tree that had stopped me. My mouth filled with the taste of blood. A pile of dead sticks and branches stabbed me from ten different directions, but I lay in as much silence as I could muster, my lungs bursting for air and my vocal cords straining to cry out from pain and fear.

The other lieutenants had kept running, and in the noise and confusion of scents, the dog handler and two soldiers passed right by me in pursuit. They captured two of the men not six meters from me, then beat the bushes and shone lights to flush me and the other one out of hiding.

I lay motionless as they crisscrossed my position, moving out as far as fifty meters only to come right back.

"There's too many of 'em; the dogs can't smell nothin'," the dog handler said.

"Try over there," the other soldier said, his voice carrying away from where I lay.

"Naw, I was just there. Clipper is onto something over here."

"Come on, Gary, I heard something over *there*!" He turned away from my direction.

"Dammit, Chuck, I'm the dog handler, and he's gonna go where I say."

The handler then turned the dog in my direction. It went a few steps and stopped, sniffing and pawing the underbrush. Right at that spot there must have been a strong scent because the animal fixed on something and came no closer to me.

The longer I lay there, the more I understood what football players meant when they said it was the first hit of the game that knocked the fear out of them. Although the hit had affected me in a comparable way via the pain of the bruises and cuts all over my body and the sweat and blood running into my mouth, it was still low on the pain scale in comparison to what I would suffer if caught. The danger from the unbearably close dog and soldiers was so critical my mind could not handle it. Before long, I noticed I had stopped fearing capture. A supreme confidence rolled over me in waves, making me foolishly indifferent to what might happen next.

Eventually my stalkers withdrew, chatting and laughing on into the night as if this was all such great fun. When their voices were fainter, my ears became hypersensitive to every noise around me. For a long while, there was no sound other than a gentle whistling through the pines as a slow wind came up. The air movement was delicious beyond words, but potentially hid any rustling that just a few moments earlier I might have heard.

I considered my next move. If I only had a process to rely on, some sequence of steps to follow, it would tell me what to do. But the exercise seemed designed to prevent us from doing any thinking, and instead to act on pure instinct.

I could not stay where I was. I was too exposed, and next time I might not be so lucky if soldiers and a dog came by. Yet this spot had saved me so far, and I was not keen on letting it go, especially since I had no idea whether there might be a better place to hide up ahead.

Out came my compass. The dial was barely visible, but it did have some of the glow left in it from when I shone a flashlight on it during the prelaunch briefing. I could see which way was north. The goal was to go in that direction and rendezvous with partisans who would take us in. Reaching them meant completing the exercise successfully; any other outcome—capture or staying hidden in the forest—meant failure, at least as far as the course scoring went.

Some deep breathing helped me to ratchet my fear level down to a tolerable level. My slow, analytical approach started to kick back in. I saw again that there was no way to build a process to reduce the danger of this situation. To find a way to get through the night without detection, I had to improvise, and that thought scared the daylights out of me.

I was convinced the whole premise of this event was an exercise in fighting the last war. The army based it on army field manual 21–77, *Evasion and Escape*, which I had read a few days earlier.

Last updated in 1958, the manual baldly stated that it derived from the experiences of World War II and Korea, which meant it contained nothing of the knowledge now emerging from Vietnam. Those earlier conflicts had quaint relics such as front lines and partisans, neither of which existed in the maelstrom of guerrilla warfare sweeping across Southeast Asia. This night would have been great training if I were behind German lines in 1944, striving to reach the French Resistance a few kilometers ahead across wooded European terrain. But this exercise did absolutely nothing to further my chances of survival in the tropical hell of a fluid war where neither side held ground for long, and the only safe way out was straight up on a rescue line from a helicopter.

As I lay in the dark, observing my thoughts, it occurred to me that I had jumped to the conclusion that the instructors' definition of the meaning of the exercise was accurate. They had said that escape was the only option, meaning we not only had to evade capture as we wound our ways north, but also had then to escape by reaching the free zone. But what if that was not true? What if there was another possibility, such as only doing half the exercise by just evading—staying hidden and not even trying to reach the safe area? That would constitute failing the exercise just as much as getting captured would, but it would be far less traumatic.

Given where I started, as a city boy who had never been in a fight, never participated in sports, and certainly never spent a night in the woods alone, success for me would simply be the evasion part—making it through the night without any of the dozens of dogs and soldiers who were prowling the forest finding me.

Giving the exercise a new interpretation in that way buoyed me with a rush of adrenaline. Just evading was so far beyond anything I could ever have thought possible that it gave me an enthusiastic goal to strive for. Some of my classmates might call me a coward for not even trying to reach the partisans in the free zone. But they would have had no idea how much courage it took for me just to press on and survive this night of horrors without a dog or a soldier catching me.

~

I closed the compass and put it back in my pocket. I waited until the wind subsided, slowly raised myself from the leaves and brambles I was lying in, and stood erect, facing north.

Hearing shouts and dog growls in the distance but nothing nearby, I took a few cautious steps, keeping my arms in front of me so I would not do any more damage to my face. I discovered that walking at night in a dark forest played enormous tricks on the mind. I would take a few steps and then freeze, certain the object looming up to my right or left was a man. Once I had stopped, I would see that the object was a tree and had only seemed to be moving because I was moving.

In the dark, I could not see any detail below the level of my knees. Periodically, I would snap a twig loudly and expect ten flashlights to come alive and swing in my direction. I would freeze and swear under my breath, and when nothing materialized, I would continue, hands out in front, groping the dark. I continued this way for a hundred meters.

Then to my right, at about two o'clock and thirty meters away, I heard the unmistakable sound of footsteps. I dropped to a crouch. Silence. Another pair of steps. More silence. Then a few more steps. They were moving away from me and pushing back brush as they walked slowly through the dark. I was sure it was not a soldier, because they always worked in pairs, or at least that is what they wanted us to believe. The only lone soldiers out here were the ones with dogs, and I heard no chain or growling. It had to be some poor schmuck like me who was out of his mind with fear as he tried to move north.

I took no chances. I settled from a crouch into sitting on my bottom to wait him out. At length he took more steps, continuing away from me, and soon he was far enough away for me to feel comfortable about resuming my own trek.

I removed the compass and checked it again. Even though I was not trying to reach the partisans, I still wanted to move north. I would be following behind the bulk of the captors, covering ground they had abandoned. At the same time, I would avoid remaining in the far rear area, where they might choose to make a sweep to look for stragglers. Staying close to my enemy in this way made sense to me, so I struck out to the north again.

Walking slowly, palpating the darkness ahead, I began to form an idea of what I was looking for. My first safe space had been at the base of a tree, which meant I was not out in the open. A tangle of fallen branches from the tree had given me quick cover. Yet it was a miserable type of cover, with sharp sticks digging into me from all directions.

Three meters ahead was a looming dark patch of brush about four meters in diameter surrounding a large pine tree. The forest floor was full of patches of thick, bushy growth like this that were sometimes waist-high and exceedingly difficult to walk through. The path of least resistance was to go around those patches. So if I hid *inside* one of them, soldiers without dogs would be likely to pass me by. Dogs would still sniff me out, but there were half as many dogs as there were soldiers, so the brush still improved my odds.

I groped my way to the edge of the growth I had spotted, listened for any suspicious noises, and dropped to my knees. I burrowed all the way in until I reached the tree trunk and patted it with my hand. Even though it was illogical, I felt safer being next to a tree, perhaps because one had saved me just a while earlier.

Once inside the burrow, I felt more secure but now faced a completely new series of concerns. I remembered the snakes. We had heard there were black rattlesnakes in these woods, but we could not trust everything the enlisted instructors told us. They loved to put fear into young lieutenants at every opportunity. Still, lying on the ground I could imagine snakes and all sorts of other creatures that might not take kindly to my intrusion. Spiders, scorpions, even ants could be a real danger. Plus, for all I knew I was lying in a bed of the poison ivy that was common throughout the Georgia woods. What was I doing in there?

~

Outside, above the brush, the buzzing of mosquitoes was incessant. They had stayed away from me because of all the repellent I was wearing, and they were the last thing I was expecting down here at ground level. They turned out to be the worst problem I faced, constantly dive-bombing into my ear.

I quickly grabbed my bottle of repellent and wiped its liquid into every crevice of my ears, eyes, and nose, putting more on my head, neck, and hands for good measure, stinging my injured lips as I did. It was crude and oily, unlike the light and fragrant repellents that would follow a half century later.

"Take that, you bastards," I whispered.

The repellent stopped the dive-bombing but not the buzzing, which continued unabated. The only advantage was that it took my mind off the snakes and other venomous beasts that might be taking over stalking duty from the soldiers.

I turned over on my back. The stress had exhausted me physically, and even more so mentally and emotionally. Little wounds pricked my arms, legs, and torso, and my lips were throbbing and stinging. I tried to avoid licking them because they had shoe polish and insect repellent all over them. But I kept forgetting and had nothing to clean my tongue with except my sleeve, which also had insect repellent and dirt on it and only made things worse. I did have a canteen of tepid water, but the mouthpiece was filthy. If I pursed my lips, I could get a few drops of clean water and swish it out amid heightened pain signals from my lips.

I listened intently for any sign of activity in the area and heard none. In the silence, I found it impossible to stay alert, and alternately dozed and awakened with a snort when I realized I had fallen asleep.

After a particularly long catnap, I awoke with a start. Jesus, I could hear someone walking *south* toward my position. Determined cracks and snaps of twigs gave a clear sign someone or something was moving toward me from the north. My heart raced with the thought that two enterprising soldiers had decided to loop back to see if there were any stragglers. I heard no dog, so maybe they would pass me by. I trained my ears on the source of the noise, and it shortly morphed into the sound of a branch tapping the tree above me from a gust of wind, then nothing. No one was coming. It had been a bad dream.

I thought of home. Four days earlier, the Watts riots back in LA had ended after close to a week of mayhem that resulted in thirty-four deaths and three thousand arrests. Yet right now, I wished I were in LA instead of in this insect-infested burrow.

I shivered. I had been still for an hour or more and all the perspiration had dried off. The breeze that tapped the branch above me had cooled me off to the point where I was cold. That amazed me, because it had to be at least eighty degrees on this hot Georgia night. However, that was almost twenty degrees below my body temperature, so a shiver was certainly possible.

On our utility belts the only equipment we had that night were the compass, the canteen, the repellent, and a plastic poncho. Still on my back, I removed the poncho from my right side and put it on my chest, unfolding it in the few inches of space between me and the top of the burrow until I got it undone. I managed to get the poncho unfolded, but it bunched up between my chest and my knees. There was no room to sit up, so I tried to grab the lower end of it with my boots and pull it flat. But my grip kept slipping. I did manage to cover myself just below the knees and decided that would have to do.

My exertion and the impermeability of the plastic supplied instant warmth—so much so that I had to lie still to avoid sweating again. The heat wave passed, the breeze brought fresh air, and I soon was fast asleep.

Later in the night, I once again awoke to the sound of someone working their way south. I knew it was another dream, but it was so *realistic*. The breaking of brush was directional in orientation and got progressively louder with each crack. I was convinced I was hallucinating like before, but this time no shiver followed the dream. I tried to move but I could not. Paralyzed, I was fully aware of louder and louder noises coming near me but could not even lift a little finger in response.

I had read somewhere that this was a normal part of sleep. During the rapid eye movement or REM phase when the most active dreaming took place, the body went into paralysis to prevent arms and legs from flailing all over. That useful tidbit supplied little comfort, however, because the noise kept getting closer, louder, and now I could hear muffled voices—no words, just incoherent syllables strung together.

I had also read that sometimes it was possible to break out of REM-induced paralysis by moving something—anything—I could extend into larger activity. I tried blinking my eyes. I could do it, but it did not stop the paralysis. I turned my wrists from side to side, or thought I did, but they were not moving. I moved my right ankle back and forth with the heavy toe-cap on my boot leveraging gravity to accelerate the movement. Gradually, I was able to move my whole leg and then come into full body control.

There were no voices, no people smashing through the growth, only the wind in the pines.

I took several deep breaths and fell back asleep.

~

The next time I awoke, it was first light. Minute by minute, the darkness lifted, and I could see straight up through the brush of my burrow. I spied the top of my large tree and a small patch of sky that started out gray and gradually turned blue. The distant shouts and growls of the night had disappeared, replaced by a chorus of birds chirping in the trees.

Despite appearances, this was a dangerous time. The exercise would continue through to 0900 hours, and now the captors had the advantage of daylight to flush out anybody who might have eluded them so far. I had no watch and could not recall how they would signal the end of the event, so I stayed where I was. I would much rather fail the exercise than get abused at the last minute.

I sat up in the burrow—now seeing that the growth was not as thick as I had thought it to be at night—then stood up and stomped my way out of the undergrowth to a clear spot where I relieved myself with joyous abandon, mosquitoes be damned.

I found a road and waited. I heard the grind of a diesel engine in low gear coming from around a corner to my right and suddenly was nervous about the consequences I might face for what I did that night. But the truck was half full of guys like me who had hidden out, and soon a small fleet of other half-full trucks joined us on the trip back to the barracks. The penalties for simply hiding might be severe, but at least I was in good company.

Despite the army staff telling us that failure to reach the safe zone was not an option, they nonetheless seemed to divide the class into three cohorts. At the top were those who reached the objective without getting caught. At the bottom were those who did get caught. And in the middle were the truckloads of guys like me who got credit for successfully hiding out all night, even if we did not reach the partisan free zone. I figured the instructors had to have been thinking something similar to this because after the course ended, they sent me a letter saying I had graduated in the top 10 percent of my boot camp class.

~

I was joyous that I had made it through the night uninjured.

But that was no thanks to my winning recipe. I had to abandon it because I knew the only way to succeed in the exercise was to be bold and daring—meaning to be an extrovert for real. I could never have been outgoing enough to triumph in this situation.

As soon as I let go of the recipe and went to the source of the fear—the idea I held that my only option was to take the terrible risk of trying to escape, rather than just to evade—I was able to cope constructively. Reframing the evasion part of the trial to be a huge potential success caused both the fear and the urgency to engage in my recipe to decline.

That was a key shift in consciousness that would stay with me my whole life. From then on, I saw that any meaning I held in my head was only an interpretation. It was not an unvarying truth, and to treat it as such closed off a whole universe of additional possibilities that might support me better as a human being. Knowing that provided me with a deeper sense of security than any recipe ever could.

WHAT I COULD HAVE DONE DIFFERENTLY

I could have tried harder to think through the coming experience instead of not doing so until I was on the way there. Yet in the end it was good that I allowed the situation to become intolerable, because out of that intensity I realized that the meanings in my head were merely interpretations that I could change.

Takeaways from Chapter 7

1. Like your recipe, your mind is a survival machine. It often defaults to whatever beliefs had an evolutionary advantage, but today can be out of date and out of place.

2. Building the habit of stepping outside your mind to watch it in operation is the best way to expose the fallacies of some of its conclusions.

3. Beliefs are interpretations, not unwavering truths. The belief that likely has most damaged your life is that as an introvert you are defective. You are free to change that.

Reflective Questions

1. What evolutionary advantage do you suppose jumping to conclusions had when humans lived on the African savannah?

2. A split second of hesitation is all you need to observe your mind. Stop reading this book for a second, and look into your head. What do you see?

3. What does your introvert "defect" look like? How would you describe it to a Martian who just arrived and is curious about what happens here on Earth?

Practical Exercises

1. The next time you are tempted to jump to a conclusion provoked by your recipe, stop before acting. Notice whether the action you contemplate serves you, or is just an unthinking reflex.

2. Sit quietly for one minute with a pencil and pad handy. Watch your mind, and write down how many different thoughts emerge one after the other after the other.

3. The "defect" lives in this thought: "As an introvert, I cannot do X in this society." See if you can change it to this instead: "As an introvert, I can do Y in this society, and it is a huge contribution to others."

~

Soon after the Evasion and Escape exercise ended in August 1965, I moved to Baltimore to complete my Army Intelligence School training, and that October met Ida in New York. We were together for eight months before receiving the devastating news that soon I would be shipped out to Vietnam.

8

Unified Awareness: Welcome to Vietnam, GI

JUNE 1966. NEW YORK CITY. Shortly after the terrible phone call from Washington that announced my alert for Vietnam service, Ida and I met at my Brooklyn apartment. We lay down together and felt the closest thing to despair we had ever known. We held each other and cried as the blackest, most irrational feelings and thoughts wormed into us in an unending stream. I pressed her body against me and felt like I wanted to die. That day, the United States had bombed Hanoi and Haiphong for the first time, and it made the danger inherent in going to Vietnam frighteningly tangible.

My forthcoming deployment to Vietnam aggravated our already-tense relations with Ida's parents. Events came to a head over the long Fourth of July weekend in Connecticut. Originally, Ida and I had planned to be engaged in a year, after she graduated from NYU, but with eight months of separation facing us we decided to have a ring on her finger in the next four weeks. Leo and Kate were firm that they did not want us to get engaged before I went overseas.

We were at a low ebb when Dad called me at the office a few days later. In his gentle, rich voice, he shared that he had been looking into a ring for us. He called to say he found that we could get a beautiful one at a reasonable price with good terms.

"And don't worry about keeping in touch with each other while you're on the other side of the world," he said. "I know buying tape recorders is probably more than you can afford, so let Mom and me get one for each of you—that way you can stay in close contact while you're separated."

He also told me not to worry about getting plane tickets for my planned three-week leave with Ida to visit with my family in California. Even if we could not go on standby status for half fare, he and Mom would pay our way to LA.

On the problem of Ida's parents, he had kind words, sober words of tolerance and patience. Having gone through tough times with Mom's father in past years, Dad said our love was the only thing that mattered. He asked us to just let go of all the issues we could not resolve with Leo and Kate.

When I told Ida about his unexpected call, we nearly cried. My parents' attitude was so diametrically opposed to that of Leo and Kate's that it hit us like a shot of adrenaline. In one chat, my father had managed not only to clear up the three things that worried us greatly—a ring, tape recorders, and plane tickets—but also to wrap them in love and support that helped to fill the void in us. I was going to war, and he and Mom would do anything they could to make things as easy as possible for us.

~

On August 14, 1966, the sun rose over the Pacific at Laguna Beach at 6:14 a.m. Ida and I stood on a rocky promontory splashed by the waves. We looked out and saw each wave rushing toward us, hitting the rocks, then withdrawing with white spray and the sound of gentle sizzling as it passed over the sand.

I placed an engagement ring on Ida's finger and held her to me. We had been betrothed in spirit since last December, and now were engaged in fact for the world to see. To me, the sights and sounds of the reced-ing Pacific had symbolized peace ever since I was a child, and in that moment, I was more at peace with life than I could remember. I was openly defying the challenges from Ida's parents and the army without any formula to rely on.

Two days later, we found ourselves enjoying three hours of delightful, childlike fun in the ocean. The lovely afternoon surf trickled off our backs in big drops. Yet at precisely that time, the fear came back. How could such a terrible thing as our impending separation exist in a world that produced the warmth and beauty of the afternoon we had just spent? We had seen it was possible to live in peace, away from violence and unhap-piness, and asked why we had to become a part of so much agony in just a few days.

Adding to my fright was the ocean itself. Especially at night, when I looked out over the dark Pacific and imagined that I had to cross every inch of it in a troop ship, then be deposited on a hostile shore where enemy soldiers and civilian sympathizers would try to kill me, it became too much to face. I knew that across that black expanse was something more sinister than anything I had ever known, and I might not come back from it. Many men did not, or they came back maimed in some way that seemed to make life not worth living. The moonlit swells of the sea, pro-pelled by the wind and forces deep within the ocean, were a living, moving reminder of the existential threat I faced by venturing out onto the water and landing in a place where life was cheap and could be extinguished with a single bullet.

~

On August 29, Ida and I were back in Manhattan in her women's resi-dence hall at NYU. It was early afternoon. We lay on her bed, holding each other. I was not supposed to be there, but nobody was enforcing the rules. At that moment, we had something much bigger on our minds. In a few minutes, we would be saying good-bye for the last time before I left for pre-deployment at Fort Bragg, North Carolina, with no idea of when we would ever see each other again.

The horns and sirens on Fifth Avenue had replaced the crashing of waves on Laguna Beach, reminding us every second that we were no longer in California.

What do two people say to each other at a time like that? Over the centuries, many men went off to war and had to leave behind a woman they loved more desperately than anything in life. When the moment came to part, the pain was so searing, so crushing, that all words failed. I have no recollection of what we said to each other. I would never wish such an experience for any of our children, or for any children anywhere.

We held each other so tightly that we felt like we were merging into one. Then the time came to go, and I gently let go of her, kissing her face and her forehead as I moved away to begin gathering my things. Starting in ten minutes, I would be driving straight through to Virginia on my way to Bragg and wanted to leave the room before both of us broke down.

We had agreed to say good-bye in her room where we had some privacy, rather than in the lobby downstairs or the street. I shouldered my gear, kissed her one last time, and walked out the door.

When I got down to Fifth Avenue, I walked no more than a few steps when I heard Ida behind me, "Ben! Ben!"

I dropped everything and turned as she ran to me, holding me tightly and trying hard not to cry. It was all I could do to hold back tears myself. It felt like we had done nothing but cry for weeks. It was the only process we had for coping, and except for talking with my parents, we had managed on our own.

I embraced her. "You are so strong, Ida. And so am I. We will get through this. I'll call you from Virginia in a few hours."

She nodded and we parted, my last image of her as I gradually backed away being that of a sad, forlorn girl standing in the middle of a broad New York sidewalk framed by tall buildings on either side.

During the six-and-a-half-hour drive to an overnight stop in Fredericksburg, Virginia, I uttered not a word to myself in the car. I dared not turn on the radio for fear that "Michelle" would come on with its piercing lyrics of love. The separation ripped out a part of me. I held an emotionless face and looked straight ahead without knowing from hour to hour where I was.

~

After weeks in North Carolina, I received my departure orders. I was to embark for Vietnam on a troop ship that would leave from the docks at the Oakland Army Base near San Francisco.

Dad, Mom, and my sisters—Carla, twenty-two, and Nan, eight—met me at the base the day my ship was to put to sea. Mom had on her pointy-ended 1950s-style glasses that somehow still looked cute on her, covering eyes swollen from crying. Dad tried to smile, but his eyes, too, were puffy and sad. Both girls were more wistful than I had ever seen them.

I was the eldest child going off to war. When it came time to go, I gave each of them a long, heartfelt hug.

I had never seen my father cry. I will never forget the sight of the tears running down his face after I hugged him and backed away to board the ship that would take me to Vietnam.

~

I hauled my duffel bag up the gangplank toward the guts of the ship that loomed in front of me.

The smell of salt water and diesel fuel filled my nostrils. The air was crisp, only in the fifties despite the afternoon sun high above. After losing my way several times on board, I eventually found my cabin. I was the first man in, so I pushed my duffel bag up onto one of the top bunks.

The *Gordon* was a World War II troop ship that the navy had pressed into duty to transport soldiers from the West Coast to Vietnam. Over six hundred feet long and seventy-five feet wide, it was a self-contained universe that looked inward to create a sense of reality as it moved through an environment of nothingness.

Fig. 4. Preparing to board the USS Gordon. *Oakland Army Base, CA, 1966.*

As I walked through the ship, I could see this humming, pulsating world of compartmentalized steel slabs was able to light, wash, and feed itself in an uncanny deception of self-sufficiency. After we pulled away from the dock, it rocked gently from side to side as a condescending gesture to the flat sea that bore it.

From Oakland, the *Gordon* sailed under the Golden Gate Bridge and down the California coast to San Diego, where it took on more troops and supplies. We then put out to sea again, all of us pressed against the portholes with our transistor radios, trying to pick up rock and roll music from the San Diego stations. The music got fainter and fainter as we headed west.

Fittingly, one of the last songs I heard was "The Sounds of Silence" by Simon and Garfunkel. The echoes of the familiar America we all knew and loved were slipping away, replaced by the incessant crashing of the sea against the hull of the ship.

This was a navy vessel, but we were still in the army—an insane world of rank and authority, of duty and abundant free time, of work ostensibly justified by its relation to higher purpose but its present context relating only to survival. We wore uniforms, spoke of the time in hundreds, saluted, begged each other's pardon with respect, and stood in line to use the head. The army functioned as it did everywhere else in the world, and I took a bit of comfort in these rituals. I ate, read philosophy, and occasionally played a guy's guitar, oblivious to where I came from or where I was going.

Soon physical malaise underscored everything I did. The sea had become more self-expressive, and while not stormy or unduly rough, it churned with life and rocked the ship. Boredom and constant motion made me too sleepy to keep my mind occupied with positive things; I felt sluggish and worthless. My appetite vanished; all I could eat was just enough to keep hunger away.

The reality of the move to Asia became clearer with each day we spent at sea. Along with the other lieutenants who were shipping out with me, I was getting worried.

"Hey, Dubchek," I said to one I had gotten to know, "do you ever think about getting hit or getting killed?"

"All the time," he said. "I can't get it out of my head. And for what? I could go home in a basket, and it wouldn't make a damn bit of difference."

Day by day, as the ship sailed farther from America, I wanted a reward for having completed the initial step of the journey. But all I had was an insane, purposeless daily routine. I tried to turn it into a process, but there was no meaningful outcome that it could produce. I felt cheated. Such thoughts swirled through my mind for hours until I was sick of them.

~

Ten days west of San Diego and four days before Thanksgiving 1966, I was sitting at a table in the recreation room still trying to accustom myself to the rolling of the ship.

A US Navy lieutenant came over and told me softly that there was a radiogram for me upstairs in the communications room. In the days before widespread satellite communications, the best way to get a message to a ship at sea was by radio. I followed him topside to a small chamber crammed with electronic equipment, signed for the message, and stepped into an exterior passageway. I looked out to sea to steady my stomach on the horizon before glancing down at the paper in my hand.

"Ben—I love you, Sweetheart. All my love, Ida." The stark, block letters moved me beyond words.

That afternoon I had listened twice to one of the tapes she sent me to hear on board. By some uncanny faculty of projection, she was able to foretell my needs three weeks in advance, offering me help as real as if she were standing beside me. She knew that I would listen to her in my bunk, that I would be conscious of the rocking of the ship and be sad about how far I was from her and my family.

Tears welled up in my eyes when she told me in words and by the ardor in her voice that she loved me. She said she was with me in thought every day and night, and she wanted me in her bed. She said I was strong, everything was all right in our world, and this separation would end before we realized it. I knew those things but still needed to hear them.

And the mail! She reminded me there would be a pile of goodwill and love waiting for me in Saigon. That gave me something concrete to look forward to on arrival.

~

After four weeks at sea, and a few days after an unexpectedly sumptuous Thanksgiving meal on board, we made landfall in Vietnam at Da Nang. We then headed south for our second port of call, Qui Nhon, but a tropical depression blew in. It prevented us from docking, so we rode out the storm in the bay.

Being captive inside an enormous steel container that moved according to powerful forces of nature was terrifying beyond words. The ship would list to the right, then more to the right, then so far to the right that bodies and belongings would slam into the opposite wall. The great steel plates squealed as they twisted in ways seemingly beyond their capacity and took a final tilt to the right, each of us knowing that surely, this time, we would capsize and die as water rushed in and drowned us where we stood.

Then, after an eternity of no further movement, in a neutral zone between righting itself and tipping over, the ship would creak, shudder, and slowly, imperceptibly, begin to tilt to the left. The whole drama would begin again on the other side of the vessel, terminating in long moments of paralysis while the *Gordon* decided, contrary to the beliefs of everyone on board, it would not tip over that time either. Then it would start to the right again.

The delay left me uncomfortable, cooped up, and thwarted in my assault on Vietnam, for which I had summoned every ounce of my courage now that we were there. I turned into a bundle of nerves as I waited for the shipboard nightmare to end and the onshore ordeal to begin.

When it did end four days later, I prepared to disembark with my shipmates sixty miles southeast of Saigon at the port of Vung Tau. As I gathered my gear, I was in decent shape emotionally. Through her tapes Ida had given me the reassurance I needed.

I wrestled my heavy duffel bag off the top bunk and dragged it with scores of other men toward the enormous disembarkation door on the lower level. A landing craft was waiting just outside to take us ashore. Its big diesel engines emitted a menacing growl so loud we could hear it through the ship's hull. As the door slowly slid open, the sound became deafening. I reflexively squeezed the handle on my duffel bag until my fingers turned white.

~

After sheltering us for more than four weeks within its thick panels of gray steel, the *Gordon* discharged us into the open sun at Vung Tau on December 6, 1966. It was a sweltering Tuesday morning.

Along with several dozen other men, I stepped onto an open barge and looked across the water to see a tall, green jungle bobbing on the horizon. We felt naked—the barge exposed our chests to any small-arms fire the Viet Cong might send our way.

Thankfully, there were no bullets. Once on land, we shuttled to a nearby airfield and avoided the dangers of the sixty-mile route into Saigon by flying to nearby Bien Hoa air base in a military transport plane.

As we drove from Bien Hoa into Saigon in the back of an open truck,

I saw a vast, disorganized complex of crooked streets, swamps, canals, and tumbled-down buildings made of everything from reinforced concrete to tin cans. The place was absurdly gaudy and shabby from the destruction and hasty reconstruction of war.

Streets were in poor repair, yet hundreds of thousands of Vietnamese dressed in plastic sandals and lightweight clothes scooted deftly around chugholes on Japanese motorbikes. Bombed-out bars stood next to new ones that appeared to have been thrown up overnight. Buses and homes had wire screens over them as protection from grenades. Women shuffled by in the ancient dress of long-sleeved, Mandarin-collared silk gowns topped with a coolie hat. Downtown, modern office buildings towered skyward with concertina barbed wire surrounding every inch of ground considered worth defending. Ruined buildings, armed men patrolling the streets, barbed wire and sandbags at major establishments, and military vehicles zipping back and forth made the war visible everywhere. The stench of garbage and putrid water seized my nose.

The compound where we had our temporary quarters in the northeast suburb of Gia Dinh was no better. Once an old villa set at the junction of the Saigon River and a major tributary, the place now had hastily built barracks, latrines, offices, and guard posts surrounding it on all four sides. Cheap red adobe tiles and cracking walls characterized the outer structures, while lofty ceilings, inlaid tile, and iron grillwork showed what remained of the former splendor of the central building.

Thirty of us moved into the second floor in what must have once been a palatial dining hall. Despite its size, each of us had little more space than on board the *Gordon*. Our bunks were comfortable enough, but the heat, the filth on the ground outside, and the unreliable running water made the space foul.

I thought of Ida. I could not wait to get my hands on the pile of tapes and letters from her that I knew were waiting for me somewhere in the compound.

I was organizing my gear on my bed when KA-BAM!!! A violent, concussive explosion ripped through a bridge just outside, deafening us and pushing compressed air against our chests. I hit the floor and pulled my mattress on top of me as they had trained us to do, terrified at not knowing if the blast was the extent of the attack or only the opening round. I was thankful my reaction had been so automatic.

All the lights on our floor were still on, and somebody's radio was blasting out "Turn! Turn! Turn!" by The Byrds.

Guys were screaming, "Kill the lights! Turn off that goddamn radio!" The lights and music persisted.

The radio continued with its plaintive refrain about a time for dying.

"The lights! The lights!"

We had only been there for a few hours, so nobody knew where the switch was. After more screaming, someone did manage to darken the room, but the radio continued on with the maddening normalcy of its tune and lyrics.

"If you don't shut off that fucking radio, I'm going to blast it!" someone yelled. We all had been issued .45-caliber pistols and ammunition, and were in a culture where shooting a radio out would have been just fine. The threat was real, and it did the trick. Silence now filled the darkness in which we lay, sweat accumulating under our backs from the unaccustomed weight and warmth of the mattresses on top of us.

The Viet Cong had loaded a river barge with explosives and rammed it into a piling supporting the bridge located adjacent to our building. The blast did not disable the bridge. Nor did the attackers follow up. But they scared the living bejesus out of two and a half dozen young American lieutenants on their very first night in the country. This gave us all a taste of what was in store.

~

With my ears still ringing from the blast, I started observing my mind. I noticed that as soon as I had arrived at the compound, I became complacent. I was on dry land, would be eating fresh food, and soon would finally have a job to do. As an introvert, I mostly lived in my head anyway, and the newfound pleasures of a setting somewhat less cramped than the one at sea made me blind to the world I had just walked into.

The explosion remade my attitude. Instead of being content, I was now wary; instead of trying to ignore the present circumstances, I dove into them with a critical eye. When I went back to unpacking, I stopped daydreaming about a fresh meal, and made sure if needed I could quickly get my hands on my ammunition.

The result was a unified consciousness unlike any I ever had. I still pondered a lot, because that is what introverts do. But I also checked every sound, every smell, and every sight around me for danger. I felt like an exterminator looking for rats.

WHAT I COULD HAVE DONE DIFFERENTLY

I might have foreseen that in emerging from the safety of a troop ship I was suddenly going to be exposed to great peril in Saigon. Still, it was extremely useful for me to be oblivious in the face of that danger, because it caused me to wake up to the need to integrate the external world into the internal one I lived in.

Takeaways from Chapter 8

1. When you're an introvert, your internal life is extremely rich. In comparison, your external world usually gets very little attention—even though it can harbor grave dangers.

2. Your recipe wants to prolong the lopsided focus on internals. Jolting it out of that practice may require a literal or figurative explosion in the outside world.

3. Make it a practice to scan your external environment wherever you go. You can do so by consciously paying attention to sights, sounds, and smells.

Reflective Questions

1. When driving, how often are you so absorbed in your thoughts that when you arrive at your destination you are suddenly surprised, with little or no memory of the trip?

2. Think back to the last time something jumped out and surprised you when you were in your head. What was the occasion? How often does this happen?

3. What physical action could you take to prepare for the unexpected? What figurative "ammunition" could you always have on hand to help you?

Practical Exercises

1. The next time you drive to a familiar destination, consciously pay attention to everything around you. Then name three things on the drive that you had never seen before.

2. Whenever something surprises you by intruding into your thoughts from the outside world, ask yourself, "If I had been watching, could I have foreseen this?"

3. Pick a place you go to often, such as a supermarket, a gym, or a doctor's office. The next time you go, what do you hear? How does it smell?

~

My gut told me that in Vietnam it was critical to stop skewing my thinking toward the internal environment and instead to unify it with the outside world. That resulted in a dual awareness that stayed with me and brought me an increased sense of security the whole time I was in the war zone.

Good thing, because at my new duty station in Pleiku, I would soon have an acute need for it.

9

Emotional Context: Pleiku

DECEMBER 1966. PLEIKU, SOUTH VIETNAM. After weeks in Saigon, I was thrilled to step down the ladder of a military transport plane five days before Christmas into the cool air of a sunny morning outside the city of Pleiku. This was my new duty station in the Central Highlands—three hundred miles north of Saigon.

I was now on a high plain surrounded by distant mountains, making it possible to see for miles in all directions. Clumps of trees did exist along the perimeter of the base where I would live and work, but even so, it was a huge improvement over the congestion of Saigon and the nearby jungle that could harbor the Viet Cong.

Here, many large combat units were in the area, including the US Fourth Infantry Division. I was no longer in an isolated compound. If anything happened, the Fourth would respond. Blankets and freedom from mosquitoes were the rule. My bed was comfortable, the water was pure (even hot on occasion), and the food far surpassed the fare at the squalid compound in Gia Dinh. And because of Ida, I had a wonderful Christmas. Her many presents, letters, tapes, and pictures all brought her presence to my side. I dreamt of her every night.

Best of all, I now had a job to do. I was working at the II Corps Headquarters of the Army of the Republic of Vietnam, one of only four such operations centers in the country. The work was clean, safe, and mildly challenging. All I did every day was combine disorganized scraps of information into larger wholes in order to produce military intelligence. Working with maps, written reports, and common sense, I tried to figure out what was happening in our area.

Sometime after midnight in the early morning of January 7, 1967, the other three officers in our room and I were sound asleep when we heard the ka-WHUMP! ka-WHUMP! of incoming mortar rounds blowing craters in the ground so close by that we feared they would hit us next. More rounds landed, and an air raid siren started to wail, directed at the thousands of men in the Fourth Division and the two hundred or so in our compound.

Our facility was in the shape of a square. The rooms formed the four sides of a grassy courtyard in the center, and each room housed four officers. The building sat right next to the Fourth Infantry Division, but rather than being enclosed within that unit, we were on the side of it, sharing a common front with the forest. A perimeter fence separated the US installations from the trees and growth just beyond.

Bedlam ensued in our room. The commander had assigned all of us defensive posts in a ditch facing the forest behind the compound, but before we could get there, we had to find our pants, our helmets, our flak jackets, our weapons, and our boots. It was pitch-black, and nobody could find anything. The incessant screaming of the air raid siren and the booms of the growing response from the Fourth Division made it hard to think.

I found my pants and shirt and got them on quickly, then put on my heavy steel helmet to protect my head in case a shell landed nearby. My flak jacket was hanging off the end of my bunk, so I easily slipped that on, but my boots were a problem. At first, I could not find them in the dark, and then when I did find a pair, I wasn't sure if they were mine.

"Hey, whose boots are these?" I said, as if anybody could see them in the dark.

"Doesn't matter!" said one of the men. "Jam your feet in and get the hell out of here!"

They *were* mine, but in the rush, I could not get my feet into them easily and had to unlace them first. Between all the noise outside and the frantic cursing of my roommates asking where the fuck was this or that, the stress was unbearable. At length, I got dressed, grabbed my .30-caliber machine gun and two magazines of shells, and stumbled out the door into the darkness.

My post in the V-shaped trench behind our compound faced the perimeter fence. I threw myself into the depression and rested my body against the side that faced the fence, with only my helmet and carbine aboveground, thankful that once again army protocol meant I did not have to invent what to do. Every few meters, men positioned themselves along the trench the same as me. In the daylight when they had assigned us to these points, it all seemed like a good plan. Now the location exposed us to any round that might be coming down upon us from beyond the fence, making where we lay feel like a death trap.

Exposing us even more were parachute flares that the Fourth Division was spreading across the sky. Those bright beacons went up a thousand feet, deployed their parachutes, and descended slowly, ever so slowly, swinging back and forth in a way that made every shadow seem to move with a life of its own. The silhouettes they created scared me out of my wits, making me see things moving in the semi-darkness.

The flares illuminated a wide area of the ground on behalf of the helicopters that the Fourth was now scrambling into the sky. The gunships had searchlights and rockets of their own. I looked left and right and saw the flares also illuminating our pitiful little defense line. If anybody in the forest wanted to pick us off, they would have no problem. I wished I had gone to target practice with my roommates over the past few weeks so at least I would know how to fire my weapon.

But then the Fourth Division fully opened up. In a colossal response, they began to pump tons of ordnance into the area beyond the fence. The flashes of light and deafening booms of shells hitting the earth showed what a systematic response of an all-army approach looked like. I felt joy and pride. But the all-consuming fear did not leave me.

The experience was doubly cathartic. First, it showed me that my recipe of handling life with stepwise processes was useless against fear, because when the fear got big enough, the recipe simply disappeared. Until that moment, I was used to having a crisis spur my recipe into begging me to launch a process. But now I realized the recipe was no match for an existential threat.

Secondly, in the trench, the attack made me believe I *was* the fear, that it was my very identity. But when the all-clear sounded, I realized I was actually the person *having* the fear. This made it easier to back away from the recipe a bit; I was able to watch it in operation from the outside and not be so stuck inside of it. In that way it helped me to escape from the prison of my own mind, something that, as an introvert, I regularly inhabited. By changing my identity in this way, shifting from fear-as-myself to context-as-myself, I got enough distance from the fear to stop shaking.

~

On the overcast afternoon the day after the attack, I was sitting in the Order of Battle section where I worked. Operation Cedar Falls had just launched in the Iron Triangle area just west of Saigon with thirty thousand American troops, and we hoped an attack that massive would shorten the war.

Major Muntz, who oversaw us, came in the next day and asked for a volunteer to transfer from Order of Battle to the Target Center, the other team in our unit. After some thought, I went for it. I knew I was not essential in my current role and did not want the commander to send me to the dangers of Kontum to the north or Ban Me Thuot to the south.

The transfer was the right decision. But it put me in conflict with the two active and experienced lieutenants who currently ran the Target Center. They resented the fact that another lieutenant, their peer but a greenhorn, was now joining their team.

They were enthusiastic about their work—locating targets for the air force to bomb—and excellent at it. Lieutenant Neubauer, compact and thickset, was from Montana and wanted to be a rancher. He had the hands and the attitude for it. He could drive cattle or men; it was all the same. Lieutenant Beadle, from Maryland, was tall and thin. He had perennially pursed lips and was strict in his work. He always gave the impression that he was hiding a riding crop behind his leg and might whack it across your backside if you gave him any lip.

The oversized room where the two lieutenants sat had one long desk running along the back wall and another along a side wall.

"Where do I put my stuff?" I asked.

"You need to find someplace else," said Neubauer.

"Yeah, someplace else," said Beadle.

Four people could have worked in that L-shaped space, but I felt like I was in *Alice in Wonderland*. The Mad Hatter and the March Hare were telling me there was no room at the tea table.

Incensed at such pettiness, I put my things down and walked over to a storeroom. There I found a small, army-issue, dark green folding table that had nicks all over it. It would do nicely. I walked back into the Target Center, unfolded the table, and slapped it down on the concrete floor in the exact center of the open space of the L behind these two jackasses. I brought out my name tag, snapped it onto the table, and arranged my papers behind it. Another trip to the storeroom produced a wooden folding chair, which I set up behind the desk. That made it official: I was now a part of the team, whether these guys liked it or not.

A few weeks later, on an unusually chilly afternoon, I was sitting in the Target Center doing my work when I saw Neubauer get up from his table and walk toward me. The hair rose on the back of my neck.

He and Beadle had been relentless for days. Even though we were now all first lieutenants working on the same team, they continued to badger me, insisting I had no idea what I was doing. The more it went on, the more I thought of lashing out. But I managed to step back and see that their aim was probably to provoke me into doing exactly that so they could pressure our superior, Captain Quigley, to transfer me out of Pleiku. At first, I was not sure how to defend myself, but I soon saw the solution could be for me to build a data-retrieval system.

The device was simple. In the days before personal computers, there was no way for the three of us to store and retrieve the large amount of data that came in each day. That did not matter too much because the reports were time-sensitive; the location of the Viet Cong two days ago was of little value today. But by breaking the reports down into categories, creating an index, and jotting down a one-sentence summary of what each report contained and where they were filed, I gained a complete understanding of the situation. When challenged, I could support myself with facts and shut my detractors up. The new process allowed me to be self-confident and more outgoing.

At times, what these predatory lieutenants told me was constructive, so I accepted the content even if the delivery was caustic. But if they made an error—if they reported the wrong area as the right target, for example—I recorded it into my little database. The screwups were valuable insights into how they thought. It also gave me more ammunition for shutting them up.

At age four, I could never have faced anybody down about anything—I was too much of an introvert. Now I needed to confront my two peers, and I believed I could not do it unless I used a process, namely organizing intelligence into a database. I had no love for it. Maintaining it was tedious, boring, and spirit-destroying. But I knew no other way to cope. And it avoided my having to call out their behavior directly.

When Neubauer arrived at my desk that afternoon, he wore both a scowl and a smile at the same time, a specialty of his.

"Plumb, you've been here for weeks and you still have no goddamn idea what you're doing. This is crap," he said as he threw a memo of mine on the table.

I stood up. He was more muscular, but I was an inch taller, so I was able to look down at him. "Look, Neubauer, remember last week when you thought the aerial photography was the problem, and just like I said, it turned out to be the infrared reports? You looked like a real dumb-ass in front of the captain. So, you might want to listen to me on this one." The scowl disappeared, leaving only a sheepish smile.

In addition to direct confrontations such as this, the duo had perfected a "stealth assault" on me. It was to champion hard opposition on something, saying, for example, that doing things my way was worthless and stupid, yet later coming around to my way of thinking. They expressed repeated, grave doubts about the value of experiments I was conducting with intelligence information, yet when they needed something in a hurry, they came to me for the data—because no one else was organizing the intelligence the way I was.

They slammed me so many times and I stood my ground with facts so often that they gradually backed off and my relationship with them improved. By outlasting their nitpicking and acid remarks, I turned myself into an authority on things they wanted to know.

Slowly, the three of us discovered we were moving onto common ground on some things. For example, I now agreed with them that our Captain Quigley was a jerk. He pretended to know things that he did not, seemed more interested in observing report protocol than guaranteeing good content, and did not have our backs. Despite that, Neubauer and Beadle had tired of baiting him, so while I now got along with him a little worse, they got along a little better, and we met in the middle.

This happened just as the room assignments in the compound changed, and I had to find a new home. The two of them were looking for a roommate, so we talked, and soon I confidently moved into their quarters. From that point on, we got along fine. True to form, a process—my database—had again produced unintended consequences. But this time they were positive—good relationships with my peers and a new place for me to live.

~

As my attention shifted away from those two clowns, I learned one of the duties of each officer in our compound—lieutenants, captains, and majors—was to serve as captain of the guard. This happened on a rotating basis every few months. As was often true in the army, the activity involved combining elements that were harmless and those that were terrifying.

Fig. 5. In front of quarters shared with Neubauer and Beadle. Pleiku, South Vietnam, 1967.

One benign item was known as the "guard mount." It involved calling to attention, at dusk, the twenty or so enlisted men who would move out to their guard posts around the perimeter of the compound and spend the entire night awake looking for signs of infiltration or attack. You had to be a real manly man to do the guard mount right, which I, as a bespectacled intelligence officer, was anything but.

Calling out "Atten-CHUN!" in as throaty a voice as I could muster, I heard the sound die away in the late afternoon heat as soon as it left my lips. Ideally, I would have done this in a canyon so I could produce a series of echoes: "Atten-CHUN!-CHUN-chun . . ." But on the plains of Pleiku, there was nothing for the sound to bounce against. After my command, the troops did not stiffen their backs one iota.

That first step under my belt, my next task was to inspect the guard. This was the other benign item of the afternoon, but it was tricky because I had no idea what I was looking for. If it were up to me, I would just check to make sure they had fully loaded their extra carbine magazines with rounds and gotten enough sleep the night before so they could stay up all night tonight.

But it was not up to me, and I had to go through the charade of standing in front of each man, looking him from head to toe and finding something negative to say. I had to address the shine on his boots, the wrinkles in his uniform, or the closeness of his shave, all of which were of course irrelevant for our mutual defense during the coming evening. Somebody who was really outgoing would do it with such passion, such conviction, and so many obscenities that he would touch the core of each man to let him know he was truly a vile human being for daring to present himself for guard duty in such a condition. But that was not me.

After the inspection, the scary part began. I stood in front of the group and said, "At-EEZE!" The men relaxed, spreading their legs apart and putting their hands behind them.

"You have all been advised what the password for tonight is. Do not forget it. I repeat, do not forget it." I could not say it aloud because only we twenty-one soldiers were supposed to know it for that night, and who knew what spies might be lurking about. The code was usually something like "RED DOG." I was always concerned about the quality of these passwords. They were bland, unoriginal, and simple so the men could easily remember them. However, that also made them quite easy to forget. I favored passwords like "RECTAL THERMOMETER" or "YO MAMA," but had to deal with "RED DOG" and the like every time.

Why was this scary? Because if one of these fine gentlemen forgot the password, and I approached him on my rounds in the dark with a word he did not recognize, or did not acknowledge back to me, we could end up killing each other on the spot. I had only a .45, so his chances of survival were good. He had a fully loaded automatic carbine and could plug me full of holes in seconds.

I dismissed the troops, and they fanned out to their posts. I then retreated to the underground bunker where the captain of the guard hung out, along with the mosquitoes that seemed to appear nowhere else in the entire compound except in that hole. Unlike the soldiers, I was allowed to sleep. The cot and pillow in that concrete hovel made it look homey and inviting. However, before I could lie down, I had to wait for dark, and then make at least two trips around the entire perimeter, hearing "Halt! Who goes there?" twenty times and answering, "RED DOG," before perceiving, "You may advance," rather than a hail of bullets coming my way.

The truly frightening part was that I was not supposed to announce my presence in the dark, but rather walk normally and see if the guard detected me. The army supposedly designed this to keep the men alert, but more likely it was to reduce the number of surplus lieutenants. If a soldier panicked and forgot to ask me who went there, or thought the password was maybe GREEN RAT instead of RED DOG, I was toast.

Fortunately, I survived the forty encounters of my two nerve-racking trips around the perimeter and was able to go back to my insect-infested cell. Yet before I could sleep, I had to complete one other essential duty of the evening.

I had to go into the Non-Commissioned Officer's Club with a bucket and withdraw all the coins out of the slot machines. The army provided them as a diversion for the troops, but only trusted officers could collect the money out of them. I carted the coins back to my hole, spread them on an aging, green folding table like the one I had carried into the Target Center, and counted them. The tallies done, I had to certify the amounts, put the money in bags, and turn them in. I conjectured that the funds were probably enough to buy a single nylon string on one of the hundreds of parachute flares that the US fired into the sky every time a Viet Cong stepped on a twig somewhere outside the fence.

I slathered mosquito repellent on my face and went back down into my dump to sleep, laughing at the madness of all this and trying to remember how many days were left before I could go home.

~

For six months, the rest of my tour passed with relatively little excitement. I thankfully faced no more attacks, and went to Singapore for a week on leave. A steady diet of tapes and letters from Ida kept me sane during long days of boredom, unappetizing meals, and post-nasal drips provoked by a string of cool and humid days.

A month before my tour ended, I climbed up to my bunk in the compound and grabbed the short-timer calendar that hung by a string over the top of my bedpost. I could smell the fresh evening air coming in through the open windows below me on the other side of the room.

Every soldier in Vietnam kept such a calendar, and mine was now getting short indeed. I had created a grid of over two hundred squares on a single piece of paper and numbered them backward to stand for the days I had left before returning home for good and getting discharged from the army. Crossing off each day was hugely satisfying, even when the progress seemed to be excruciatingly slow. One by one, the days fell away, and this evening there were only thirty left. Nice!

When I was down to nineteen days, I began to feel overwhelmed with everything I had to do before I could get out of Vietnam. There was another depressing all-night tour as captain of the guard, the assumption of all Neubauer's duties while he was gone for a few weeks, and the impatient wait for the port call paperwork that would take me home. In the days before email, I then had to figure out a way—quicker than the regular mail—to relay my arrival date to my family and Ida. And, at the very end, I had to spend three miserable days in Saigon to complete exit procedures.

I also needed to get mentally prepared for the huge transition that would await me when I got home. I had to get ready to be a civilian again and to be close to Ida physically, not just metaphorically. I had been admitted to the Harvard Business School in the class entering in September 1967, which meant I would only have two months to make the psychological change from Pleiku to Boston.

On my last night in Pleiku, July 4, 1967, I recalled the final night Ida and I had spent in Laguna before beginning our long ordeal almost a full year earlier. The white fluff of the tide and the golden descent of the sun had captivated me. Sitting at my writing table back then, I thought about how subjective the experience of time was. I had written, "Perhaps our long separation will be made short if we can adopt the proper attitude . . . [and] live at peace in the long months ahead."

It was hard to wrap my mind around the knowledge that we had traversed virtually every day of that huge monolith of time. So far, I had not suffered any of the harm I had feared I might, and had done so with no process to guide me other than the small database I had used to defend myself from Beadle and Neubauer.

Ida and I had triumphed over our separation, and now it was time to go home to her. The only remaining obstacle to our being together was that her parents still had the upper hand, but I was confident we would eventually find a way to change that.

With only a few days left, I flew to the Bien Hoa air base near Saigon. The hassle of processing wore me out. I rushed about, carrying my bags and records from place to place, then found myself sitting with not a thing to do for hours on end, waiting for a ride to somewhere else. Luckily, I ran into Les Gorman, my skinny South Georgia roommate from intelligence school in Baltimore.

"Les! I can't believe it! Why aren't you in jail?"

He laughed. "*Je suis moi, d'ailleurs.*" ["It's me, by the way."] He said it with his toothy grin, as if putting that nonsense into French made it have deep meaning.

Cooperative as always, and swearing in his South Georgia French, he joined me in working through the out-processing, and we got it done a lot faster. But it still came down to what we all said: "You're never short enough," meaning as long as you had one hour to go, you were still a prisoner of that wretched war and had to suffer all the attendant discomforts of being there.

After two more days of waiting, my short-timer calendar expired. At dusk, I stood on the tarmac in a long line of soldiers pinching themselves to make sure they weren't dreaming as they saw a gorgeous Continental Airlines Boeing 707 jet waiting just ahead of them.

A beautiful American girl—the first any of us had seen in months—stood at the top of the stairs by the open door in her crisp flight attendant's uniform, smiling and beckoning us to come aboard, and my eyes welled up with tears. Our job was over, and America was calling us home.

The flight from Saigon to San Francisco took seventeen hours. When we touched down on American soil, every soldier on the plane erupted in cheers and high fives.

~

I took a plane to LA, and as soon as I stepped off the airstair, I saw Ida running out onto the tarmac with tears in her eyes, joined by half a dozen other young women who were rushing to welcome their soldiers home. Ida and I kissed and cried, finding it hard to believe our long separation was finally over and I'd come home safely.

Inside the terminal, I had a joyous round of hugs and kisses with my parents and sisters. Above our smiles and laughter, we were all choking back tears.

I had experienced no fears about going back to Ida; it felt good to be with her again. But after we spent several days together at my parents' Van Nuys home, I began to feel a bit distant from her.

Part of that was my fault. In Vietnam, to cope with the ever-present possibility of a Viet Cong attack, I shut down my emotions more than I had realized. Now, sitting next to Ida on the side of the small swimming pool at the house, our feet in the water, I realized that I had little spark. She saw that. We talked about it and decided it would just take time for me to abandon a war mentality and reenter the civilian world.

But another part of the distance was due to Ida's having grown. The whole time I was gone, she was finishing up her senior year at NYU. She had now graduated and seemed more self-assured than before. She had been on her own for so long that she had firmer opinions and was more willing to speak up.

The distance was not due to a reemergence of my doubts about her; those would appear much later. For now, we gradually got used to each other without being gripped by the passionate level of neediness we both felt when I was preparing to go to war.

~

One month later, Ida and I sat on a quiet, secluded picnic ground just outside Avalon, thirty miles off the coast of Southern California on Catalina Island.

She looked radiant, her complexion pink from the sun and her eyes squinting with happiness every time she smiled at me.

After arriving on the steamer from Long Beach, we cycled to the picnic grounds on a contraption made for two and were enjoying long moments of rest on a hill overlooking the Pacific. As we gazed out to sea, the water and the air were crystal blue. The sun was clear and hot, the ocean breeze fresh. The searing brown California countryside was dotted with olive-green patches of oak and palm and somehow reminded us of how free and alive and in love we were. We owned the world now. Our lives together were just beginning, and at that moment we felt washed and clean.

Three weeks later, we were in Boston. We were busy getting Ida into an apartment in Brookline, and me into an on-campus dorm at the business school.

Ever since we returned from California, her parents had been meddling in our affairs, telling us how to go about getting set up in Boston and voicing disapproval at our modest achievements as we got one thing settled after another.

One afternoon, when we were at their house in Connecticut, Ida's mother came to us unexpectedly and asked us to sit with her at the dining room table. The house had no air-conditioning, but a breeze was blowing in off the lake, cooling us despite the heat outside.

"I'm beginning to see," Kate said while looking down, "that I've been trying to slow the process of Ida leaving home. The thought of my first child going away really made me uneasy."

She paused and looked up at us. "I'm sorry for being such an obstructionist."

We were floored. In so many words, she said she realized Ida's going away was not a rejection of her, but rather an affirmation of Ida's healthy self-expression. She asked us to bear with her while she readjusted her thinking.

Her self-analysis required not only profound care and skill, but also great courage and no small amount of humility to voice. We never expected such a positive approach from her and were overjoyed at what this could mean for the quality of our relationship with Kate and Leo in the coming years. We had vanquished not only our long separation, but also the opposition from her parents that had troubled us for so long.

~

My winning recipe had been a big success in dealing with Neubauer and Beadle. It spurred me to create a database process that not only earned me respect from them, but also the beginnings of friendship. After so many failures in using processes with women, this was the first time a procedure had actually improved relations with people I was trying to influence. I saw that under the right conditions, the recipe could work outside of academia.

But as a guide to living, it had been powerless to provide me with safety. It was no help in reducing my terror during the Evasion and Escape exercise, my anguish after the Vietnam alert, my fright after the blast in Saigon, or the scare of the night attack in Pleiku.

WHAT I COULD HAVE DONE DIFFERENTLY

I could have gone to target practice with my roommates to get familiar with firing my .30-caliber carbine. Yet the unfamiliarity served me well, because under the glaring lights of the parachute flares it increased my fear to an intolerable level. That pushed me to create distance between myself and my emotions, seeing that they were not my identity—I was simply the receptacle in which those emotions occurred.

Takeaways from Chapter 9

1. Recipes are useless against extreme fear. They are not capable of mounting an authentic response, because they themselves are not the authentic you.

2. You designed the recipe to avoid emotional overstimulation. But in the face of fear, it can actually make you more overstimulated because it is likely to vanish and leave you feeling defenseless.

3. You are not your emotions; rather, you are the environment in which they show up. Seeing that creates distance between you and them, helping you to avoid being overwhelmed.

Reflective Questions

1. The last time you felt seriously frightened about something, was your recipe any help at all? Or like mine, did it simply disappear? Or perhaps even make things worse?

2. During that fear episode, how defenseless did you feel? What action did you take to defend yourself emotionally? For example, did you call on your recipe or do something else?

3. Also during that fear episode, did you have any distance from the terror, or was it so pervasive that it felt like it consumed your whole being?

Practical Exercises

1. Write down what most scares you in your immediate future. Then below it write down what you would do if your fear materialized. Is the planned action based on your recipe?

2. As you contemplate that future fear episode, write down what makes you feel most defenseless about it, and how possibly not being able to call on your recipe is part of that.

3. Look directly at that future scenario from the outside. That is, picture yourself going through it. Notice the distance that that creates between you and your fear.

~

I had survived the war and now faced a whole new problem—one potentially more perilous for my self-esteem than anything I had just faced in Vietnam: how to survive the Harvard Business School. As I would soon discover, the program as designed was a highly intrusive form of introvert hell.

10

The Little Voice:
The Snake Pit

SEPTEMBER 1967. BOSTON, MASSACHUSETTS. On a crisp, chilly morning, my sixth day at the Harvard Business School, I approached the entrance to Aldrich Hall. The 105,000-square-foot, red-brick behemoth in front of me had heavy wood double doors that must have been twelve feet high. It was all I could do to pull one of them open.

Inside, I reported to the classroom for Section C. Like the sixteen other amphitheaters in this cavernous facility, it was horseshoe-shaped and held about one hundred students. Seven rows of swivel chairs and continuous writing surfaces descended into a hollow at the bottom. Each row was broken by two aisles that ran from the top down to where the professor stood.

Students called it the Snake Pit.

Every weekday, the school assigned three business cases, each one a sanitized real-world situation typically described in twenty to forty staple-bound pages of text and financial data. We picked them up from a cave in the catacombs under the school. For a guy used to the bright sunshine of California and Vietnam, the place was uncomfortable and foreboding.

There was no assignment other than "What should Mr. Brown do?" The case rarely even identified what the problem was; you had to figure it out for yourself.

There were no textbooks or lectures, just a relentless flow of cases five days a week. We might be reading about how to market the first indoor winter tennis court in Kansas, or how to produce the lowest-cost combination of stocks and corporate bonds to finance a mine in Peru, or how to create a win-win solution to a conflict between departments in a retail chain in California. Occasionally we would get a note on production or some other topic that might describe a few general principles, but that was it.

In each of the three daily classes, the professor cold-called on a student to present his or her analysis of the unique case written for that class. Half the course grade was based on class participation, which meant that when called on, you needed to give a cogent, convincing analysis of what the issue was and how to solve it. And when not the presenter, you had to join the snarling, noisy debate that immediately followed the student's presentation. At that point the class became a pack of hyenas ready for a kill.

This was an introvert's worst nightmare. The loudest, most incessant voices often prevailed, regardless of how shallow the thinking might be. Whether presenting or commenting, the premium was on projecting certainty and confidence even if you barely had time to read the case the night before. Because even when you did read it, there was rarely enough information in it to justify much confidence in a decision. Appearing unsure of yourself or, worse, rarely speaking shunted you to the lower reaches of the class and put your social status in the cellar.

The school purposely designed the workload to prevent students from ever being prepared. I could not take my time with anything or think through a problem in any more than the most superficial way. A slow and steady approach—the way I preferred to approach things—was a recipe for disaster.

The shock of all this drove me deep into my shell. I sat all the way at the back in the very top row of the Snake Pit, just inside the door as if ready for a quick escape. I prepared for each case by trying to resurrect the safety of the same process I had used so successfully in my undergraduate days—taking notes, memorizing them, and rehearsing what to say. But in the end, I never spoke a single word into the cacophony of unrestrained extroversion all around me in every class. I watched it from my perch high above the brawl, looking for—but never finding—a way to say anything at all. As I sat up there, my heart pounded. Every time I thought I might raise my hand, I trembled.

~

In contrast to the stress at school, being with Ida after so long a separation was soft and comfortable. I had now fully made the transition to civilian life, so I loved being with her again. Jointly we were able to smooth out the rough edges of the new world we faced in Boston. And given the threatening environment I faced in grad school, she provided the only security I had.

She lived in a nice hillside apartment in Brookline, and I had a small dormitory room on campus so I would have a place to study between classes. I spent every night at her apartment, enjoying the taste of her delicious home-cooked meals and going back to my room only the next morning before class.

Ida could not find anything that would make use of her psychology degree, so she bought a new skirt suit and took a job as a receptionist at Liberty Mutual Insurance. I bought a pair of tan wingtip dress shoes to complement the suits and ties I would be wearing to class each day so I would fit in with the formal dress code in the 97 percent male atmosphere.

Outside of the Snake Pit, I kept to myself, getting to know none of my classmates. The one exception was an Englishman who had observed my comings and goings from the dorm. He was bunking down the hall with a roommate and had no place to spend time with his fiancée, so he asked if he could use my room at night. When I gave him the key, he was the happiest Brit I ever saw.

~

"Mr. Plumb, please present today's case."

It happened in Marketing two months into the term. I had not uttered a word in that or any other class. A bolt of fear pierced my midsection when I saw I was onstage with a hundred faces turning up to look at me.

My college-based study process had been sputtering. It was a high-performance engine that relied on a steady flow of textbooks and lectures as fuel to drive my note-taking. At Harvard, any notes I could get from cases were thin and sporadic, making my engine close to useless. But I knew no other way to cope, so I kept at it.

A few days earlier a background document on marketing had shown up, and I devoured it using my standard techniques.

Fortunately, I had applied what I learned from the note to the case the professor asked me to present. It was about market segmentation, figuring out how to divide the customers for a product according to their preferences for things like convenience, reliability, selection, and service.

An occasional feature of my old approach was to create little tables of information as a mnemonic device. I had done that here, creating a matrix of sixteen cells, four columns of preferences for four categories of customers that I could discern in the case.

As I reeled them off, the professor turned to the blackboard and kept up with me, frantically writing to capture the contents of every cell as I spoke. He filled the board, then pushed it way up with an audible *swoosh* to reveal a second board beneath it and kept writing. He was silent the whole time, except for questions about what I meant, so I thought for sure he was setting me up for the hyenas. They were already restless.

"What kind of numbers would you put on each of these segments, Mr. Plumb?"

More stirring from the audience.

"That's as far as I got, sir."

A stern look in my direction. "All right, who has done the numbers on this?"

The room erupted. That was normal, but in the case that I was presenting, numbers were central. In contrast to the qualitative thinking many people had trouble with, and I excelled at, they had all run the numbers. As different students spoke, all with characteristic bravado, the professor kept writing.

I noticed that nobody was challenging my matrix. When the professor had had his fill, he ended the discussion, reached the back of his hand up to me, and said, "Mr. Plumb, that is the kind of analysis we want to see in this class." In two months, the professor had never acknowledged anyone in that way. The guy sitting in the row just below me looked up and said, "Wow, roses!"

~

In the following months, I was never able to duplicate that win in Marketing or in any other class. Instead of helping me, my undergraduate study process was so far off track for this environment that in almost every class it made me virtually unable to function. The tension was almost unbearable.

One valuable takeaway from the experience was to pay attention to the numbers of a case, and thereafter I always did. But otherwise, even though I understood the material, I still did not have the confidence to speak up in class.

I came away with exactly the wrong message: I doubled down on trying to take notes, because doing so had saved me once in Marketing and might again. That reinforced my dependence on the now-gasping system that had served me so well at Stanford, and it blinded me to any possibility of change.

I knew many of my classmates were meeting for an hour before class to hash out the day's cases. But from afar it just looked like more grandstanding and the thought of joining them turned my stomach. I continued alone, reinforcing a lifelong pattern of staying comfortable as a loner, prioritizing my own process over benefitting from collaborating with others.

The stress of the caseload became intolerable. The more I took notes, the further behind I fell. In Written Analysis of Cases, I was pulling all-nighters to turn in my reports by the 6:00 a.m. deadline, sliding on the ice in the predawn darkness to reach the designated turn-in chute before it closed. In Decisions Under Uncertainty, I got called on and had to admit I was not prepared—I did not read the case the night before.

Everyone felt pressure; it was part of the teaching model. What I did not know was that it also affected the instructors who were trying to gain tenure. I discovered this when the young assistant professor of our Human Behavior in Organizations class went into the attic of his residence, put a shotgun into his mouth, and blew off the top of his head. I recall little or no reaction among the students. It was as if the professor had jumped out of an open boxcar door on a moving train, and the cars had just kept rolling down the line.

In January 1968, I crunched across the snowy walkway to my dorm and found a letter from the dean waiting for me. It was courteous but blunt:

"Mr. Plumb, if you do not significantly improve your performance by the end of March, the university will have no choice but to ask you to leave the program."

My undergraduate study process had failed me so disastrously that I was now in danger of getting thrown out of Harvard. By yielding to my winning recipe in such an inappropriate way, I had stuck with something that was utterly unworkable. I was now more concerned about my ability to survive as a person than I ever was in Vietnam.

I considered giving up and seeing if I could reactivate the admission to the Stanford Business School that I had received while in Pleiku. But on reflection, I saw that if I could not make it at Harvard, the other school was not likely to let me in.

When I calmed down, I decided there was no way for me to improvise my way through this. So, over the next few days I met with every one of my professors. I walked up and down the long, dark halls of the school seeking advice. My Managerial Economics professor was particularly candid.

"Stop being a loner, Mr. Plumb. You need to go join a discussion group with some other students. You have been here for four months. Why haven't you done that yet?"

"It's hard for me, sir. I'm not used to learning that way."

He pulled back and took a long look at me.

"Well, you better get over that. Otherwise, you'll never make it. Your isolation from the other students is unhealthy both academically and socially. Maybe you don't belong here."

I left in despair. Joining a group was so far outside of who I was that I could hardly stand to think about it. I *was* a loner, and they were asking me to pretend to be somebody else.

I agonized over this, but only briefly. If I wanted a Harvard MBA, I had to do it. Otherwise, I would have to drop out. Within that stark frame there was no choice. I held my nose and approached a guy named Lloyd who had been nice to me once. He was happy to have me join his group.

~

The first few times I met with Lloyd and his group, I felt awkward and said little. I was preoccupied. The recent deaths of Gus Grissom, Ed White, and Roger Chaffee were on my mind; they had just been killed in a fire that swept through the Apollo 1 command module in Florida. I shuddered at the unimaginable pain their families were going through and at the management failures that likely caused such a disaster. It showed that if we got something wrong in the profession we were being trained for, it could have life-and-death consequences. This was personal, because for all I knew I might end up in mining, construction, health care, steel manufacturing, or some other industry where people's lives were at risk every day.

I looked from man to man in my group. I saw that some, like me, wore suits from JCPenney and sounded like they went to public school.

Others wore silk ties and tailor-made Italian ensembles and talked like prep-school patricians.

As I had feared, a few in the group did beat their chests and waste everyone's time. But I noticed that overall, what mattered most to these guys was quality, not volume.

We continued meeting day after day, and I started making two important contributions to the group. The first I expected: being able to make insightful, subjective analyses, much as I had done that day in Marketing. The second was a surprise: I found that I had an easy facility with numbers and could use them to distill points that some of the others had missed. I also was able to use figures to bolster the qualitative arguments I was already competent at making.

By listening to the group, I got deeper insight into cases and as a bonus went through them faster than on my own. Most importantly, I received the confidence I needed in order to speak up in class. I became surer of my arguments after trying them out on the others because I learned of any pitfalls before looking like an ass in front of a hundred people. And, best of all, I had dry runs of speaking before a group. I slowly learned to condense my sharing down to a few key points and make them with more confidence than I actually felt.

The impact on my performance was measurable. By March, my grades had come up so fast that there was no more talk of asking me to leave. And by June, I had had a strong finish to the first year.

All the while, I was doubly uncomfortable with the frequent and intense experience of being around others and with having to fly blind so often, just as I had that night in the Georgia woods.

But as the year drew to a close, I saw that while I would rather work in a cave with a single light bulb hanging from a wire in the ceiling than go to group meetings, those guys were not so bad. They were smart, committed, and occasionally funny. I was learning more from them than from the professors.

I also saw that far from being without a process at this school, I now had a shiny new one. It was different from anything I had ever built. Now the only notes I took were scribbled reminders of things the other students in my group said. Unlike at Stanford, my fuel for achievement was no longer memories gleaned from textbooks and lectures, but memories of the insights from my peers. The system geared itself to their perceptions, as well as their reactions to my own thoughts and number crunching. In just a few months, all that had reversed my slide into disaster and positioned me for even more success in my second year.

The good news was, it made me feel safer. The bad news was, I was ignoring a danger even more serious than expulsion: the reality that I was not temperamentally suited to be either a senior executive or an entrepreneur. To succeed in the executive suite or in the marketplace, I would need to repeat my Harvard peer group experience every day for the rest of my career.

If I had heeded the tiny voice that was warning me about this, I would have had to admit that I simply did not have the stomach for it. For now, I certainly felt more secure. But for decades afterward, the mismatch between my disposition and the realities of the business world would prevent me from ever feeling completely okay with myself.

I belonged in research or writing, but with such slavish devotion to my recipe, I could never have chosen those careers. The processes leading to success were far too amorphous; by comparison those in business were crystal clear. The solution to the danger would have been to tell the truth about who I really was. But I was so focused on getting through business school—and so immature and unaware—that I did not even stop to think whether business leadership was the right career for me.

~

On June 8, 1968, in the glow of a good Harvard report card, Ida and I were married in a little New England church resplendent with white flowers. By now, her parents had accepted me. But a major wrinkle was that one week before the wedding I missed a step while rushing down a flight of stairs at Leo and Kate's house and broke the outermost metatarsal bone in my left foot. Ida's father took me to the local hospital where an osteopath set the bone. I limped out on crutches and in a plaster walking cast that extended up to my knee.

Another issue was that despite the success of my new peer-based system at school, I could not find any groomsmen among my classmates. I had no friends, even among our discussion group, because I did not participate in the drinking and dining they all enjoyed at night. Ida and I had devolved into an unhealthy dependence on one another; my wanting to spend every free moment with her justified my not socializing with classmates. I learned years later that I was not considered to be a wholly successful Harvard Business School graduate because I had not used after-hours socializing to build a robust social network.

At length, Sam Horowitz from my Brazil group, Lieutenant Beadle from Vietnam, and Ida's brother, Leo Junior, as best man, kindly came as groomsmen to Ida's church in Connecticut for the ceremony. Beadle in particular surprised me. Now that he was out of the army, he was friendly and supportive. In Vietnam I was so focused on running my little intelligence-gathering database that I had completely missed seeing that side of him.

I split my pants leg to accommodate the cast during the wedding ceremony and did a passable job with a cane to peg-leg my bride down the aisle.

~

During my military service and graduate business education, the recipe had short-circuited and almost prevented four realizations from coming to light. Instead, fear had forced me into a crash course in self-awareness, and I now had the foundational Tools of Detachment to draw on for the rest of my life.[4]

---

4   For all twelve tools, please see the Appendix.

- **Observing the Mind:** In Chapter 7, I related that being chased by dogs and men with clubs during the Evasion and Escape exercise in the deep woods of Georgia taught me to watch my mind in operation, and thereby observe that all the meanings in my head were merely interpretations. I saw that to support my well-being, I was free to change those meanings.

- **Unified Awareness:** In Chapter 8, the Saigon River explosion unexpectedly sent a terrifying blast into the barracks my shipmates and I had just disembarked into. The experience embedded in me the desire and ability to increase my own safety by unifying my internal focus with the external world.

- **Emotional Context:** As described in Chapter 9, the night mortar assault in Pleiku left me and my fellow officers exposed to potential enemy fire under the swaying lights of parachute flares. The incident taught me to see myself not as whatever emotion I was having, but rather as the context for all of it. I was not the emotion. I was the person who was having it.

- **The Little Voice:** Here in Chapter 10, I ignored the quiet little voice that was warning me at Harvard that I did not have the personality needed to succeed as a business leader or an entrepreneur. It would be half a century before I would listen to that message, and use it to help me transform my life

Underlying all these understandings was my growing skill in being able to step outside my mind and simply watch it operate.

WHAT I COULD HAVE DONE DIFFERENTLY

If I had listened to the little voice whispering to me, I might have avoided decades of unhappiness in my future career, and likely become a writer fifty years before I finally did.

Takeaways from Chapter 10

1. A quiet, persistent little voice inside you often speaks inconvenient truths. Your recipe does not want to hear them, because instead it wants you to be committed to *its* agenda.

2. When you are in a hyper-extroverted environment, all your recipe can do is hunker down and insist on its own program. That is likely a formula for failure.

3. At a critical juncture in life, paying attention to your recipe instead of the little voice, which is the fourth Tool of Detachment, can cause long-term problems in your relationships, career, or personal development.

Reflective Questions

1. Recall the last time you heard a calm, persistent inner voice and disregarded it. What was the outcome? How would things be different if you had acted on what you heard?

2. When you are in a group of highly outgoing people, you cannot hear the little voice, only your recipe. The last time that happened, what did it urge you to Be, Do, and Have in the situation?

3. Recall a critical choice you made years ago based on advice from your recipe. What are some of the costs you have incurred as a result? For example, hooking up with the wrong marriage partner? Enduring an unsuccessful career? Being dissatisfied when developing a skill?

Practical Exercises

1. Write down a repeated, quiet, and inconvenient message you are getting from your inner voice. Then write down how it would change your life if you implemented it.

2. Next time you're in a highly extroverted setting, go to a quiet place and sit. Write down what the urgent voice of your recipe is saying in the situation, and see if you can hear a soft, recurring voice saying something different.

3. Write down a life-changing choice you are facing now, or will face in the future. Then write what contrasting choices the loud recipe voice and the quiet inner voice would advise you to make.

~

Ida and I had a brief honeymoon in the Poconos, then boarded a flight—cast, cane, and all—for the wilds of northeastern Brazil. For months, I had planned to go there to do research for my second-year master's thesis at Harvard, and I was damned if a broken foot was going to stop me.

Three Deeper Costs of the Recipe

11

Insensitivity:
A Testicular Engineer

JUNE 1968, 10:32 P.M. SOMEWHERE OVER THE AMAZON. Ida and I clutched each other's hands so tightly that our fingers were white.

Our Boeing 707 was on its final approach into the Atlantic port of Belém near the mouth of the Amazon River in Brazil. The thunderous lightning storm outside our window had buffeted us to the point of nausea.

We could not look at each other or even speak. It took all our concentration to just keep breathing and avoid losing the dinner we had eaten on board an hour earlier.

We hit an air pocket. The plane plummeted twenty feet, stabilized, then plummeted another twenty. It felt like twenty thousand. My mind raced with the thought that below us were two possibilities. Either we would try to land on the river and hope the incoming water did not include the flesh-eating piranhas that swam in the Amazon, or we would crash into the jungle and a fire would race through the cabin to kill us all where we sat.

The plane whined, creaked, and shuddered, making snapping noises that sounded like pieces of it were falling off.

I thought back to the map of Brazil I had looked at months earlier when choosing a destination for my master's thesis. The chart was clean and pretty, immobile on a tabletop at Ida's parents' house in Connecticut. It was simple to trace a route from New York to Belém and then on to São Luís farther east down the coast. It looked like an easy trip.

I had chosen São Luís because it was so godforsaken. It was the small capital of one of the poorest states in Brazil, and I saw opportunity there. It sat between the Amazon proper to the west and the Northeast rump of the country to the east, two regions investors had been targeting for years. I was hoping I could launch an agribusiness project halfway between them based on oil from the *babassú* (ba-ba-SOO) palm tree. It would help to transform the economy, put money in the pockets of poverty-stricken people, and in time provide a good living for Ida and me. As such, this could turn out to be more than just a research project, so I was glad Ida had made good progress in learning at least a conversational level of Portuguese.

To go into a foreign city where I knew no one and come out with measurable results, I needed to be more extroverted than I was used to being. Today, I am surprised I chose to put myself in such a situation. To meet key people, I would have to improvise, which meant I would be uncomfortable. But I guessed that my success with the peer group at Harvard would give me the energy I needed to reach out once we got to São Luís. I was sure I could figure out a process that would bring a good outcome. And thankfully, my Portuguese was still good.

I had chosen agribusiness because it was central to the pet theory of my thesis advisor, Professor Nelson Pettigrew. He believed helping people produce and market their agricultural products could lift them out of poverty. Tall, lanky, and handsome, he was the Brahmin son of generations of Massachusetts congressmen. Pettigrew had left Harvard to run for the House himself in 1958, but he lost and was now back at the university.

"Ben," Ida cried, her voice shaking as she shouted above the roar outside, "shouldn't we be there by now?"

I had made the same calculation. "Yes, we should be. Maybe we have to land someplace else."

"Oh God, I just can't stand this," she said. "I really think I'm going to be sick." She withdrew her hand and put it on her stomach.

With my newly freed hand, I reached down to scratch the top of the cast on my left leg, trying to relieve a persistent itch that jabbed me from deep inside.

Belém
São Luís
Rio de Janeiro

Fig. 6. Map of Brazil.

I forced myself to recall once again why we were there. One of Professor Pettigrew's consulting clients was Herbert Cornuelle (pronounced "Cornell"), the CEO of the United Fruit Company, a firm headquartered near our campus in Boston. At the time, United Fruit was one of the largest corporations in the world, the iconic owner of the "Great White Fleet" of refrigerated ships that for decades had brought fresh bananas from Central America to the US.

United Fruit was massively unpopular in Latin America. The company owned land, railroads, and company towns. As such, it had a reputation as *El Pulpo*—the octopus that took more out of each country than it put in. Cornuelle desperately wanted to change all that and was looking for a novel approach. Knowing this, Professor Pettigrew convinced him to grubstake me for a summer of research in any poor location of my choice. I chose São Luís with a goal of building a revolutionary new model that United Fruit could scale up.

One of the things the business school drilled into every student was a concept I called "Environmental Scanning 101," even though there was no actual course by that name. It meant that an integral part of any decision-making process needed to be a visceral, aggressive look at the business setting a company was in. What forces were on the horizon that might upend the current situation? What threats existed, and what opportunities? What strengths did the firm have in the face of those, and what weaknesses? In my excitement to get to Brazil and get on with the research, I skipped over doing that. Instead, in thrall to my recipe, I focused on all the steps I had to execute between now and the time my thesis was done.

I had happily bought two suits, one blue and one dark green, along with white shirts and a few ties, all of which could be thrown in the sink and washed to rid them of the tropical stink that would no doubt saturate everything we wore in São Luís. I was an experienced international traveler, but this was Ida's first trip outside the country. She no doubt was wondering what she had gotten herself into.

A plunge through a third air pocket made us gasp. We lurched down, and down, and down. Ida was close to tears, and I was close to vomiting. We heard the wheels screech and felt them hit the runway. The engines roared to reverse thrust and slowed us down, pushing the smell of kerosene through the ventilation system. Weak applause rippled through the cabin.

~

Shaken, we took a cab to a modest hotel in Belém. In our room, I was surprised to find glorious, dark hardwood doors and cabinets that normally would grace a much more expensive inn. No doubt they were products from the rainforest that surrounded the city.

Ida was in no mood to appreciate them. She was disoriented and frightened, her discomfort made more acute by the exhaustion of the long trip and a terrifying landing. She wanted to talk, but I was impatient, silently wondering why she could not suck it up like I had. I forgot how unsettling an alien environment could be to a first-time foreign traveler. In retrospect, I was a real shit. She just wanted to be held and comforted, and I was so insensitive to that need that I could only think about getting us both to bed so we could catch our early flight to São Luís in the morning. Just a few minutes of caring from me could have made such a difference for her, but I was too small and immature to offer it.

Decades later, I realized this was an unintended consequence of my devotion to my process-driven approach to life. All I could think about were the steps I needed to follow for my thesis. We had to get to São Luís, meet people who could provide me with data, and capture the information. I then had to organize it, run numbers based on it, prepare a business case, and so on. I was thinking about all of this so constantly that in Belém, it put the first crack in our relationship.

The next morning, Ida felt better. We boarded a small two-engine plane for the three-hundred-mile trip east to São Luís. The day was sunny, but the heat welling up off the land below us kept battering the small craft. Once again, we felt nauseated.

When we landed, we found our hotel to be even more modest than the one in Belém, but it still had a full ration of gorgeous hardwoods on wall panels, armoires, and doors. Spare but clean, it had a decent bathroom, plenty of space to spread out, and an effective but noisy wall unit air conditioner that kept the room cool.

First thing the next day, Ida donned a nice dress while I put on a coat and tie, and in the blistering heat we walked to the local library. This was long before the days of the internet, and there was not even a copy machine in the building. So we spent hours writing down production and sales figures for babassu palm oil on lined notepads. This gave me data on the size of the market that at the time was available no other way.

We then walked over to the Brazil–United States Institute in search of data. The institute taught English and promoted understanding between the two countries. As soon as we arrived, the staff treated us like heroes—here were real live Americans in São Luís! Olivia, the administrator, gushed all over us in decent English, asking dozens of questions and wanting to help us in any way she could. She had no statistics I could use but did know of two people who had given her a standing invitation to house any Americans who might need a place to stay—a professor and a businessman.

Never expecting such a windfall and happy at the thought of being able to live more comfortably than in a hotel, we readily agreed to move into the businessman's home if he and his family would have us. Soon, we and Olivia were in a cab driving toward what passed for an upscale neighborhood in this humble town and found ourselves outside the gate of a fortress—a large two-story concrete-block house surrounded by a high wall. We rang the bell, a housemaid answered, and Olivia explained to her that she had brought some Americans who wanted to speak with the owner.

The young woman nodded and led us through a spacious courtyard that had a mammoth hardwood tree growing in the middle of it to block the broiling sun. An upstairs balcony loomed over the space; we could hear yelling and scurrying around from beyond its open French doors. The housekeeper told an unseen senhora who we were. The lady called her husband at work, and within minutes, he joined us in the living room.

Tall, swarthy, and well-built, William Nagem (NA-zheng) was an affable, outgoing, fortyish entrepreneur of Lebanese-Brazilian descent. He spoke excellent English that he had learned when studying engineering at a textile institute in England in the early 1950s. He owned a cloth-making factory in São Luís that obviously supplied a good living. He introduced his small, attractive, and garrulous wife, a son about eight years old, and a daughter about five, all of whom said hello and then left us alone with William and Olivia. An air conditioner on the wall growled to life, pushing a delicious, cool breeze onto our faces.

When Olivia told him that we were from Boston doing research on babassu oil for a program at Harvard, his eyebrows went up. She said we were looking for a place to stay and knew he had expressed interest in helping any Americans who might show up at the institute. He nodded and quickly offered us our own apartment—a bedroom and bath located above the detached garage on the other side of the courtyard.

We thanked him for his generosity, shook on it, and were about to return to the hotel to get our belongings when he expressed keen interest to know the nature of the project I was working on. I told him it would be a venture to use US capital to fund a babassu oil processing plant, as well as any other agricultural ventures that might make sense. This heightened his attention even more, and it was only when Olivia said she needed to get back that we left—in William's car, no less, with his personal driver at the wheel.

~

Over the next few days, I thought a lot about William. When I started on this trip, I was not looking for a local venture partner, but after meeting him I began to entertain the idea. It would smooth things politically, bring in local knowledge, and in general get us off to a faster start.

That said, I concluded that William was not the guy. I would want someone who was a disrupter, a development-oriented partner who would not focus on earning money to the exclusion of supplying social benefits for the local people. This, William was not. On the contrary, I saw him as having all the signs of a patriarch, a man with an entrenched interest in the status quo.

He owned a factory that used an ancient technology; textile manu-facturing had been around for two hundred years. In his home, he had at least four full-time, live-in servants—a maid, a cook, a driver, and a houseboy. And he was something of an outsider, although as a Lebanese Brazilian, he did have a wide network of Middle Eastern contacts.

Yet he had good political connections. A childhood friend was Edison Soares, the governor of the state of Maranhão where São Luís sat. And William was a funny guy. He told me that in this city, people were not familiar with *engenheiros têxteis*—textile engineers—and he sometimes got mail addressed to *William Nagem, Engenheiro Testicular*. So, I now considered him to be our friend, the Testicular Engineer.

The apartment William kindly offered made our grubstake go a lot further. He would not accept a penny for rent or food, even knowing that United Fruit was footing the bill. But the place had its challenges. Foremost was the lack of air-conditioning or any screens on the windows. To stay cool, we did have a ceiling fan, and we could get a cross breeze by keeping the windows open all night long. But to do so, we had to sleep under a mosquito net. That cut down the air circulation and was a pain to get in and out of in the dark.

All the odd night sounds of São Luís came directly into our bedroom. Motorbikes buzzed on the street outside. Vendors cried, "*Jornal do Rio!*" announcing the arrival of newspapers that had just come in by air from Rio de Janeiro fourteen hundred miles to the south. Roosters crowed at 4:00 a.m. Competing roosters crowed at 4:01 a.m. But otherwise the apartment was clean and comfortable, and Ida was content with it.

She continued to go with me to the library, which had a surprising amount of useful information for us to copy. She had studied Portuguese at NYU before we came down and tried to speak with William's wife. But with language issues on both sides and the woman insisting on simply speaking louder when Ida did not understand something, there was not much companionship. Especially when Ida saw the lady standing on her balcony every day screaming at the housekeeper and houseboy in the courtyard below. Ida hated that.

To help ease her isolation, I read to Ida in the evenings, translating articles about America from the Rio newspapers. That July in 1968, Vassar College began admitting men, the first Special Olympics were held, and Virginia Slims launched a new cigarette brand using the slogan "You've Come a Long Way, Baby."

Since the day we arrived in Brazil, Ida had had an upset stomach from the unfamiliar bacteria in the food. Fortunately, a test showed no infection, and eventually her discomfort passed.

Each morning, we had breakfast with William and the family on a picnic table in the courtyard, under the giant hardwood tree; for lunch and dinner we ate inside by ourselves, with the cook or the maid serving us. At Sunday breakfast, we all ate a huge spread of eggs, fruit, and wonderful Brazilian coffee. For some reason, the meal always included tapioca pudding, a delicious but strange addition. Sunday evenings, William treated us and the family to dinner at the best restaurant in town, which improbably was at the airport. Our favorites were broiled chicken and a dessert of chocolate or vanilla ice cream covered with *ameixas cozidas*—stewed plums. William ensured us with a grin that we could eat as much as we wanted, because nothing we consumed on a Sunday would make us fat.

William often spoke of "the interior" as if it were a place of mystery. São Luis was a civilized little city of 200,000 people on an island just yards off the Atlantic coast. But the rest of Maranhão was a wild and untamed wilderness where most of the state's 3.75 million people lived. Periodically, he drove his pickup there to buy cotton for his cloth factory and see to some of his other ventures. He always came back filthy, with red dust on his truck and his clothes from having driven for hundreds of kilometers over washboard dirt roads. Once, he lent us his truck so we could go to a beach that could only be reached by a half-hour drive over the washboards.

Ahead of time, he told me how to drive on them. "Go slow," he said, "and it jars your teeth loose. Go fast, and you skim over the top of the bumps."

"Won't that hurt the truck?" I asked.

He laughed. "It hurts it worse if you go slow. If you drive fast, it's bumpy but still smoother."

His was the voice of experience. I tried it, and it worked.

One night, William took us to an astonishing *macumba* ceremony in the backlands. *Macumba* is an Afro-Brazilian form of witchcraft widely practiced in the interior. He was not sure where to find the event because it moved around from night to night. So just after 10:00 p.m. he drove into the darkness with Ida and me sitting beside him in the pickup. He cut the engine and lights and listened. After doing this three or four times, we all heard the syncopated rhythm of drums beating, and by homing in on that, we soon found a wooden structure where the ritual was taking place.

We were nervous about interrupting a quasi-religious ceremony, but William assured us nobody would even notice we were there. We walked into a sizeable room and looked across it, seeing thirty or forty people milling around in a circle with a large opening in the middle, and he was right—we were invisible. Four African-Brazilian women dressed in white linen were in the middle, spinning, their eyes looking straight up as if hypnotized. A fifth woman lay on the floor, rigid and quivering. Shortly, a woman standing next to us let out a yelp and threw herself into the circle on the floor, rolling and shaking as if in the grip of an epileptic fit. William said they were all being possessed by spirits but would be fine in the morning.

~

Over the ensuing weeks, I spent many hours with William and gradually came to see him in a different light.

He had been born and raised in São Luís. Twelve years earlier, when he returned from England, he started his own small textile factory from scratch, using his technical knowledge to compete in a way new to Maranhão—based on low costs, thin margins, and high volume. As his business grew, he generously offered technical and financial aid to friends and competitors alike. Now, just about anyone of influence in the state was indebted to him in terms of gratitude or money.

He was fascinated with my project and asked me many questions about it, offering suggestions that made sense.

"Why just focus on babassu oil?" he asked. "It's true that we have over a billion babassu palms, and there is strong demand for the oil. And, yes, supply bottlenecks are keeping the market artificially small."

He paused, looking at me intently. "But there is a lot more you can do here."

"Such as?" I asked, my curiosity piqued.

"Well, rice milling. And cotton ginning. I have small operations in the interior doing both of those, and they are very successful."

This struck a chord in me. In my research, I had learned that Maranhão cotton was of low quality and improperly cleaned, but that the soil would support high-grade varieties. It had done so in colonial times until it began to overshadow the industry in Portugal, leading the colonizers to shut the Brazilian industry down. Rice, too, could stand to have its seed quality and handling improved. William's local knowledge seemed right on target.

As he spoke, I thought of the families in the interior who were gathering the babassu nuts and growing the rice. I had discovered that they lived in almost total deprivation, earning under one hundred dollars per year. They were semi-nomads, moving their families every two years because the slash-and-burn technique that they used to clear the land depleted the soil. They were constantly in debt to local traders, which was another reason for moving. The traders were intermediaries between producers and customers; they worked for the *grande comerciante* or big business owner who controlled the economy of the municipality. Because Maranhão was so isolated, the families still regarded the *comerciantes* with some affection; elsewhere in Brazil, rural violence had been directed against those oligarchs.

Among the families, illiteracy was close to 100 percent, and health was staggeringly bad. Their diet consisted of rice, beans, and manioc—a great deal of starch. They drank polluted water and walked barefoot. Worms, malaria, and schistosomiasis were the main conditions they suffered from, but they also had to deal with tuberculosis, pneumonia, leprosy, gangrene, and snakebites.

I contrasted their health situation with my own, which at that moment consisted of only one problem: how to get my cast off now that the required six weeks had passed. I was leery of a doctor in this town using a circular saw to remove it, so I plunged it into the bathtub until it got soft and ripped it off with my bare hands.

I began to see that William was more of a disrupter than I had imagined. He did not do business like a *grande comerciante*. One of his best friends was a French-Canadian priest named Edmund Pouliot, a man who had been working in the interior for over seven years organizing and motivating the families to form self-help groups. Pouliot used a painstaking process of "self-inventory" to help the locals become agitated about their poverty and self-organize to fight the conditions they lived in.

After learning about how people lived in the interior, I could not wait to add a community development piece to the project. When I told William, he got excited and said Father Edmund would probably jump at the chance to lead it using techniques he had already mastered. Recently, the padre had risen to program coordinator for twelve interior parishes and seemed to be looking for a bigger challenge either with local families or back in Canada. We went to see him, and he, too, became thrilled over the possibility of doing work on a larger scale than he had been. A serene man with curly brown hair and a cherubic face that belied his interior drive, he surprised us a few days later by reporting that his archbishop had already given him tentative approval to work with us.

I say "us," because by now I was convinced William was indispensable to this project. We had talked further, and he was now openly willing to join me in any way he could be helpful. As if to make good on that promise, he asked if I would like to meet Governor Soares. I said yes, since I was on a roll. I had already reached out successfully to William and Edmund and did not shrink away from visiting the governor, despite my strong introvert traits. The energy of dealing with my peer group back at Harvard still pushed me forward.

"Edison is the first development-minded governor we have ever had," William said. "He is looking for projects that will bring money, technology, and good management into Maranhão."

"That sounds too good to be true," I replied.

"In a way it is. Soares does not like private foreign investment. Most of his power comes from the *caboclos* [the subsistence families in the interior], not the *grandes comerciantes*, so he may not be too enthusiastic."

William went on to balance out his advice. He said the governor had the power to grant virgin land to us in the interior, reduce taxes, and cut red tape. "The first year of the project, he would probably make us build dirt roads and drill freshwater wells," he said. "But that would not be a big deal."

William reported that despite Soares's progressive interests, he still had some old-time oligarch ways about him. I knew from photos in the paper that he had slick black hair and eyes set close together that peered out over a bushy black mustache. He certainly looked the part. I laughed when William said that whenever Soares called a *caboclo* to speak with him at the governor's residence, he brought the man into his bedroom and sat with him on the bed. This was intimidating in the extreme, since most people in the interior did not have even so much as a mattress to sleep on in their mud-and-stick shacks.

When we met Soares—not in his bedroom, but on the second-floor veranda of the governor's mansion under a slowly turning ceiling fan—I found that William had correctly sized him up. The governor was mildly interested, but openly skeptical that I could do anything. I looked out across his manicured grounds, then watched a trickle of sweat drip down the side of a transparent glass pitcher of iced tea on the table in front of us. I assured him we would have the backing of United Fruit. But he said he had heard many promises of such foreign largesse before and would have to be shown our project was real. He would not oppose us, but we had our work cut out. After we left, William said once our deal was more mature, he was sure he could bring his friend Edison around.

Now we went to work on the project in earnest. Based on William's cost and revenue figures, I built financial projections for an $8.5 million venture: $2.5 million from United Fruit and the rest from local investors and government incentives. A synthetic cloth manufacturing facility in São Luís would take 70 percent of the money, and a self-supporting complex of agricultural projects in the interior—a babassu oil mill, a cotton gin, a rice mill, and a community development program—would take 30 percent. The textile factory would provide a nice return on investment for United Fruit, while the other projects would help to transform people's lives.

At a 125-acre site, Father Edmund would organize and train one thousand families to change from subsistence to commercial agriculture, raising crops that they would sell to our company, the Maranhão Development Corporation. At Edmund's suggestion we would supply only roads, fresh water, and training—via seventy-five full-time professionals in health, literacy, home economy, agriculture, and community organization. It would be up to the families to stop slashing and burning and fix themselves to the seventy-five acres of land they would buy over time.

I would be managing director for up to five years, and William would be president. Initially, I might have been concerned that William was taking part only to enrich himself and would pocket much of the investment money. But there was nothing in his background or his personality that even remotely suggested he would be dishonest.

It came time for Ida and me to leave Brazil. William, Edmund, and I agreed that we now had to put everything on hold until I got back to the States and could work with Professor Pettigrew to get the funding we needed from United Fruit.

~

By late August, Ida and I were back in Boston and moved into married student housing in a tower on the Charles River. My foot had healed. We got a gray tabby kitten that we named Babassu, and on his first night with us, we laughed as he curled up in one of my tan wingtip shoes to sleep.

Soon, we settled down into a normal life as I went back to my second year at the business school and Ida got another job. She was relieved to be back in the US, but neither of us realized how hard the summer in Brazil had been on our relationship. She craved stability, and with me she was getting anything but.

Professor Pettigrew was thrilled with the progress William and I had made on the project. It showed how private business could change centuries-old ways of doing things and lift people out of poverty.

He wanted to meet William. One freezing night in October, I welcomed the sturdy Brazilian at Logan Airport, finding him shivering in the light topcoat he had worn. The next day, we met Pettigrew in his office on campus, and the chemistry was excellent. William's sincerity, passion, and executive presence were obvious. The next step was for the three of us to meet with Cornuelle, the CEO of United Fruit, to present our case and convince him to show the project to his board.

But that never happened. Unknown to the three of us, United Fruit was being pursued by companies that wanted to take it over. Just as we were ready to meet with Cornuelle, he revealed that he was in late-stage negotiations for United Fruit to sell itself to AMK Corporation of New York, a conglomerate. He could not focus on our project any longer and refused to meet with us.

We were devastated. William returned to Brazil and resumed his duties as a testicular engineer. Professor Pettigrew and I continued on, meeting with the new owners in later months, but found they had none of Cornuelle's social consciousness. Their only interest in Brazil was to see if their A&W subsidiary could open root beer stands there.

~

I had been so focused on the internal processes needed to get the Brazilian project off the ground that I was insensitive to the danger existing in the sponsoring company's external environment—its economic situation.

It was clear that before going to Brazil, I should have looked at the company's balance sheet. United Fruit was a public company. The records were easily available at the business school's Baker Library, and it would have been a simple matter to walk in and review them. Their current assets would have shown me immediately that because the firm was awash in cash, it could be in peril as an attractive takeover candidate. Armed with that knowledge, I could have gone to Pettigrew with a concern, and we possibly might have lined up a backup sponsor.

As it was, when AMK showed up I got blindsided. Now it was too late to do anything about it. I had forgotten the painful lesson I learned after the explosion that first night in Saigon: that despite being an introvert, I always needed to take the external environment into account. In this case, it was not a matter of failing to be omniscient, just one of failing to do the homework I had been trained to do.

In 1969, Nelson Pettigrew published the Maranhão Development Corporation as a Harvard Business School case study. He taught it to students to illustrate his view that business could have a productive role in helping societies advance.

Cornuelle resigned within a few months and moved to Hawaii to work for an international construction firm. He died in 1996.

The main shareholder in AMK Corporation—United Fruit's new owner—was a man named Eli Black. He mismanaged the company by crippling it with debt, and in 1975 committed suicide by jumping out of his office on the forty-fourth floor of the Pan Am building in New York.[5]

Edison Soares left the governorship of Maranhão in 1970 and was elected president of Brazil in 1987.

Father Edmund Pouliot returned to his home in Victoriaville, not far from Montreal in Quebec. Ida and I drove up from Boston to visit with him there while we were still working with AMK to continue the project. But we had little hope of success, and our lunch was melancholy. We lost contact with him, and I later learned that he died in 2017.

William Nagem continued expanding his local businesses. He was diagnosed with Alzheimer's disease in 2001 and died in 2014 at the age of eighty-four.

~

Thanks to my peer-based study approach, I graduated in the top third of my class in June 1969.

Given where I had stood just eighteen months earlier, that was a joyful outcome. But the successful process I had followed concealed an inconvenient fact: I had gotten short-term results by joining a peer group and

---

5   Peter Kihss, "44-Story Plunge Kills Head of United Brands," *New York Times*, February 4, 1975, https://www.nytimes.com/1975/02/04/archives/44story-plunge-kills-head-of-united-brands -united-brands-head.html.

ended up feeling safer at Harvard by doing that. But I simply did not have the outgoing personality required to survive long-term, let alone prosper, in the aggressive and confrontational world of top executive leadership in business. Far from giving me financial security, a business career would put me in decades of economic jeopardy.

I now had an MBA but had done no interviewing because I had felt so reassured by the way the project was coming together. Consequently, I was in a dangerous financial bind for months. I eventually landed a job as assistant director of planning for Castle & Cooke, Inc., in Hawaii. As the owners of Dole bananas, they were the main competitors of United Fruit. After I joined them, I saw firsthand that a project such as mine would have sparked zero interest there, so I let go of it.

WHAT I COULD HAVE DONE DIFFERENTLY

I could have been much more sensitive to Ida's needs in Belém, and, instead of rushing us off to Brazil so quickly, could have checked the sponsoring company's external environment. Had I looked at their balance sheet, I would have seen they were cash rich and a prime target for acquisition, which would have led me to seek a backup firm.

Takeaways from Chapter 11

1. We introverts tend to form first impressions of other people based not on who they are, but who they appear to be through the filter of our recipes.

2. Recipes often rush us into doing things, because they make us feel so certain that we can handle them. Beware of doing that, because the situation may contain hidden problems.

3. Recipes frequently lead us to devalue the needs of the people around us. We are driven to achieve, not necessarily to relate.

Reflective Questions

1. The first time you meet someone, what criterion does your recipe urge you to use to judge them? How often have you found that impression to be wrong?

2. Recall a time you rushed into something without thinking it through because your recipe made you feel confident you could manage it. What was the outcome?

3. Due to urgings from your recipe, when was the last time you overrode or ignored something your significant other needed? Maybe it was deciding on a move, holding off on having a child, or something else. How did that impact the relationship?

Practical Exercises

1. Consider the opinion you hold of a person you just met. Then ignore that opinion. What impression is left? Write it down, and how it differs from the view through your recipe.

2. Think of a choice you are facing at work. Write down three problems that could occur if you rushed into it based on advice from your recipe.

3. Think of a decision you are facing in a relationship. Write down what your recipe suggests, and what the other person truly needs from you.

~

Ida was ecstatic that we were not going to be roughing it in the interior of Brazil; in retrospect, I see a life like that would have been tough on both of us. Instead, Castle & Cooke had hired me for a whopping $11,000 a year, and soon the three of us—Ida, Babassu the cat, and I—were on our way to company headquarters in Honolulu.

I was now twenty-six years old. It was late 1969, and we were excited about the new world that lay ahead of us in Hawaii. But moody clouds surrounded the plane as we descended into Oahu.

12

Obsession:
Chaos in Chile

OCTOBER 1969. HONOLULU, HAWAII. When Ida and I stepped off the plane with the other passengers, a line of women in brightly colored dresses placed leis of live fragrant flowers around our necks and welcomed us to the islands.

Our cat, Babassu, received no lei. Instead, the airline shipped him and his cage directly to an airport holding facility and a few days later to the permanent quarantine station just outside Honolulu. The islands were free of rabies, and to keep it that way, the state required pets to be held for 120 days.

The animals lived in luxury. On our first visit to our cat, we looked up and saw that his outdoor, screened-in enclosure was at least ten feet tall and big enough for both of us to walk around in. A leafless tree trunk led from the concrete floor up to a platform and a covered box where he could sleep. Every day, Ida went to see him by herself; on weekends we went together. He was her baby, and she could hardly stand to be away from him. This was a sign that she was not getting everything she needed from our relationship, but it did not concern me enough to do anything about it.

My own obsession was my new job. I worked for Elijah Chan, a native of Hawaii and the director of planning at Castle & Cooke (C&C). Ours was the largest company in the islands, the owner of enormous pineapple plantations whose output they marketed under the Dole brand. Our office building rose far above the nearby Aloha Tower. When I mentioned that to my parents, they were amazed—that old tower had been the tallest building in Honolulu when they honeymooned there in 1939.

Elijah was fortyish, handsome, intense, and brilliant. A chain smoker who often had small white clouds of smoke wafting up into his coal-black hair, he was also kind and somewhat of an introvert, committed to developing me in a gentle way. On my first day, he took me to a Chinese restaurant and introduced me to dim sum, a Cantonese dish of steamed dumplings that I had never heard of and found to be deliciously exotic.

In one week, he taught me more about financial forecasting than I had learned in two years at Harvard. Our department's main job was to evaluate companies for acquisition, so it was critical to build an accurate model of how much cash we would have to invest and when it would come back to us.

We did everything by hand on buff-colored thirteen-column sheets of accounting paper. The only tools we had were electronic calculators and slide rules; personal computers powerful enough to do the job were at least fifteen years in the future.

The work was excruciating, but Elijah made it come alive. He likened each analysis to a detective story. When we projected income into the future and subtracted expenses, we exposed precisely when the acquisition would run out of money, and by how much. But that information was hidden and had to be dug out.

Elijah had two approaches for doing that. A private learning experience with him was a salve to my heart after so much forced extroversion at Harvard, and I was eager to absorb both of his methods.

First, he said, project everything weekly. If you did it monthly, you would not uncover the actual cash shortage that lurked inside the month. Second, keep a running total from week to week. If you simply picked the week with the biggest *one-week* shortfall, you would likely be wrong—perhaps fatally for the business.

I was thrilled. Here was a robust, practical process I could use to face the real world head-on as my primary contribution to success. I latched on to it with steely-eyed determination.

One of the acquisitions Elijah had already decided on was Erdesa, a builder of earthquake-resistant steel-and-concrete houses in Chile. The struggling, two-bit operation belonged to Art Kipke, the manic-depressive president; Bill Warneke, the perpetually angry field manager and the only one of the owners currently living in Chile; and Bruce Fraser, the grounded and energetic executive VP. Bruce was of Scottish descent and had a twinkle in his eyes above a graying beard; I took an immediate liking to him. It was mutual—he probably saw in me an ally who could help him provide coherent thinking in the small company.

Elijah wanted his own man in Chile on the inside of Erdesa as VP and controller, and after I had been in Hawaii for just nine months, he gave me the job.

My first task before I left for Chile was to buy a money belt. As soon as I had it, I went in to see him as he had asked.

"Here's a present for you," he said, reaching into his desk. He took out $55,000 in negotiable cashier's checks and handed them to me, saying, "Fold these in half the long way and see if you can get all of them into the belt."

"What is going on here, Elijah?"

"You're going to smuggle these into Chile when you and Ida move down there. The clowns at Erdesa illegally took that much *out* of the company by using Chilean escudos to buy US dollars on the black market. So, there is a gaping hole on Erdesa's local books. The only way to fill it is to reverse the process—black market and all—and you're the only one I trust to do it right."

He watched as I crammed the heavy, bulky checks into the belt. If I had needed to burn off any fat around my midsection, that would have been a great way to do it.

~

C&C had shipped our household goods and our blue 1965 Chevy Nova coupe from Boston to Honolulu and now had to ship all of that again from Honolulu to the port of Valparaiso, near Santiago in Chile. In preparation, I had heavy-duty shock absorbers and springs added to the car so it could survive the local roads.

C&C also paid to ship our long-suffering cat on the plane with us when we departed for South America in June 1970. Babassu was only a few months out of Hawaiian quarantine after his five-thousand-mile trip from Boston. Now he found me once again propelling a tranquilizer pill down his throat before we all got on the eight-thousand-mile flight to Chile.

We stopped during the day in LA and again at night in Lima, Peru. There we had his cage lowered onto the dimly lit tarmac amid the roar of jet engines. Every hair on the cat's body was sticking straight up, but likely not from the noise: A bear was also in the plane's animal compartment. Babassu seemed unusually eager to accept the tranquilizer I offered. On arrival we had no worries about going through another quarantine because there was none; rabies was widespread in Chile.

Our living situation was far more comfortable than it had been two years before in São Luís, and Ida adapted well. The nice wood-frame furnished bungalow we rented in the Pedro de Valdivia section of Santiago felt to me like it was in a middle-class part of LA. The warm, dry weather was similar since the two cities were roughly the same distance from the equator. Except here we were in the shadow of the towering and snowcapped Andes Mountains, and June was the start of winter instead of summer. On cold days, we were thankful for the kerosene stove in the hallway. It smelled of fumes but heated the whole house nicely.

We hired a full-time housekeeper named Conchita. Squat, good-natured, and cheery, she called us Don Benjamín and Doña Ida, which she pronounced as Ben-ha-MEEN and EE-dah. She cooked, ironed, shopped, and laughed a lot, smoothing our introduction to local life. Ida especially appreciated help in running the house and having someone friendly to practice her Spanish with.

Only three of the four executives of Erdesa moved to Chile. Art Kipke remained in California. Bruce Fraser and his wife moved down to Santiago when Ida and I did. Bill Warneke was already living seven hundred miles to the north in Antofagasta to run our project there. I was glad he was so far away because he was a pain in the ass to deal with. Bruce, on the other hand, was upbeat and great fun to be around. He and I set up a small office in the leafy Vitacura section of town. He focused on chasing new projects while I managed the cash flow and kept Elijah Chan up to date on our progress.

Another bright spot was Maximiliano "Max" Soto, our lead civil engineer. A Chilean in his thirties, he had extraordinary competence and a gentle, patient air about him that made him a natural leader. Squinty-eyed from the smoke of the frequent cigarettes in his mouth, he was slightly extroverted and always a source of fun and good advice. Once, when I proposed that we postpone paying a bunch of small bills instead of a few large ones, he said, "*Son las cuentas chicas que friegan*, Ben," meaning it was the small accounts that grated on us. I took his suggestion and paid them, letting the big ones fester instead. I did not regret it.

I quietly got the $55,000 into the country and contacted our insurance broker, a Brit in his sixties, to convert the funds on the black market. Jolly, overweight, and a bit befuddled, his name was Jerry Bell. Before each transaction, he liked to receive a phone call with a coded request. Exchange controls were not yet being enforced, but he was nervous, so he asked us to call ahead and let him know how many holes of golf we wanted to play for how many days (the amount of US dollars to exchange, in thousands), as well as the hour we wanted to start (the exchange rate we would accept).

"Hello, Jerry, this is Ben Plumb from Erdesa."

"Hello, Ben! Bruce told me you might call today."

"Yes. We'd like to play eleven holes of golf for five days [meaning

$55,000] and are looking to start at about eight p.m., which is twenty hundred hours [meaning a rate of twenty escudos per dollar]."

"Fine. That is fifty-five holes. Could we play them all today?"

"Umm . . . sure."

"Give me a minute to see what I can do." Long pause. "Good news. I can play at twenty-one hundred hours. Is that okay?"

"Sure, Jerry, that's even better." The escudo was already depreciating, so we were getting a few more of them for each dollar than I had expected.

"Okay, fine. Bring it in, Ben, and I will make a deposit to your account."

If anyone was listening in, that last comment exposed the whole call as a farce. I told Bruce about it, and he fell over laughing.

Early on, Bruce had five new projects in the pipeline. I calculated the expected revenue, costs, and cash flow for each one using Elijah Chan's method, then prepared a summary into which I fed the results of each project. This took weeks and filled more than a dozen thirteen-column pages of accounting paper. I shipped them air mail to Honolulu, and Elijah was astonished. He pinned all of them to the wall of his office so that as he looked from left to right, he could trace the money flow from each project into the summary. He approved only a few of the invest-ments, but now at least he and his boss no longer saw Erdesa as a flaky outfit run by guys who didn't know what they were doing.

The exercise also proved to Bruce that I was the financial authority in Erdesa. Both Bruce and Art Kipke were highly extroverted and therefore prone to have less patience with detail than I had. My financial forecasting work focused their attention on the specifics in an engaging way.

~

It was not long before an unfamiliar, dark side of Chile started to appear. Overall, it would require more extroversion to confront than I could muster.

The triggering event occurred in November 1970, five months after our arrival, when Salvador Allende became president. A far-left social-ist who got only 36 percent of the vote, he rapidly nationalized copper operations owned by US companies, and gave zero compensation to three of the five of them.

The action was popular with voters, as were the achievements of his first year in office—economic growth, lower inflation, less unemployment, and increased pay for workers. But Allende professed Marxism. A visit by Fidel Castro gradually led many Chileans to fear the president was putting the country on the same path as Cuba. Soon, sporadic riots started to occur.

Despite that, Chile was a beautiful place. The cost of living was extremely low, the food and wine delicious, and the scenery magnificent. At one point, we drove the Chevy six hundred miles south on the Pan-American highway to Puerto Montt, the capital of Chilean Patagonia. The forested mountains descending toward fjords made us think we were in British Columbia. We boarded a moored fishing boat owned by a local artist and bought an original oil painting called *Merienda*, meaning "lunchtime." It showed a family gathered in the dark hold of a small boat like the one we were on, their faces illuminated by a lantern in the center of their mealtime circle.

From the day we arrived, Erdesa struggled to survive. My cash projections helped us to stay afloat, but for me, the work soon became miserable. Our main projects were building earthquake-resistant, low-cost houses out of steel and concrete in the Atacama Desert in Antofagasta and even farther north in Arica. When I went up there and looked across the terrain, it was so dry that I felt like I was on the moon.

To put correct forecasts together, I had to go on-site and, in so doing, clashed regularly with the white-haired, irascible Bill Warneke. He did not appreciate my long sideburns or the bell-bottomed suits I had bought in Singapore when I was on leave during my Vietnam days.

Copper was Chile's main export, and during 1971—President Allende's first year—the world price fell. That, plus Allende's populist policies, soon led to rampant inflation, shortages of consumer goods, and more riots.

The stress of all this was acute, especially for Ida. I was totally focused on the business and was in Antofagasta for days at a time. She was now pregnant, and at one point, things got so bad we packed up our household goods and planned to leave the country. The situation calmed down and we did not leave, but around that time, Ida developed a pain in her abdomen. During a visit to a local clinic, she bled a great deal and ended up losing the baby. To add to the growing public chaos around us, we now had to deal with our own private grief as well.

Strikes and demonstrations became so common that Ida and I each fell afoul of them separately. One morning, she was shopping downtown when a riot erupted in the street, and police used tear gas to disperse it. She fled into a nearby shop just before the owner rolled down the heavy steel curtain that usually protected the store only at night. Tear gas fumes found their way inside under the bottom of the curtain; Ida, the owner, and his salesladies retreated as far as they could to the rear of the building as the fumes kept advancing. There was no back door. Fortunately, the tear gas stopped just short of where everyone had huddled. When Ida finally was able to leave, she was shaking.

On another day, I was driving by the University of Chile on my way downtown for an appointment when students dragged a coiled row of barbed wire in front of my car. I quickly looked along the length of it and saw it crossed all four lanes of the two-way boulevard I was on. I wheeled the car to the left, bumped up over a curb, drove across a grassy median, dropped into the street on the other side, and high-tailed it out of there with screams and shouts following close behind me. The tension kept my heart pounding until I got miles away from the scene.

These incidents terrified Ida and left me unsettled. Neither of us had ever been through anything like this. The unrest threatened our safety and left us with a feeling of helplessness. We did not want to think about what would have happened to Ida if she had not been able to escape the tear gas, or to me if I had not been able to outrun the mob.

We talked about the physical side of what happened to us, but rarely spoke about the psychological impact. Fortunately, she had majored in psychology and knew she needed help. She started seeing a local psychologist every few weeks, and it eased her mind a bit.

The cat was a lifeline for her, a link to happier days in Boston, but she worried about him. He loved to sit on an eight-foot cinder block wall in the backyard, hissing at a ferocious German shepherd below. It drove the dog so insane that when he growled and jumped up at the wall, the whole thing shook, and we were afraid Babassu would fall off.

He never did, but once he got stuck in a space between the roof and the overhang on the outside of the front of the house. I was in Rio de Janeiro with Bruce chasing new business. Ida managed to get a call through to my hotel and was in tears, asking me to come home to get him out. I was so concerned for her that I packed up and flew back, getting to Santiago the next day. By then, the cat had freed himself and all was well. But imperceptibly, the incident rekindled my initial concern about whether she was the right girl for me. My chosen career was in international business, and Ida needed more stability than I could provide. I did little to address that.

The loss of the baby weighed much heavier on Ida than it did on me. We kept trying for another one but so far were having little success. I was either out of town or so preoccupied at the office that we had little time together for intimacy or even to talk.

She spent every day going out to shop for necessities. That was a challenge in an economy where supermarkets were rare and supply shortages were starting to appear. So, it took her hours to find the simplest things. Otherwise, she was at home with Conchita, whose chattiness and good humor did help Ida's sagging morale.

It was clear that because of the political unrest, our business would not last long in Chile. The economy was sinking fast and taking us down with it. Despite support from C&C, our company had never been that strong to start with. By now, supplies were getting short, skilled labor was hard to find, and inflation grew every day. The currency seemed to depreciate by the hour.

~

When the one-year lease was up on our little wooden bungalow in Santiago, Ida and I moved into a modernistic concrete home in Vitacura, not far from the office. It was more spacious and sat on a beautiful half-acre lot. The owner, Orlando Marcos, turned out to be a construction manager who, like so many in Chile, had fallen on tough times. Ida and I felt sad that he had to move himself and his six children elsewhere, but Bruce ended up hiring him to fill a vacancy on one of our projects.

Ida loved the new place and decorated it well. She was homesick, so we brought her youngest sister, Naomi, down to Chile from Connecticut for a two-week visit that helped Ida's spirits immensely. Unfortunately, her optimism did not last.

A few weeks later, in the middle of the night, the sound of an approaching freight train woke us up. At this house, we had never heard a train before and there were no railroad tracks near us. What we heard approaching was an earthquake.

The roar grew so loud we could hardly talk over it. We jumped out of bed and groped our way barefoot across the undulating floor to an archway just outside the bedroom. It was a strong point likely to endure if the ceiling started dropping around us. We huddled under the arch; the noise became deafening, and we could barely keep our balance. We heard crashes across the house as plates and knickknacks fell to the floor.

The movement stopped as quickly as it began. The electricity was out, so I got a flashlight from my night table and surveyed the scene. I happened to point it upward at a heavy ceramic teapot that was on a shelf jutting halfway out of the arch we had stood under. The pot had turned completely around. If it had fallen, it would have thrown shards of glass all over our legs and bare feet. In addition to all the violence in Santiago, it scared us even more to realize we could not even count on the ground beneath us.

Not long afterward, Ida had a sharp pain in her groin that doubled her over. She was pregnant again and we feared it was another miscarriage. We rushed to the closest hospital. The doctor told us it was her appendix and that he needed to operate immediately. Ida was so frightened that before the staff took her away, I asked him if I could be present. To my surprise and Ida's relief, he said I could. He would give me a complete surgical getup and introduce me to the operating room team as "Doctor Ploom."

I suited up and came in just as the anesthesiologist was injecting an intravenous needle into Ida's arm. Duly introduced to the staff, I went to her and held her hand until she became unconscious. Shortly afterward, and before the doctor began cutting, Ida started flailing her arms and legs so violently she almost fell off the table. Nurses rushed to contain her; she was still out and thankfully unaware of what was happening. The surgeon was relaxed, saying that happened sometimes, and he would wait until he was sure she was calm before operating. At that point, my faith in Chilean medicine was pretty shaky. But the operation went well. The baby was safe, and in a few weeks, Ida was mostly back to normal.

In the middle of the night, a month or so after the operation, someone broke into our house. We heard it; I grabbed a flashlight and rushed toward the living room. Footsteps hurried out the kitchen back door. I flipped on the outside floodlights just in time to see a man scaling the side wall and jumping onto the property next door. I recognized him as one of the workers our housekeeper Conchita had recommended to do some repairs. When she found out, she was mortified. He was a relative and she never thought him capable of such a thing, no matter how bad the economy was getting.

We believed she was telling the truth and we never had another break-in. But with the public violence, Ida's surgery, the earthquake, and now the burglary, I felt great anxiety, and Ida descended further into fear. With a trembling voice, she asked if we could get a golf club to put under the bed to defend ourselves. I got one right away.

Today, I am aghast and ashamed that I let things get to that point. We talked little about what really mattered, namely our emotional safety, which was threatened almost daily by the events around us. Instead, I saw to her physical comfort as best I could but rushed about dealing with urgent problems at work by running my financial projection process. I hoped it would fix everything in the business and, by extension, fix everything at home. But it did not, and we gradually became more anxious and more distant from one another.

~

In mid-1972, it became too difficult for Erdesa to function. We could not get materials. And the workers, egged on by the socialist Allende government, expropriated our most valuable piece of equipment, the high-volume concrete pump we had imported at great expense from the United States. Unable to build, and under pressure from C&C to get out, we made plans to abandon everything.

Because the government had implemented strict export controls, we had to leave with only the clothes on our backs plus the contents of one suitcase apiece and just a few hundred US dollars. A trip to the black market netted us several thousand dollars in hundred-dollar bills, so a most important question became how to get the money out. Ida was now six months pregnant, and we would need the money wherever we went to make a new start.

We knew Allende had inspectors at Santiago's Pudahuel airport who went through everyone's luggage and presumably checked their wallets before they boarded an international flight.

So, to get around that, I improvised and came up with a way to take the money out. It was risky because, if caught, I could be detained and funneled into the Chilean justice system. But out of desperation, I devised a little process to hide the funds.

In the office, I flattened the bills into two stacks. I put each one in a letter-sized envelope and folded the sides to reduce the envelope to the size of the bills. I then took off my shoes and socks to do a trial run. I placed one stack on the bottom of my right foot and put my sock over it and did the same with the left foot. I then put my shoes on and stood up.

My Chilean partner Max was watching this whole charade. "What do you think?" I asked.

"I don't know. Show me one of the packets," he said.

I retrieved it from my sock and handed it to him. He put it up to his nose.

"OOOOFFF," he said with a frown, squinching his face up like it was the worst thing he had ever smelled in his life. Then he broke into a huge grin.

On the day of our flight, Ida and I headed to the airport in a cab. Once we were there, the inspector searched our suitcases. When finished he stood in front of me and looked me up and down. The bills were so hot against my feet that I was sure steam was rising out of my shoes. He must have decided I looked too geeky to try anything risky, because after a long moment he waved us on to the boarding gate.

~

Obsession with my Elijah Chan–inspired cash forecasting model had not prevented our demise in Chile. Instead, it had distracted me from seeing how bad the situation outside our door really was. Far worse, I was so deeply into the model that I failed to provide enough psychological comfort to a wife who was enduring terrifying experiences thousands of miles from home.

In all of this, the relentless demands of my winning recipe kept me focused on the future instead of on the present reality we were facing. The solution to the danger would have been to "be here now," in the New Age parlance of the day—to pay attention to the current situation instead of always concentrating on a future state that never came.

What is so devastating for me to realize in retrospect was that the two giant issues I missed were right there in front of me. Ida and I could not even go downtown to shop or do business without potentially having a run-in with a mob. What was I thinking? How could I possibly assume my cash flow machinations could overcome the train wreck that the Chilean economy had become? As it was, we were lucky to get out with a few clothes and some US dollars hidden in my shoes.

In addition, Ida's stress was right on the surface. She had trouble sleeping; we lived in a nice part of town, but she feared another home invasion. When her sister Naomi had flown down from Connecticut and then returned to the US, I had been sure Ida wished we could be on that plane with her. Yet I plodded on, continuing to hope my cash management process would provide the financial security the business needed. In the end, we simply had to flee.

The Chilean story illustrates a truism: Even when the whole world is burning down, you will die in an effort to save your winning recipe.

~

By now, my family back in California owned a little house on the beach in Malibu, and they offered it to us as an interim stop after Chile.

That meant I had three choices: quitting Erdesa and trying to find a job in the US while living on the beach, transferring within C&C to an opening they had for me on a banana plantation in Honduras, or going with Bruce and Max to the Republic of Panama for a new project he had secured on the Atlantic side of the isthmus at Colón.

Given all Ida had been through, she wanted to have the baby in the US. But my career ambitions based on my financial forecasting method eclipsed everything else. Art Kipke, the president of the company, was ill, so Bruce was now leading Erdesa and reporting directly to Elijah Chan in Honolulu. The prospect of riches—baronial splendor, as Bruce described it—by building steel-based housing in a stable and prosperous country like Panama captivated my heart. I was sure in that setting my financial forecasting method would finally pay off. And I knew that after Chile, Ida's Spanish was fairly good, so she would be able to get around well.

Even though it further increased the distance between Ida and me, I selected the third option. She was six months pregnant, but I allowed her very little say in it. It was cruel and unforgivable of me to treat her like that. It might have extended our marriage if we had gone to Malibu. But we did not, and we would pay a harsh price for my choice.

WHAT I COULD HAVE DONE DIFFERENTLY

I did irreparable damage to my marriage by not taking Ida's needs into account. And I became so fixated on financial forecasting in order to survive in Chile that I did not see how hopeless the situation in the country was. We could have gotten out sooner in an orderly way, but instead we hung on until we had no choice but to flee.

Takeaways from Chapter 12

1. From day one your recipe has been trying to ensure your survival. The paradox is that the recipe can be the very thing that reduces your chances of surviving.

2. You cannot control the external circumstances of society. But beware of ignoring them—the allure of your recipe may cause you to do so and put yourself in peril.

3. When you face several options at a critical point in life, do not let your recipe make the choice. It will not do so based on your overall best interests, and could trigger a disaster.

Reflective Questions

1. Recall a time when following your recipe actually increased the danger you were in. What was the situation, and what was the outcome?

2. What external conditions of the society you live and work in are you ignoring? This could be anything from politics to economics to social conditions. How is that potentially putting you in danger?

3. What critical choice in the past did you let your recipe make for you? Did it serve your overall best interests, or do just the opposite?

Practical Exercises

1. In the situation in Question 1, write down what you could have done to avoid the peril that your recipe helped to put you in.

2. In the situation in Question 2, write down what you can do to stop ignoring the conditions and reduce the risk you are facing.

3. In the choice in Question 3, write down the decision you could have made to override your recipe, and what the likely later results might have been.

~

We took off from Santiago with the cash still in my socks. I did not remove it until we were safe in Panama some seven hours and three thousand miles away.

With us also were Babassu the cat and a stray black-and-white cat named Baba Junior who had adopted us in Chile. With them in tow, we were eager to make a fresh start.

We had no idea that in Panama, we would face a new and even more serious physical threat to our safety than we had in Chile.

13

Blindness:
The Noriega Incident

JUNE 1972. PANAMA CITY, PANAMA. When we came off the plane at Tocumen airport, a hot blast of tropical heat hit us in the face, telling us we were now in a place totally unlike the temperate Santiago where we had lived for the past two years.

Around 2:00 p.m. each afternoon, it rained with such fury that the water bounced off the streets to a height of two feet, creating a knee-high horizontal line of water to walk through if we were foolish enough to go outside.

Unlike Chile, Panama had no public unrest and no inflation. The economy was bustling and the American influence was everywhere. The city butted up against the American-controlled Canal Zone, a strip of land five miles wide on each side of the Panama Canal in which thousands of Americans lived. Life there was like any small community on the US mainland. In Panama City itself, many people spoke English, and shops accepted US dollars, which they called *balboas*. Ida and I felt relieved.

That said, I was so desperate to get out of Chile and get a new forecasting process set up in Panama that I jumped at the chance to move there without looking closely at the business setting we were stepping into. Manuel Noriega, the country's hidden puppet master, was a grasping, venal thug who, as the country's unelected chief of military intelligence, sat unofficially atop the national bank that was to be our paymaster. I was so frantic in service to my recipe that once again I had not scanned the environment as I was trained to do in business school. If I had done so, I would have seen that while Panama looked stable on the surface, its underbelly was rotten. I might have insisted that Bruce try to locate a new project somewhere else, or at the very least have thought about how we could protect ourselves if Noriega tried to squeeze our company.

That said, Ida was thrilled to be in a place that felt so familiar it was almost like home. We rented a brand-new, two-story town house off Calle 50 near the upscale Punta Paitilla part of town, and she loved it. Our venerable Chevy Nova was stolen by the Chilean employee we had asked to sell it for us there, so we used our savings to buy two new cars—a tiny green Datsun hatchback for me and a silver Mitsubishi mini station wagon for her.

Like Hawaii, Panama was free of rabies, so Babassu and Baba Junior went into quarantine, this time for ninety days. The feline digs were not as sumptuous as in Honolulu, but they were adequate, and Ida got to see the cats every day.

Fig. 7. Bruce Fraser and myself. Panama City, Panama, 1973.

As soon as we left Chile, C&C bowed out, transferring the stock to Bruce, Max, and me. We formed a Panamanian company, Erdesa International, Inc., so we could continue to do business. In running it, the three of us got along great, balancing each other's skills well—Bruce promoted new business, Max oversaw the construction work, and I managed the finances. Bruce bought a little Alfa Romeo sports car; he was happy that in Panama he did not have to worry about it being damaged in a riot.

Despite the disruptive effect on my relationship with Ida while we were in Chile, I at once started running the cash forecasting method again. I believed that surely in this more familiar, more American context my financial processes would thrive and provide the security I sought. Bruce had made a deal with an American developer for us to build our earthquake-resistant housing in Colón near the Atlantic entrance to the canal. It was only an hour away from the Pacific side where we had our office, so I was sure I could easily get the data I needed to keep my process fed.

The developer, Al Oberlander, was a short, middle-aged, and confused American salesperson whose signature possession was a six-foot-long, four-inch-wide tan leather tube that held rolled-up plans of the project. In the tropical heat it smelled like fresh cow dung. He took it everywhere, often in the company of his partner, Tito Vazquez, a thin man with a heavily creased face whose level of incoherence fluctuated hourly depending on how much scotch he had just nipped. The two were so incompetent that they bordered on being morons. In the company of such fine gentlemen, what could possibly go wrong? I was too focused on the numbers to care.

~

When we emigrated to Panama, we knew the medical care would be excellent. The country boasted many US-trained physicians and had hospitals with good reputations. This put our minds at ease as we waited the three months after our arrival for Ida to have our first child.

With steam rising from the streets of Panama City after an epic downpour on the afternoon of October 2, 1972, Ida gave birth in the Clínica San Fernando. She endured nine hours of labor followed by a cesarean section to deliver a girl, whom we named Hannah. We were out of our minds with joy. The baby was beautiful, healthy, and a portent, we thought, of many wonderful things to come.

After we took her home, our first responsibility was to get her registered as an American citizen. I completed the paperwork at the US Embassy and the Ministerio de Relaciones Exteriores of Panama, secure in the knowledge that she could now live permanently in the US.

We had hired a full-time housekeeper named Cora, a skinny African-Panamanian woman who cooked and cleaned but would not iron because she was convinced that doing so in the heat made people sick. She loved Hannah and was an immense help to Ida in caring for her.

Ida blossomed like I had never seen. She adored being a mother, nursing the baby, cooing and talking to her in a little voice that previously she had reserved only for the cats. We alternated nighttime feedings, with me heating up the formula in the kitchen when it was my turn.

A month after Hannah was born, my father, Neely, flew down for a few days. She was his first grandchild, and he was entranced. We took a now-graying Neely to the canal at the Miraflores Locks, sat in the bleachers there, and looked across the concrete to see a massive ship slowly rise up, up, and up right in front of us. He had spent several years at Georgia Tech and marveled at the engineering that made it all possible. When he saw a sign that said "Miraflores Locks—1914," he noted that he had been born in 1912. "Geez," he said, "I'm older than the Panama Canal."

Shortly afterward, Ida's mother, Kate, came down for a week. Hannah was her first grandchild as well, and the baby completely captivated her new grandmother. Having her cheery, perennially smiling mother there kept Ida's spirits high.

When little blond-haired Hannah was old enough to walk, she followed Cora around the house saying, "¡*Chuletas, Cora, chuletas!*" Chuletas were pork chops, one of Cora's specialties. Hannah's dietary preferences were broad. For example, she loved to go onto the patio and eat dirt out of a potted plant before grinning through a large patch of soil around her mouth.

We had to be careful about our backyard. Our patio faced a small lawn that had six-foot concrete walls on three sides and backed up to an overgrown creek. Near the water were iguanas so huge we feared they might be a threat to Hannah. One day, a thirty-six-inch-long reptile came across the patio and through the open sliding doors into the house, flicking its forked tongue in all directions to see what might be available to eat in our living room. I grabbed a broom. When it saw me coming, it turned around to run but struggled to get traction on the terrazzo tile floor. It finally did, swerving its tail back and forth until it hit the grass. It went straight up the wall and disappeared into the growth on the other side.

One of our favorite pastimes was to take Hannah to the beach on the Pacific side of the isthmus and stay in a rustic cabin for a few days. There was no bathtub, so Ida bathed her in a plastic dish tub.

During the day, we put a beach umbrella in the sand just at the water line so Hannah could hold on to the pole as the gentle surf came in. She would squeal with joy as the cool water hit her, and in seeing that, we bathed ourselves in happiness.

~

At the start of our project in Panama, the company did well financially. We always prospered at the beginning of a construction job because in its early days it was cash-rich. But as soon as the work advanced a little, we began surviving from one progress payment to the next.

The initial bloom of optimism we felt after moving to Panama gradually wore off in other ways as well.

The heat was stifling, and we had no central air-conditioning in the town house. The window units were too expensive to keep turned on all the time, so we only fired them up when we needed them. Cora lived in a four-story wooden tenement with arcades around each floor, and I felt terrible taking her back to such a place each day. Once, we went to a wedding in a nice part of town and came back to find that the left rear tire of the Datsun had been stolen right off the car, leaving it and us in the lurch.

In quick succession, I caught both amebic dysentery and malaria. The dysentery had me ejecting material at both ends and so thoroughly emptied me of fluids that all I could do between episodes was lie on the bathroom floor. To get help, Ida had to carry the baby as she ran next door because Cora was off that day. An elderly neighbor put me in the back seat of his car and drove me to the Clínica San Fernando, where an intravenous solution of glucose soon made me feel better. I recovered in a few days.

The malaria, however, was insidious. It appeared not long after I left the hospital, causing spikes of fever and shakes every few hours. I could work, but I never knew when the fever would hit. As I began to feel it mounting, I would rush home to sweat it out, then possibly go back to the office. The case turned out to be light. My doctor had treated it at once with antimalarial medication, and after a year, it disappeared.

No amount of financial process work on my part could make Erdesa International survive in Panama. The project was too small, and payments tied to progress came in too slowly. In addition, Al and Tito constantly inserted themselves, gumming up our efforts to make headway.

Bruce was unfazed. Somehow, in 1973 he connected with people in the Middle East who expressed interest in our earthquake-resistant building technology. We still had some cash in the bank, so we left the work in Max's capable hands and bought plane tickets for the seventy-three-hundred-mile trip to Beirut, where we picked up a flamboyant promoter named Farid Shaheen. The three of us then continued to Bahrain and Saudi Arabia.

Thanks to Shaheen, we met with two Saudi princes. One was an elderly man who listened to our pitch with dignified respect, nodding and occasionally saying, with perfect diction, "I see." He said that about forty times. Later we learned he did not understand a word of English.

Then we met with a young prince who did speak English and was excited to go into business with us. He was obsessed with the idea of opening an office in London, which we saw no purpose for but did not oppose. Afterward, we found out he just wanted to get away from the strictures of Saudi society to a place where he could drink and whore to his heart's content.

After returning from such a pointless trip, we decided to look for work closer to home. Bruce again beat the bushes and in 1974 came up with a real project—a big one—in Jamaica. It was with the Ministry of Housing, which, like all our former customers, loved our earthquake-resistant construction.

They wanted to build several hundred units in Port Antonio on the eastern tip of the island. Some were single-family structures like we were used to building; the rest were multistory units that we had never constructed but figured we could build if we modified the technology a bit.

We decided to hire a third party—a New York construction management company called ADA—to keep a project manager on-site in Jamaica and do all the reporting.

I worked overtime preparing the financials. This was by far the biggest job we had ever bid on, and I did what I could to make sure the numbers were right. I traveled to Kingston several times to meet with Ministry of Housing officials in musty offices piled high with yellowing paper files. Thanks to Bruce and Max's meetings on the technical side, we got the contract.

Unfortunately, the project manager ADA sent was an alcoholic more interested in consuming gin than generating correct data. ADA just added overhead without improving performance, so the burden fell on Bruce, Max, and me to get things done.

This was difficult because of the distance and because Jamaica had become a gangster economy. A mobster once approached one of our own project managers from Panama and said he was going to slit the man's throat and suck his blood if he did not pay a bribe. Somehow, we scraped through without the thugs cutting anybody's throat.

~

By mid-1975, my cash forecasting systems in Panama and Jamaica needed a great deal of attention just to keep my partners focused on the money so we could stay afloat. In concentrating on all of that so fixedly, I continued to be inattentive to Ida and damaged the relationship even further. I also completely missed a sinister, looming threat that would soon consume us.

Manuel Noriega put the squeeze on us. Jowly, pockmarked, and ruthless, he was the power behind General Omar Torrijos, the Panamanian president who had overthrown his predecessor seven years before. Noriega was a key information source for the American CIA, as well as an operative who quietly supplied illegal guns, equipment, and cash to CIA-backed counter-insurgency groups in Latin America. Noriega had made a fortune in drug trafficking, ran the gambling business in Panama, and, despite being largely hidden from public view, was the most important man in the government.

Noriega's power affected our business as an everyday, indirect threat because as a small foreign firm, we were a visible target. He had his hand in everything in the country, and soon it reached out to grasp us.

Our Colón housing contract was with the government, via the Banco Nacional de Panamá. To make sure funds got to us in a timely way, instead of via the unreliable mail service, I stuffed down my introversion and reached out to the bank's paymaster, a diminutive, mustachioed bureaucrat named Señor Bonilla. He was always pleasant and received my detailed progress reports with courtesy and interest. Disbursements to us were based on the physical progress of the job. We were often behind schedule, so it took some convincing to get him to release partial funding if we did not qualify for the full amount.

One day, I went to see him for a $50,000 disbursement we had legitimately earned the previous week, but he balked. He said there were irregularities. The bank was looking into them, and until they finished, there would be no more money.

Confused, Bruce and I tried to get an appointment with the president of the bank. He would not see us, and Bonilla would not tell us what the problem was.

At first, we thought it might be related to the Panama Canal negotiations between President Carter and General Torrijos. But that made no sense. The last thing Torrijos needed was the bad publicity of appearing to pressure a small American company.

We then thought the bank might be having financial problems and needed an excuse not to pay us. But again, that would not have been smart. The bank wanted the houses and the windfall of positive news they would generate for the people of Colón.

In the end, we concluded that it was simple, heavy-handed extortion. The bank would refuse to pay the $50,000, thinking we would be too intimidated to stop the job, and they would still get their houses. Because little happened in Panama without Noriega's consent, we guessed that he had to be behind the ploy.

The accuracy of this interpretation came home to us one evening around 7:00 p.m. when Bruce, Max, and I were working in the office. Two Panamanian soldiers with crew cuts, thick necks, and green fatigues pressing tightly against their biceps walked in and demanded my passport. With no smiles on their faces and outsized revolvers hanging from their army-issue web belts, they were serious.

Shaking, I opened my briefcase, took out the passport, and handed it to them. They left with it as quietly as they came.

They had not taken Bruce's passport, or Max's, because I was the face of Erdesa International at the bank. We at once called our lawyer, a young man named Jorge Antonio Rojas. Slick, mustachioed, good-looking, American-educated, and the grandson of a former president, Jorge Antonio was politically well-connected. Although now that the soldiers were running everything, we were not sure how much that still mattered.

He came right over. With the relaxed air of an aristocrat and sporting a fresh coat of Old Spice on his cheeks even at that late hour, he told us not to worry. He would fix it. Seeing we were not convinced, he walked over to the window and pulled back the curtains to reveal the darkness outside.

"Uh-oh," he said in a somber tone. I looked at Bruce and Max. They had turned as white as I had, thinking the police had come back to haul us off to rot in a Panamanian jail.

Jorge Antonio whipped his head around. "Gotcha!" We gave him a nervous laugh.

"Look, you guys need to loosen up," he said. "I will look into this and get it handled quickly if I can."

On the way out he chuckled to himself and winked, saying, "Better keep a watch on that window . . ."

He came back a few days later wearing a silk tie and one of his many Italian suits. After doing some checking, he was convinced not only that Noriega was behind it, but also that the best way to get out of the situation was to sue the man, personally, before the Supreme Court of Panama. Noriega was not expecting that and would not want the media frenzy Jorge Antonio gleefully expected to launch just as the canal negotiations were becoming serious. He loved the idea of doing that because he considered Noriega to be a criminal and an upstart not worthy of the influence he had.

The easy confidence with which the words rolled off Jorge Antonio's tongue made it all sound so simple. But my mind raced with images of sitting forever in a Panamanian jail while the legal system made glacial progress. I told him I needed to think about it.

When I related all this to Ida, she asked what our options were. I saw two. The first was to follow Jorge Antonio's advice and embark on a risky course in a country where the rule of law still existed but was shaky. The second was to flee. We would not need a passport to get back to the US since there was free passage from Panama into the Canal Zone. We would find a way to get ourselves on a military flight to Florida.

She did not like either choice, especially running away, and the more we talked I saw why. Fighting Noriega was hugely risky, but trying to escape might be even more so. For all we knew the government was watching me and could arrest me if we tried to cross into the Canal Zone. We would have to leave everything behind except what we wore and two suitcases, just like in Chile. Plus, there was no guarantee that the American military would let civilians on a flight, particularly if one were under a cloud in Panama and had no passport to prove he was an American. We had a little girl who was not yet two years old, and Ida was six months pregnant again.

I listened to what she said and the next day talked it over with Bruce and Max. I told them that for Ida and me, the only way ahead was to take Jorge Antonio's advice and bull through. They agreed, and soon Noriega had a case pending against him at the Panamanian Supreme Court.

~

That did nothing for my peace of mind.

A pang of fear went through me every time I saw a police officer. They all wore military uniforms that were like those of the Panamanian Defense Force goons who had taken my passport.

Weeks passed, and we heard nothing. Jorge Antonio made the rounds of his contacts, letting everyone within earshot know he was going to create a huge stink about this case if Noriega did not return my passport and pay us the $50,000 we had justifiably earned. The canal negotiations were continuing. We hoped Noriega was getting the message, but Jorge Antonio could detect no movement from the other side.

One Saturday, we put Hannah in her car seat in the Mitsubishi and drove toward Colón for an outing. The shortest route to the Atlantic side was a two-lane highway through the Canal Zone, but before entering it, while we were still in the Republic of Panama, a police car appeared behind me with its red lights flashing.

If this was it, I stupidly decided I was not going to let them catch me when we were all so close to freedom. Without thinking it through, I punched the gas and went as fast as the curving jungle road would allow. We drove for five miles before I noticed the cop was gaining on me. There were still ten more miles to go before reaching the Canal Zone, and I knew he would not follow me in there, so I kept on. But the cop was a more experienced driver, and after another few miles, he pulled up right beside me and pointed for me to pull over.

I did so. He came up behind and stood by the door. He had the familiar green Defense Force fatigues, bulging biceps, and huge hip pistol. I rolled down the window. The pungency and humidity of the surrounding jungle air flowed into the car.

In my best Spanish, I asked what the problem was. He asked me to step onto the road. My heart pounded. I got out and looked up and down the highway. No cars. If anything were to happen, there would be no witnesses. The police officer motioned for me to come with him to the back of the car.

Once there, he pointed to one of the taillights.

"Señor, this light is not working. It is dangerous. You must have it fixed. Have a nice day." He turned his car around and sped off. I wished there was a good place to clean out my pants.

Now more rattled than before, I almost fainted from a hyperactive heartbeat a week later when our secretary told me a lawyer from the Corte Suprema was on the phone. He would not give his name and said one of the justices wanted to see me, alone, that very morning at 11:00 a.m.

I had no idea where the Supreme Court building was, and as I drove, looking at the directions our secretary had given me, I could not find a building that was stately enough for such a facility. At length, I matched the address to a squat, aging structure that could have been a warehouse. Waist-high dirt and scuff marks colored the yellow walls on both sides of the door.

I walked in and told the man inside who I was. He ushered me into a small office where a middle-aged gentleman in a black robe was sitting. His desk looked like it had just been delivered from a garage sale. His manner was grave and dignified.

"Señor, there has been a misunderstanding," he said in Spanish. "Please accept this."

He opened a tiny drawer and pulled out my passport.

He held it toward me but did not release it. He looked straight at me, and with every ounce of gravitas he could muster said, "This did not happen."

I looked back at him and agreed wholeheartedly that none of this had ever taken place. My passport resting in my pocket and a huge release of breath now exiting my lungs, I walked out, silently thanking Jorge Antonio Rojas and his aristocratic ways.

Because of him, we also recovered the $50,000 Noriega had unfairly withheld from us. We had applied the law and used the magnetic pull of possible adverse publicity at a time when canal negotiations with the United States had become critical. Jorge Antonio was masterful.

~

When Hannah found out that another baby was going to come out of Mommy's tummy soon, she started calling us by our first names. "I want a cookie, Ida," or "Ben, I have a poopy." We read that was normal behavior for a two-year-old, so we did not make a big deal about it, and eventually she stopped.

Panama was causing much less stress for us than Chile had. But the Noriega episode made us acutely uncomfortable, because now we had so much more at stake with one and soon two little children to care for.

Bruce and I had also soured on the place and on overseas living in general. The Colón and Port Antonio jobs were winding down after having supplied an adequate, but not baronial, level of financial returns. We now looked to Miami for our next venture.

In Panama, we had set up an international trading arm within our company to bring in goods in bulk, break them down in a duty-free zone in the republic, then reship them to customers throughout Latin America. The business was prospering and had generated a comfortable cash cushion for the three of us. Max loved that business and would stay behind to run it in Panama, while Bruce and I would set up a branch in Miami to do the same kind of work. We looked forward to doing more trading deals and leaving the problems of the construction business behind us.

The prospect of returning to the US after the baby was born made Ida happy and excited. In that mindset, she scheduled a cesarean delivery on September 22, 1975, in the brand-new Paitilla Medical Center just a few blocks from our town house. I was not allowed to be present, so when I saw the obstetrician wheeling the baby out at the end of a long hall, I ran up to him and asked in excited English, "What is it?" A little flustered since English was his second language, he hesitated and said, "It's a baby!"

In Spanish, I clarified what I meant. "It's a boy," he said, "and look how pink and beautiful he is. He did not have to go through the birth canal."

We named him Conor and were beside ourselves with happiness at having two such beautiful children. After Ida and Conor came home, I made the rounds of the embassy and the ministry again to collect the paperwork for registering him as an American citizen. And in December, as soon as Ida was well enough to travel, the six of us—two cats, two kids, and two adults—flew the eleven hundred miles to Miami. I was thirty-two years old, and Ida was thirty. For the first time in five years, we would be living again on American soil.

~

Some might say that in Panama, I was a victim of circumstance and coercion that I could not have predicted. While it is true that I could never have foreseen the exact form in which events would unfold, from the perspective of today, it is more probable that *something* rather than nothing would have happened to us.

In addition to lobbying Bruce to move us elsewhere after seeing how dangerous Noriega was, I could have implemented a risk mitigation plan— something else I had been trained to do at Harvard. In Jorge Antonio we had a powerful spoiler, a well-connected political operator who probably could have thrown an effective ring of protection around us. Through intermediaries, it would have been easy for him to let Noriega know to keep his hands off us. "Touch these gringos," he could have said, "and I will sue you, publicly, before the Supreme Court. They are not worth it. Go somewhere else to make your money." That was exactly what he ended up doing. Only he did so *after* Noriega made his move, not before-hand as we might have preferred.

I again had suffered from an extreme case of selective perception, seeing only the accounting ledgers in front of me and thinking they represented the whole situation.

Psychologists suggest that many things can cause such a narrow view—beliefs, past experiences, mood, gender, age, race, and religion among others. But for me, an introvert, my winning recipe surpassed all of those. It had me willingly relying on a step-by-step cash-flow process to ward off danger instead of looking beneath the surface to detect the real peril.

Paradoxically, getting insight into underlying facts often requires not a microscope but a telescope, stepping back to get a wider view. I could have only done that by going outside of my recipe to assess the nature of the man who ran the swamp that my partners and I were in, and then using the potent political force represented by our lawyer and his contacts. But I did not, and as a result, we again were abandoning a country for which we formerly held high hopes.

~

The recipe had performed no better with danger than it had with fear.

I escaped from the peril of expulsion from Harvard only by being will-ing to push past my discomfort and join a peer group, all the while being blind to my unsuitability for a top-level role in business. The Brazil project got canceled because I was more focused on the weeds—financial details—than on the situation at United Fruit Company headquarters. Physical danger in Chile and Panama threatened us because I paid more attention to my recipe-induced financial forecasting system than to the hazardous situations we lived in, or to a marriage that was falling apart bit by bit.

In all these situations, the recipe itself had been one of the main reasons I failed to find security. It had actually helped to *increase* each of the dangers I faced.

WHAT I COULD HAVE DONE DIFFERENTLY

As in Brazil and Chile, I was so obsessed with a survival process that in Panama I also disregarded the external environment I was in. I could have foreseen that the thug who ran the country might try to extort my company, and taken steps to block him before he acted. I could easily have alerted our talented, aggressive lawyer to my concerns about Noriega ahead of time, prompting him to deliver in advance the same blunt, pointed message that had worked after the fact.

Takeaways from Chapter 13

1. Most recipes are not helpful for looking below the surface of a situation. Instead, they simply call you to execute their way of being and do little else.

2. When your recipe is faced with a risky choice, it tends to lead you blindly into whichever option is most compatible with it, rather than the one that most supports you overall.

3. You designed the recipe to distance yourself from relationships, but often the best way out of a dilemma is to consult a trusted person.

Reflective Questions

1. What is a recent situation that surprised you because you didn't see something below the surface? How was your recipe implicated in that blindness?

2. Describe a risky choice you had to make recently. What did your recipe urge you to do? Did you follow that advice, and, if so, what was the outcome?

3. Describe the last time you asked for advice from someone to resolve a dilemma. Did it conflict with what your recipe suggested? If you took the advice, what was the result?

Practical Exercises

1. Write down a difficult challenge you are dealing with, and put your recipe aside for a moment. What do you see lurking beneath the surface of the challenge? Write that down too, and think about how to deal with it.

2. Note a risky choice that you see on the horizon. Then write what your recipe normally would advise you to do, and what a better solution might be.

3. Describe an either/or choice you recently made, and whether you followed your recipe, or asked someone for advice. Then note what the outcome was.

~

In Miami, we would no longer have to be preoccupied with danger. The move there was the shortest in distance that we had made yet, but despite our best intentions, it would not be the sweetest.

Part 4

Four Breakthrough Tools for Detaching

14

Living Life Forward: Upside Down in Miami

DECEMBER 1975. MIAMI, FLORIDA. We arrived full of hope. We rented a pretty little house on Key Biscayne for a few weeks, and had two white cribs brought in, one for three-year-old Hannah and the other for one-month-old Conor. Even though we were in a subtropical climate, the air was drier and cooler than we had felt in years.

Bruce and I and our families loved being back in the United States, but over the next four years we could not make a go of the trading business. As a construction salesman and a financial guy, he and I did not have the instincts or the skill sets to broker deals that would provide value to all parties.

For me, the worst part was that there was no new methodology that would make a difference. My financial projections were useless because we had no cash coming in.

The impact on our marriage was heavy. After leaving Key Biscayne, we moved into a nice rental home with a pool in the Kendall area of Miami and started to build our own house based on the promise of trading deals that had not closed yet. Babassu, who had survived Boston, Honolulu,

Santiago, and Panama was now in Miami but soon disappeared; we looked in nearby vacant lots reeking with dead grass clippings that people had dumped, but could never find him. By the time the new house was finished, we could not afford to close on it and had to move out of the rental into a much smaller one. While there, Baba Junior got deathly ill, and we had to put him down.

Ida now focused on our two toddlers and took the pet losses in stride. But the forfeiture of the new house broke her heart. She had worked for six months to make selections for it, and to have to move into an old place that had none of the conveniences she was looking forward to was hard.

By 1977, we had exhausted our savings. Big trading deals always looked enticing, so we kept chasing them, but there was no income. To keep my end going, I started borrowing money from my family every few months.

Bruce and I had an office in the Dadeland Towers office complex at the southern end of the Palmetto Expressway in Miami. At one point, we could not pay the rent. In fear of the landlord changing the locks, I moved all the files to my car. I had a 1976 Cadillac Coupe de Ville and was always amazed at the size of its trunk. Each day I opened it and panned my vision across sixteen large open boxes of files, four across and four deep, before selecting the papers we needed for the day. When the management eventually told us to leave, we set up in Bruce's house and moved all the files there.

Ida openly questioned my business judgment at staying so long with Bruce. She did not blame him for our troubles, but me for not recognizing that despite his best efforts, and mine, we had failed. I could not hear this and angrily let her know. I did not say it to her, but I was a Harvard Business School graduate, and what did she know?

Despite that, in the spring of 1979, I told Bruce I could no longer continue with him, and he understood. Max was doing reasonably well in Panama, and at his request, I signed over my shares in Erdesa International to him.

Bruce and I parted as friends and sought income elsewhere. He ended up hiring on as international VP for a company that made interior folding panels. He had a successful twenty-year career there that took him all over the world signing up foreign licensees. He happily retired with his wife in central California, and passed away at ninety-seven years of age in 2024.

Meanwhile, Ida and I were now living in a third Miami rental. The events of the nine years since we left Honolulu had so badly shaken my self-confidence that in trying to get a job, I did not even try to trade on my Harvard MBA degree. Ida had been right; my business judgment was terrible. Any large employer was bound to see that as well. For almost a decade, I had produced no track record of achievement whatsoever.

By 1980, our marriage was falling apart. Long-dormant issues—ones I had detected when I first met her—now came up to complement the money problems that increasingly divided us. She wanted our kids to be exposed to some kind of traditional church, and I did not. I was interested in occasional sex, and she was not. And neither one of us wanted to talk about it.

To distract from my problems, I started watching a twenty-four-hour news station called CNN that began broadcasting as the first ever such network. One segment covered the premiere of the movie *Urban Cowboy* and its launch of the "mechanical cowboy" craze in country and western bars across the nation. I wondered why anybody would go to such places. Another segment covered the former B-movie actor and governor of California, Ronald Reagan, who was gunning for the Republican nomination for president.

One day in early 1980, I met a guy my age who owned a business called Filterco that made oil refiners for truck and car engines. Short and wiry, with thinning hair, Grant had invented the device himself. It avoided oil changes by constantly cleaning the oil as the engine ran. He was having trouble managing his cash flow, and when he heard what I could do for him, he hired me.

Instantly, I was back in business. In the front office of the company's cavernous factory, I stocked up on thirteen-column paper, resurrected the Elijah Chan cash projection process I'd learned in Honolulu, and, despite not being familiar with manufacturing, I put the finances of the company in order in just a few weeks. The company attorney and two board members took note, thanking me for turning things around and privately confiding in me that the owner was in over his head. Until they said that, I was too focused on finance to think much about the owner. But on reflection I had to agree.

I enjoyed the security of successfully being able to keep food on the table at home. But the income was less than we needed to pay our debts. My singular focus on handling creditors and keeping my job kept my attention from Ida and our relationship.

I was also not focusing on the children. I was not as close to them as my father had been to my sisters and me, and it hurt. I did spend time with them, taking them on rides with Ida on little seats on our bikes, going to the beach, and even joining a father-daughter club known then as the Indian Princesses—since adopted as part of the YMCA Adventure Guides program—where Hannah and I had loads of fun. One of our favorite games was for the fathers to bend over, place their foreheads on baseball bats that rested perpendicular to the ground, walk in three complete circles while staring at the ground, then stand up dizzy and stagger around like drunk men until they fell at the feet of their giggling daughters.

I loved that Hannah and Conor were getting acculturated into the US instead of Panama. But my preoccupation with my new job and our continuing lack of money—despite having some regular income—had to have had an impact on them.

When I got out of survival thinking long enough to look at my life, I saw unmistakably that it was not working. The company I had been part owner of for the better part of ten years had recently failed. Any sense of intimacy with Ida, my wife of twelve years, was gone. On both accounts, my self-confidence was in the cellar.

A member of Filterco's board of directors was Dick Bertram, owner of Bertram Yachts and a legend in the boating industry. Silver-haired, craggy, and fit, he invited me to lunch one day but would not say what he wanted to discuss. I was in such grief that I jumped at the invitation.

I thought it might be a promotion that he and the other directors were engineering at the company. But it was something far different.

~

Over mayonnaise-rich tuna sandwiches, Dick told me about a personal development program he had recently completed called the Erhard Seminars Training (known as the est Training, with a lowercase "e"). It had been founded in 1972 by a former car salesman named Jack Robinson, who had changed his name to Werner Erhard and become a sensation on the seminar circuit.

Dick was a hardheaded, successful businessman, and I respected him a great deal. He said the four-day training showed people how to put their past in the past instead of using the past to drive their present. In so doing, things they had been struggling with would clear up just in the process of life itself.

Despite admiring Dick, I was skeptical. The New Age movement was in full swing, and this sounded like pure woo-woo.

"Will this help me be a better manager?" I asked.

He nodded. "Absolutely. My experience is that whatever you have not been able to overcome will clear up."

"But how? You can imagine that sounds a little glib."

He looked right at me. "You will be able to take a position outside of yourself and see how you are making choices. That gives you the ability to make changes rather than be on automatic pilot all the time."

I had discovered something like that during the Evasion and Escape exercise back in 1965 in Georgia. I saw then that I could make a choice to just evade rather than automatically try to escape. I was intrigued that a whole program was now being dedicated to mastering that skill. My life was a mess, and I definitely had been on automatic pilot with everything I had striven to implement since Vietnam. When Dick said the program was for people who were well and wanted to take their experience of life to a higher level, he sold me.

I took the course in June 1980 with about two hundred other people of widely different educational, income, and age backgrounds in a hotel seminar room on Miami Beach. The training consisted of the participants holding a microphone and relating experiences in their own lives that connected to points the seminar leader was making. It also involved eyes-closed, guided "processes" that asked everyone to consider times in their lives when X or Y had happened. Those two vehicles exposed cascades of insights for me.

We all sat in chairs tightly packed together facing a raised platform where the trainer stood. From there, he delivered the meat of the course, its "distinctions"—a dozen or so key insights about human behavior that had an unsettling impact on me. They were not intended to do so, but they challenged my default position of being a loner.

I already knew that at age four I had invented myself to be an introvert. I did so before I ever knew the word, based on a judgment that I did not want to be around other people because they were so loud and disruptive. Ever since then, that past decision had governed my present. In the est Training, I realized that even though I was afraid of being more open to stimulation, I could have my fear and go ahead with things anyway.

All this got triggered inside my head as I sat in my chair and listened to the seminar leader and the other participants talk about things that were seemingly unrelated to me. It gave me a pounding headache that lasted for days, both during and between the two weekends of the training. On breaks, I went outside and stood at a railing watching the surf hit the beach that separated our hotel from the next, hoping the cool salt breeze and negative ions would relieve the pain. They did not.

For me, the distinctions were a new way of thinking, a novel approach to life and to interacting with other people. Just to take part in this training was an exercise in extroversion, because it instilled an irrepressible desire to share insights with the group. I did so twice. I took a microphone that a runner handed to me and looked out across two hundred expectant faces, strangely unafraid of making eye contact with so many people. For a guy as reluctant to be in a large crowd as I was, this was momentous. For the first time, the stimulation involved was not painful but exhilarating. It was opening me up to other people and another way of being.

I went back into the session, and more realizations hit me. I did not know it at the time, but the most important of them would be something they called "Be-Do-Have." The trainer asserted that we were all living our lives backward, from Having to Doing to Being. That did not work, because transformation does not begin with the circumstances. It begins with identity, with life flowing from Being to Doing to Having.

This certainly applied to Ana Maria and her fantastic skills in singing and playing the guitar. As a little girl she had started out with a cheap instrument and little support from her parents, but had practiced every day until she slowly became accomplished. She had begun not by Having equipment or lessons, but with her identity, her Being—namely a conviction that she had real musical talent and that someday it would manifest. By Being a capable musician and Doing the things that musicians did, namely practicing intensely, she ended up Having the phenomenal voice and accompaniment that sent cold chills down my back every time she picked up the instrument.

Contrast this with another little girl, an imaginary one, who Had an expensive guitar from the very beginning, along with costly lessons that her parents supported. This allowed her to Do recitals, but not very good ones, because she did not practice much. She was not committed to Being a musician, so she never became one.

As you will see in the Conclusion, I used Be-Do-Have to transform my own life, but not for almost forty years.

~

Things between Ida and me were not good, and I had not taken steps to address them. I had not yet decided that the marriage was unworkable, nor that I wanted a divorce.

But the more I sat in the training, the more I did see the possibility of being completely blown away in a relationship with a woman. I realized I did not have a relationship like that with Ida and needed to work with her to make a change for the better. Ida was a fabulous mother, but any sense of intimacy or partnership between us was long gone.

I saw I was directing a great deal of anger toward my mother for her drinking while I was growing up. This came up when we were asked to pick the parent we felt most distant from and write down one hundred things they had done for us. As I wrote, I got in touch with how deeply she loved me, how tenderly she cared for me, and how gladly she would have given her life if it would have saved mine. I was crying so hard the ink started to blur on the paper. I resolved that no matter what it took, I was going to clean up my relationship with her.

I took responsibility for my failures in business. I saw that the past decade had been less about the circumstances themselves than about how I had not faced up to them. In Chile, I put my attention on plans and processes instead of admitting that the chaos we were in was unworkable and getting out of there sooner. In Panama, I did the same thing, focusing on my ledgers instead of using my business training to ferret out the risk Noriega might pose to us and putting in a plan to mitigate it. I saw that given the nature of the owner of Filterco, where I now was working, the unwillingness of the board to remove him, and the precarious cash flow coming in, my current job was a dead end.

Further, the course astonished me by putting my reliance on processes into perspective: *Everybody* did something like that. Not specifically to be methodical, because that was just one of the thousands of different paths people chose. Rather, they did it to overcome their childhood belief that they were not already good enough to succeed in life in some way.

The trainer referred to the phenomenon as having a "winning formula."[6] It was one or more ways of being that we all had hit on to be successful in life, to "make it." The formula could be anything and was compensation for something we could never be when we were young. It often prevented us from relating to people, since it was about achieving

---

6   Today the successor to est, the Landmark Forum, calls it a "strong suit."

success, not getting close to others. Even though I was not sure all of that applied to absolutely everybody on the planet, I noted that it eerily described exactly what I and virtually every one of the two hundred people in the seminar room had experienced.

~

By the time I emerged from the four days and a follow-up evening session a few days later, my world was upside down. Despite my headache and having to take two five-hundred-milligram Tylenols every six hours to deal with it, I was joyous. I saw the possibility of inventing a whole new life and felt I had the tools and the motivation to make it happen.

I soon realized, however, that the distinctions I got exposed to during those four days were a two-edged sword. On one hand, they provided an alternative to my winning recipe as a source of security. They called me to focus on integrity, commitment, responsibility, and engagement—things that could alter my reality for the better if I delivered them well. But on the other hand, the trainer specifically called us to be "unreasonable," meaning not to settle for the status quo or let anyone or anything stop us by offering a "reasonable" argument. For someone as safety conscious as I was, that tended to undercut the very distinctions I had just learned.

That said, the training woke me up. I realized I was victimizing myself, beating myself up over having terrible judgment in choosing a business opportunity and in choosing a woman to spend my life with.

The solution, I came to realize, was to take responsibility for where I was in life. The program leader said three things on that issue that struck me:

- Responsibility begins with a willingness to be the cause of a matter, meaning to admit your participation in the issue.

- Responsibility is something you take on by declaring it.

- Once you take responsibility for a complaint, it will disappear completely.

These realizations turned my head around.

I called my mother in California and told her how deeply I loved her and appreciated everything she had done for me. I acknowledged I had been a shit to her and asked if she would forgive me. We both cried, and from that moment on, I had my mother back during the last fifteen years of her life.

I took responsibility for my business judgment by quitting my dead-end job and starting to seek whatever was next for me. After I resigned from Filterco, I called Dick Bertram to let him know I was sorry that had to be an outcome of the training he had recommended. He laughed and said he guessed that might be a possibility but knew whatever I decided would be best for me. He supported my leaving.

I took responsibility for my relationship judgment by trying to rebuild my marriage with Ida. A particularly powerful exercise we had done in the training was to sit knee to knee with a stranger and look into their eyes for ten minutes, only blinking and not averting our gazes. We did that with multiple people and in each case were so moved by them that we hugged and cried when it was over, even though we had never met until then.

Ida agreed to try that while the kids were asleep, so we set up two chairs in front of a pile of dishes drying on the kitchen counter. About a minute into it, she said she could not continue; it was too hard for her, and she got up. Years later, I realized that at that point, she probably did not recognize me. For a decade and a half, I had enrolled her in my being a hard-driving introvert, and now I was more relaxed and outgoing.

After I did est, Ida lost me as her partner in introversion. My genetic makeup had not changed; I was not now an extrovert. But after the training I gained self-confidence and felt less inclination to withdraw from others. That, plus the scars from many years of financial struggle and inattention from me, made it almost impossible to reconnect with her.

Not long afterward, she said she wanted a trial separation and took the kids to her parents' house in the Del Water Gap area of western New Jersey for six weeks. After the est Training, I felt more love for Hannah and

Conor than ever before and missed them terribly, even as I was relieved to be away from Ida for a while.

A few weeks into her trip, I got a call at work from our brother-in-law Rob, who was a Lutheran minister.

"Ben, Ida and I have been talking. I just wanted you to know that if you and she are to stay married, things are going to have to change."

"I agree, Rob. What things did she mention?"

"I'd prefer not to get into that. Ida will let you know when she returns."

A month later, she and the kids came back. Her thinking had apparently evolved since the day she spoke with Rob, because now she said she wanted a divorce. I had not seen this coming so soon, but readily consented. Her reasons included our inability to communicate, her having to join a church without me because she knew I was not interested in doing that, and her exasperation that I was not using my education to get hired by a big company.

The conversation was cordial. We agreed that the well-being of the children was paramount in this, and that no matter what happened, we would never disparage each other in front of them.

We called them into the living room and sat with them on the cheap green carpeting that covered the floor in the rental where we lived. Conor was now five, busy playing with a toy truck. Hannah, eight, was looking down at the floor. When we said the word "divorce," she whipped her head around to look at us. She knew extremely well what that meant. We hugged both children and told them we would always be their mommy and daddy, not sure in our own minds how we were ever going to do that successfully if I did not live with them.

WHAT I COULD HAVE DONE DIFFERENTLY

I could have guessed that the years-long experience of prioritizing my recipe over my marriage would likely end in a divorce. Even before that happened, I realized that my life did not work. In the resulting est Training, my growth in awareness was one of the most powerful learning experiences

I ever had. It helped me to decrease the frequency of three experiences that regularly triggered my recipe: futility, complaining, and drama.

Takeaways from Chapter 14

1. Living from Being, to Doing, to Having is the mechanism of your recipe, which is one reason why it has survived for so long in your life. But its form of Being is inauthentic, so it does not help you to avoid futility. On the other hand, if you used Being-Doing-Having in every aspect of life, instead of the Having-Doing-Being approach that you normally employ, you could eliminate much of the futility you deal with now.

2. Your recipe is useless against most of your complaints. To end them, take responsibility for them—ask yourself what being responsible means in each situation, and act accordingly.

3. Your recipe is also useless against drama, and in fact is the source of much of it in your relationships and career. Keep your agreements and much of the drama will disappear.

Reflective Questions

1. Where are you experiencing futility in your life? Could it be because you are focusing on Having things as I did—Having my recipe of being methodical so I could Be more comfortable with myself in our extroverted world? What if you focused instead on Being a certain way? How could that bring better results?

2. What major complaints do you have? How could you take responsibility for them, meaning owning them and taking effective action instead of just complaining? For example, if you and your spouse have different ideas about how to keep the house

clean and complain often about the other's behavior, taking responsibility might involve deciding on a compromise that you can both live with, even though it doesn't meet the most extreme expectations of either one of you.

3. What agreements with other people are you not keeping? How is that causing drama in your life?

Practical Exercises

1. Pick an area where you are trying unsuccessfully to Have something. Write down how you would need to Be about it so you could Do something that would actually allow you to Have it. Try it, and see what results you get.

2. Write down a major complaint you have, and what taking responsibility for it would look like. Perform the resulting action, and see what outcome you get.

3. Pick an agreement you are not keeping with someone and that consequently is causing drama in your life. Clean it up by either adhering to the agreement, or remaking it with the other person. See what the result is.

~

The divorce was only the start of the changes I was beginning to make in my life. I was about to slide into a dangerously intense depression, but would come out the other side in a completely new career.

15

Intention: On the Brink

APRIL 1981. MIAMI SHORES, FLORIDA. The divorce from Ida was finalized on April 28, ten months after I completed the est Training.

At first, I reveled in the freedom of my new life. I picked up the kids twice a week—on Tuesday night and on Saturday—and loved spending time with them at the mall, the library, and anyplace else that did not have an entrance fee. Oddly, I felt closer to them now than when I lived with them, helping to assuage some of the guilt I had whenever I compared myself to my own dad as a father.

I found a place to live just north of the city in Miami Shores—a single room in a trim stucco bungalow built in the 1950s. I had a nice tile bathroom and a private entrance from the side of the home. My only furniture was a burgundy velvet sofa bed on one wall, a door supported by wire legs that I used as a desk on the opposite wall, and a futuristic leather armchair beside a sliding glass door that looked out on an overgrown backyard.

My landlords were two guys who kept to themselves and had decorated my space with tuck-and-roll padded walls. It was clean and comfortable, and I made sure I kept it that way.

Beyond the weeds in the backyard was a tiny in-ground swimming pool under some shade trees. Twelve feet long, six feet wide, and four feet deep, it was the best pool there was as far as the kids were concerned. On Saturdays, they would spend the night, sleeping in my sofa bed while I slept on the floor. They had a ball splashing around Saturday afternoons and again on Sunday mornings before I took them back to Ida.

Now a ten-month veteran of the est Training, I had stayed enrolled in weekly seminars that solidified the insights I had gained during the event. They also helped me adopt a less reserved, more open approach to life. The desire to invent processes to compensate for being an introvert went underground as glowing embers; I still felt their heat but did not act on them.

At a post-training meeting, I met a young guy named Henry who owned one of the first Apple computer stores in Florida. Curly-headed with fleshy cheeks and a growing midsection, Henry talked about the power of these new devices in a way that excited me. I drove the five hours from Miami to his store in Tampa to check them out and see if I could get a job there.

He was not hiring, but his talk captivated me with what personal computers could do for a small business. Out of that realization, I resolved to learn how to sell them. When Henry told me about a new computer store called International Computer Systems (ICS) that had just opened in Coral Gables back in the Miami area, my brain started working intensely on how I could join them.

I came back to Miami Shores just as the long Memorial Day weekend began. After so much exuberance in Tampa, I was disappointed to return to my empty room. After a few hours, it hit home that I was now totally alone, and I started to sense my newfound sociability might be only a veneer. As more long hours unfolded, I realized I had nowhere to go and nothing to do and slowly descended into what would turn out to be the most devastating depression of my life.

~

When it washed over me, I rolled a blank piece of paper into my portable typewriter and began to write.

"I run my life out of 'take care of me,'" I wrote. "I want people and companies to tell me how great I am and save me. I'm always looking for someone or a formula to rescue me. The world doesn't care."

Stunned, I lifted my fingers off the keyboard. This was a new insight. I had never thought of my processes as something I had invented to take care of me. But when I looked, I saw that awareness was blazingly accurate. Processes provided security, and from the very beginning I had sought to use them as a shield against intrusions from an extroverted world.

I continued. "The lack of intention in my life is staggering."

I was thirty-eight years old and had been out of work for over a month. I was not keeping agreements about money. I had no sense of direction. I reacted to every newspaper ad about a job and every acquaintance who had a deal. I tried to fit everything together, to figure it out, to force it to work. I resisted participating with people. I blasted them for being how they were being. I looked only for comfort and rest. I had no satisfaction whatsoever from my life. I feared I would not survive. My mind absolutely dominated me from the early morning until I went to sleep, and even in my sleep, it ran me. I was physically thin but emotionally heavy. I was no fun to be with.

I had a tremendous sadness about my money situation. I was sad that I could not support the kids and Ida. I could not put food on their table. I could not give them any advantages in life. They were barely making it, and I was so broke that I might have to discontinue providing what little I had been giving to them.

I was sad about my relationship with my father. It was emotionless and filled with survival. I was perpetuating my own dependence and bleeding his resources. He would absolutely have given me the last dollar in his pocket and starved, and I was causing him to do it because of my own lack of intention. I loved him so very dearly. I loved my kids so very dearly.

My most cherished images were when I was little, and Dad would hold me. He took me everywhere. He took care of me at the barber, picked me up from the school bus stop with a towel when it rained, went to bat for me in high school when I almost got screwed out of being co-valedictorian, and brought me hot water bottles to lessen the joint pain when I had rheumatic fever.

My mother was absent from those memories. She was small and beautiful and wore high-heeled shoes. When I was two years old, she crossed her legs and bounced me on her free foot. She scared me. She was so vibrant, alive, talkative, and pretty. I could not stand the noise and ran to Daddy to save me from her. He would take care of me no matter what. Mom's taking care of me had a hook in it. She wanted me in some way, and I could not deal with it. Yet she stayed with me in the hospital when I was fourteen and had my appendix out. She scratched my back countless times at night to relax me. She took care of me at home when I was sick with measles.

I got up from the table and walked over to the sliding glass door at the back of my room. I looked across the backyard and saw the grayness outside. A slow drizzle was coming down, putting circles all over the surface of the tiny swimming pool and a sprinkling of droplets on the tufts of weeds and the scruffy St. Augustine grass that my landlords had not cut in months. Somewhere in the neighborhood, a dog on a porch barked to be let in.

Back at the table, I went on typing. The cups of the keyboard letters felt comforting on my fingertips.

I closed up inside when Mom came at me to listen to her chatter. I shut down and turned to Dad for love that was pure and unconditional. Except his had a hook in it too—his desire to play the role of the daddy he himself never had. He could not be just himself, and that was all I ever wanted him to be. Sometimes he *was* himself, but most of the time he was acting out of his conscious role of giving me the attention he never had.

He rewarded me for needing him. We played an elaborate game and were doing it now. I created circumstances where he needed to take care of me so he could care for me like no one ever cared for him. My whole life had been about this and my processes.

Dad took care of me because he needed to be the father who was missing from his own life. Mom took care of me because she wanted to give me the kind of nurturing that would prevent me from ever becoming like her father. He was a successful businessman, but he drank, neglected her, and physically abused her mother.

Because of those agendas, I did not get that they took care of me for *me*. I did not get a sense of safety out of all that. I spent my whole life trying to find it by having another person or some kind of a process take care of me so I could feel safe.

I saw that the only times I had money were when I successfully found situations where others could care for me. At Castle & Cooke in Honolulu, I had a big company to take care of me. Then my partner Bruce took over, and my other partner Max made a big pile of money for all of us. It was only when the party was over and I had to contribute on my own that the money stopped. I drove deeper and deeper into Bruce and Dad to take care of me. They played their roles magnificently. They took care of me, isolated me from the world until they could not do it anymore.

Now for the first time ever, I was completely alone. After ten years, my close partner Bruce was gone. After twelve years, my wife Ida was gone; I married her to take care of me, and she got tired of it. She was her own person now. Only the kids were around to take care of me, and I was using them for that purpose every weekend. Rather than contributing to them, I was setting things up so they would take care of my emotional need for love. I was not making a damn bit of difference in their lives.

~

I wanted to die. I wanted to end this and get on with something else.

I was holding on to my crummy circumstances by my fingernails so that the person I was would not die. Yet what I really wanted was for all this to go away. If I just let go of everything and allowed it to be, most likely a new person would emerge. If I had intention—a deliberate focus to move toward something meaningful or valuable—living would become purposeful. From the ruins I was walking through, intention would call forth an awareness of a purpose and a willingness to act on it.

The more I wrote, the more I began to feel the stirrings of a nascent willingness to take responsibility for my life again. With a clear intention, the circumstances would be okay enough for me to face them. If I had a framework of intention, if I knew what I was committed to regardless of the circumstances, then declaring bankruptcy, being cited for contempt of court for nonpayment of child support, and losing my car—all of which hadn't yet happened but I knew were staring me in the face—would be merely the contents of my situation.

The key to the whole thing, to my life, was to have intention. What did I intend?

I got up again and looked out the sliding glass door. It gave me a CinemaScope view of the wet gloom outside. I panned my eyes across the weeds and overgrown grass. The thousands of tiny droplets of water clinging to their sides somehow made them look hopeful. I opened the door a crack and got a whiff of fresh rain on grass, but quickly closed it to keep out a blast of humidity.

In that moment, I realized my intention was to have influence in the lives of people around me. But how?

Back at my familiar typewriter, I wrote that I had always thought making a difference had to look a certain way.

"But I could make a difference at any time," I wrote. "And in any place if that were the framework of my life. Whether I sell encyclopedias door to door, sell personal computers in a store, or work for a construction company in an office, I can make a difference if that is what I intend to do."

For me, making a difference meant empowering other people to become all *they* could be. It would be unique in each situation. I would do whatever they wanted and needed so that I could contribute to them.

Satisfaction all around would be the main product. Money would flow out as a byproduct.

What was it that was wanted and needed that I could provide? I thought of my experience with Henry, the Apple computer guy in Tampa, on the previous day and rephrased the question.

"How could a personal computer make a difference in the life of a small businessperson, and thereby help me provide for my kids?"

Traditionally, people used the machine for the dog work of keeping track of the general ledger, payables and receivables, inventory, and sales. How could it be used to transform the business and blow it off the map?

The small business owners would figure it out. When they bought an Apple II and had the experience of making better decisions, they would empower themselves to transform their businesses. My job was to show them how to use that small computer to blow away themselves and their companies.

~

Through my writing that weekend, I got to the point where I was ready to experience what I intended to be—a person who would make a profound difference in the lives of small business owners. To do that, I would need to become an ace salesman for personal computers, even though I knew nothing about them.

I visualized myself learning the products—not how to program them, but how to get them to produce output. I saw myself focusing on the key decisions business owners regularly made and on showing them how a computer could improve their thinking and their self-image in the bargain.

I then looked down, as if I were hovering high above the floor of a computer store. I saw myself talking with walk-ins, sitting down and doing demonstrations, listening actively about their decisions, collaborating with them to figure out how the computer could improve those choices, and encouraging them to share themselves. I saw myself writing up the order and shaking the customer's hand, then following up after the sale to learn about their experience.

I created a meaning around all of this: It meant that I was *already* an ace salesperson. I *already* had it within me. All I needed to do was to manifest it in a place where the product and service were right, and my customers and coworkers supported what I was doing. This was not about them taking care of me. It was about me empowering myself to have influence.

This was not noble, it was not a crusade, and it was not "right." It just was. It was a vehicle for satisfaction in my life and in the lives of my customers. It was desperately wanted and needed in the uncertain and chaotic business environment of the day.

What about International Computer Systems, the Apple store in Coral Gables that Henry had told me about? Yes, I was a non-computer person. But I did not need to sell what was true. I had been a small business owner for ten years and knew what the problems were. I spoke the language. I had a burning desire to be effective in the businesses and lives of the ICS customers. I could do it. I was already successful. All I needed to do now was to play it out.

Henry had told me that the ICS sales manager's name was Johnny. I was now writing on a Sunday; Monday was Memorial Day. I would go see Johnny on Tuesday and enroll him in my joining ICS. I would tell him that what the company was doing absolutely inspired me and would say that I wanted to be a part of it. I would work for no salary, only a commission as a rookie salesperson starting at the bottom. I would do whatever it took to learn the business and succeed. My intention was to help customers by encouraging them to introduce a computer into their businesses. I was totally convinced of its power and that we had only begun to use it. I learned fast, and as far as I was concerned, I was already a successful ICS salesperson.

That Memorial Day a professional acrobat, dressed in a Spider-Man costume, climbed the entire outside of the 110-story Sears Tower in Chicago using suction cups on the windows. If he could do that, I could be extroverted enough to succeed with Johnny.

~

First thing that Tuesday morning, I drove down to Ponce de Leon Boulevard in Coral Gables and walked into ICS cold, brimming with pure intention. I asked for Johnny, and when he walked into the showroom, he did not look anything like the technical expert I had expected to find.

Johnny was a thin, fortyish old hippie. He had shoulder-length blond hair, tinted glasses, and an open-collar silk shirt more proper for barhopping than for business. Bell-bottom pants and brown boots completed the California image, except that when he opened his mouth, out came pure Brooklynese.

Kindly and attentive, Johnny listened to my pitch. I told him I was his most successful salesperson, and it just had to manifest. As I spoke, I demonstrated a big part of the est Training—verbally declaring a framework and then stepping inside it.

It worked! Johnny hired me on the spot and had me start the next day. To my surprise, the job included a small salary of $150 a week, and commissions were a generous 10 percent of retail. In those days, an Apple II with a pitiful four kilobytes of random-access memory, two five-and-a-quarter-inch floppy disk drives that stored only 160 kilobytes of data, a boxy black-and-white monitor, and a huge dot-matrix printer would set you back about $10,000. And at that price, they were flying off the shelves.

We shook on the deal. "Come into the back with me, Ben," he said as he started walking.

"This is the order machine," he said as he swept his hand over some equipment pushed up against a side wall. "It is configured exactly as you will be selling it."

A blinking dot sat in the top left corner of a black-and-white monitor.

"What's that?" I asked, pointing to the dot. "I realize how dumb that question is."

He laughed. "That's the cursor. It is where you start typing. Watch."

He showed me how to key in anything I sold. It was mindlessly simple. He entered a four-digit product code, and the system automatically priced it and asked if he wanted to print an invoice.

I loved his cheerful outlook. The next day, he put me on the floor to talk with walk-ins and volunteered to help me close any sales. I was so enthusiastic about what the Apple II could do and was so quick to learn how to demonstrate its power that I was able to answer everything but the customers' technical questions. Johnny kindly did that for me.

The following day, and with only a minor assist from Johnny, I sold my first hardware and software package. It came to over $11,000, which put a commission check for $1,100 into my hands the following week. It is hard to overstate the positive impact that check had on my self-esteem and on my eagerness to do more of this work.

~

Selling as a profession was alien to me, so for security I quickly built a process. Sales was a numbers game. For every hundred phone calls to local small businesses, a certain percentage would make an appointment to come in. Only some of those would show up for a demonstration, and of those who did, a certain number would buy. It was just a matter of getting the percentages right at each level.

This was known as the sales funnel. I constantly had to get in touch with the est distinctions to be outgoing enough to guide customers through each stage to a sale. But the sales funnel reduced the anxiety around doing that. I could get by with less extroversion by just focusing on the funnel and the numbers.

Coming out of the est Training, I had guessed my compulsion for processes might lessen or go away. But now that I was selling computers, I was again relying on a process—more strongly than ever.

This brought out something the trainer had said about winning formulas that, at the time, did not register with me: They never go away. No matter how much you are aware of them, no matter how much you see through them, they tend to stay with you for a lifetime. Yes, you can mitigate them and lessen their hold over you. But they are always there as a default when things get tough.

~

In service of the sales funnel, I worked the phones relentlessly. I tracked the fractions at each level, compiled the data, and reliably produced sales at such a rate that within one month I was the top floor salesperson in the store. It helped that we had a hot, unique product, and that nobody else on the sales staff was milking it the way I was. They could not match my levels of determination or production.

After a few months, I graduated from cold-calling businesses out of the phone book to managing a stable of large clients, some of whom were my customers and others the store had turned over to me. The store called my area the Business Analysis Group, so inevitably I became known as the B.A.G. man. The repeat business was lucrative, the work fairly easy. It was enough to live on and pay off some small debts.

How I was able to create that out of nothing was no mystery. In the est Training, I had learned that in life, you do not get what you want; you get what you intend. And if you want to know what you have intended until now, look around at your life.

I also learned that creating intention was not complicated. All it took was for me to make repeated proclamations about what I intended, backed up by an unwavering commitment to make it happen. In time, that would offset whatever unconscious default intention I had created.

A deliberately driven intention was the product of passion. And a great way to kindle it was to ask how I could contribute to others in some way. As soon as I did that, a vision of the Apple II appeared in my head, and I was on my way. It was completely "unreasonable," and it worked, helping to restore my confidence in the training. Plus, it added some much-needed, long-sought security to my life.

WHAT I COULD HAVE DONE DIFFERENTLY

Had I thought about it, I might have seen that simultaneously ending my marriage and a long-term business relationship would make me despondent. But to override the recipe, I needed to experience a deep and dangerous depression. It allowed me to discover that the critical ingredient missing from my life was intention.

Takeaways from Chapter 15

1. Your recipe is not the authentic you, and is useless against your depression. To pull yourself up emotionally, rely instead on discovering an intention that you have.

2. When your life is not working, you will hang on to your recipe by your fingernails as if you were suspended from a cliff. The best thing you can do is simply to let go, and see what happens.

3. When you discover a passionate intention, it will be outside the recipe. Act on the intention before your recipe shows up again, which it will.

Reflective Questions

1. Recall the last time you were seriously depressed. How would discovering a passionate intention have pulled you into a more positive state?

2. What unworkable situation are you hanging on to? For example, this could be a job, a relationship, a belief about something, or any other circumstance that consistently upsets you. What if you just let go of it? What would that involve, and how would it feel?

3. When was the last time you had a passionate intention about something? Did you act on it, or did you allow your recipe to modify it or even shut it down?

Practical Exercises

1. Write down something you are depressed about right now. Then write down an intention, a purpose that would be highly exciting for you to commit to. Finally, write down the impact the intention had on your depression.

2. Find another unworkable situation, and let go of how you are Being about it—for example, being angry, being frustrated, being sad. Then find another way of Being about it and Do what comes out of that. Write down the results. If your recipe is "being curious," you might try to figure out a solution. If it is "being diplomatic," you could make a new approach to someone. "Being funny" might lead you to laugh the whole thing off.

3. Write down a passionate intention that you have, or create a new one. Listen for the approach of your recipe, and block it by planning how to act on what you intend. Write down the result.

~

All that intention was wonderful. But it was not effective enough for me to keep my children close by enough in distance so I could ever see them again.

16

Accepting Acute Loss: Good-Bye, My Sweet Children

JULY 1981. MIAMI SHORES, FLORIDA. I now had success in sales and a few new friends at work, but by Fourth of July weekend, I was lonely. Hannah and Conor were up north with Ida's family and would be there for weeks. I missed them desperately.

On Saturday, I went to the beach at Key Biscayne by myself and spent almost ten hours there. When I arrived, I looked out to sea. Even after years in Florida, I could not get used to how calm the Atlantic surf was compared to the crashing waves in California. But the salt air blowing in smelled just the same, and it was bracing.

In the three months since the divorce, I had not intended to find another partner. At thirty-eight, I was too broke and too preoccupied with trying to make a living. Now that I had some success in selling computers, I began to think of reaching out. I was more alone than I could ever remember being and longed for the feeling of safety that a loving relationship could provide.

But lonely as I was, I was no longer looking for someone to take care of me. As I discovered with Ida, that did not work. More importantly, after the est Training I was now committed to being fully responsible in any new relationship, coming at it from a position of accountability rather than one of need.

My mind had a full set of criteria worked out. She would be as busy as I was. She would have her own life but also be looking for a relationship after someone had burned her. That part was key, so she would not be willing to settle for the first guy she found. She would be available to me in the exact proportion to my availability to her. We would have only a limited time to be together. We would make love passionately during brief intervals, then after charging our batteries would retreat to our respective lives.

I expected that the appearance of a woman in my life would closely parallel the appearance of money. Not because money made women possible, but because both women and money were a function of intention. Until I created intention, I did not have a job. And so it would be with a new partner. If I put myself out there, was willing to make mistakes, and had a high level of intention about a relationship, it would appear.

What did putting it out there look like? There were a lot of beautiful and interesting women in my post–est Training seminars. But I always felt so transparent. And gawky. And uncool. The wonderful thing about est was that you got to be however you were. Putting it out there would be going up to someone and sharing that I wanted to meet her but could not think of anything to say, so there I was. In est, somehow that worked.

I soon found myself checking out the ring finger of every attractive woman I saw in the est seminar to see if she was available. I had already spotted three or four I wanted to talk with.

Yet I was torn. I knew that seeking love did not work. What might work was to encompass a new woman in the exuberance and spontaneity of my own life. If a new activity had as its main purpose the expansion of my inner self, then it would work.

~

A first step was to practice sharing myself with people in general. Fortunately, my positive experience in doing that during the est Training eased my anxiety about reaching out. And that Monday, July 6, a brilliantly sunny day, I had the opportunity to practice.

I went back to Key Biscayne and this time took my skim board. It was the same circular, laminated piece of plywood Ida and I had used in Laguna before I went to Vietnam. I looked up and down the coast to find a flat part of the beach and started using it to ride the slush of sand as water retreated back into the ocean. It gave me a chance to talk and share with a lot of people, even though every one of them was a stranger.

First was a guy with a crew cut named Joe who was coming in from swimming and stared at me with wide eyes as I skimmed over the sand. I asked him if he wanted to use it, and did he ever. It reminded him of when he did the same kind of thing as a kid in Miami streets after a big rainfall. He called it "womping" instead of skimming. His girlfriend tried it and fell down a few times, getting her long red hair full of sand; we all three had great laughs when she tumbled into the surf with a splat.

Then there were two kids the ages of Hannah and Conor, except that the blond boy, Todd, was the older one. Katrina had a great smile and followed Todd around like a puppy. At first, they were scared to ask, but then they got brave. I threw the board for them a few times so they could learn to jump on it and stay on. Pretty soon their super-fit father, Craig, came over and tried it. He owned two clothing stores, one in Coconut Grove and one in South Miami. I even got in a pitch for an Apple computer. I gave him the specifications on the skim board, and he said he would make one with Todd.

After a while, two little black-haired Colombian kids, Maria and Tomasito, began to use the board. He threw it on the slush and promptly fell.

"*¡Ay Tomasito, qué pena!*" Maria said, laughing—"What a pity!"

The second time he threw it, he got a good ride. They were not surprised that I could speak Spanish, because this was Miami, and people everywhere could speak it.

"*Ahora me toca a mí,*" she said with authority—now it was her turn. Same result: a fall on the first try but a decent ride on the second.

They used it for a long time, running with it, hopping on it, and sitting down. I went into the deeper water, and they followed me in with the board, which I knew would be dangerous if a wave caught it.

"*Ya niños, regresemos a la playa*"—"Okay, kids," I said, "let's go back to the beach."

Tomasito then put the board in a shallow pool, and a one-year-old kid, a gringo with blond hair, seemed quite delighted with himself just to sit naked on it. His young mother, Nicole, was with him. We sat and talked for a while with the Colombian kids looking on. She was from Buffalo and had been in Miami for less than a year. I was not sure if she was married (no ring), but after a while the conversation became distant, so I moved on.

The world was such a rich and varied place. I got a lot of satisfaction by reaching out from love and acceptance. Doing that was so unfamiliar to me. But it gave me a sense of safety, and of connection, to everyone I spoke with.

Unfortunately, it did not last. Within a day, the ache of loneliness returned.

~

Ida's situation was getting desperate. She had no job, needed to move soon, and was pressuring me to take off from work to help move her up north, as last year I had said I would so she could be near her parents, sisters, and brother. I was not keeping my agreement with her on this, and I needed to clean it up.

I could do so by giving her money, but I was finding all sorts of excuses as to why I could not do that. I did not have any spare cash, and why should I help her take the kids away from me? Plus, it would probably not matter; with or without my help, she most likely would go anyway. I was not earning enough by selling computers to help her financially to the point where she might consider staying.

I recalled that I had played "take care of me" not only with my father and Bruce, but also with Ida. One night in Brooklyn in 1965, I had come up from my army post in Baltimore to see her at my aunt Rae's brownstone. Outside, it was freezing. We were alone on the couch in the downstairs living room. I had my head in Ida's lap, something we had never done before. She stroked my head, she kissed me, and she took care of me. That was it. She overwhelmed me with love. I had found what I wanted. I did not have to be alone anymore. She was the first woman I had ever met who did not scare me in some way, and I married her.

We got married to take care of one another to forbear the other's idiosyncrasies. To be mutual crutches. I wanted someone who would hold my head in her lap and always be there for me to lean on.

She wanted the same thing, but I could not provide it. I pushed her away. I could not bear taking care of her, because I thought I deserved for her to take care of me. I became bitter and aloof, condescending and cold. She became the same way, and we got a divorce.

Nowhere was there an intention to have an experience of Ida as Ida, to accept her magnificence exactly as it was. I tried to remake her, and in the last year of our marriage, I got the same treatment back. We were like two mirrors reflecting each other. Now she was alone, frightened, and wondering if she could possibly cope with everything. I had the same feelings, but after the est Training was beginning to crawl out of my hole.

The most painful memory of the divorce, which usually occurred first thing in the morning while I was getting dressed, was that I did not have Ida's familiar presence to take care of me anymore. To iron my shirt, fix me breakfast, be there all day so I could relate to her and make excuses for not wanting to relate to anyone else, be there when I got home to fix dinner and support me in thousands of ways. For twelve years, I played that game, and she wearied of it. So did I, not realizing it brought diminishing returns. Now I had no one to take care of me, but there was progress; I was slowly increasing my level of satisfaction on my own.

I had always seen women as filling a gap in my life, performing a personal and social function, rather than a balance of being who we both were. It was as if I was hiring her for a job rather than making a difference in her life with the expectation of nothing in return.

That seemed to be what Prince Charles was doing late that July when he married Diana Spencer. She would look great at royal receptions.

When I walked into International Computer Systems after Memorial Day, I created a job out of pure intention. I was not up to doing that yet with a relationship. Instead, I was creating loneliness so I could have *that* experience first and then clear it up.

~

Despite my refusal to seek another new relationship, I tried to fight the feelings of loneliness that threatened to overwhelm me.

I filled the hours with work. When it got too bad, I went to my room, held a picture of the kids in my lap, and cried for a while. I loved them so. I loved the experience of being with them, of holding them close to me, of feeling their little arms around my neck. That was the only form of skin contact I had with another human being, and now that they were up north temporarily for the summer, it was virtual. In my imagination I held them to me and told them how much I loved them, smoothed their clothes, and played with their hair, then squeezed their hands and sent them off again, satisfied with having had an experience of their love.

At work, Johnny occasionally brought in his daughter Abby, who was eleven. Happy and alert, she said one day that I was beautiful. She was so fresh and sincere that I believed it. I never expected anyone would say something like that to me. She penetrated right to the core of who she thought I was. She let me see that all there was in life was love, and we were all here to experience that.

A few days later, I was working a chiropractor convention in a high-ceilinged room in a Miami Beach hotel overflowing with tourists and the smell of suntan lotion. Abby came in with Johnny and a little cousin and told me they were playing Cinderella. The hotel was the palace, and I was the prince because I was so beautiful. It made me cry to think of that. There was so much depth to life, and little children were in touch with something special that we, as adults, had forgotten.

Ida's brother Leo Junior would arrive in a few days with a rental truck to move her to New Jersey. She had decided it was time to move permanently and live with her parents until she found a job and an apartment so the kids could start school there. Her sister Naomi had just gotten married and lived in the neighborhood with her husband and her son Thomas, who was Hannah's age; the two of them and Conor had always gotten along well. Ida's brother and other sister lived only a few hours away, so Ida would have plenty of family support to draw on.

As Ida's departure date approached, she softened her stance toward me. She wanted to talk, so we met one night in the parking lot of a Publix supermarket on South Dixie Highway. We sat on the shabby front seat of my aging AMC Hornet two-door for our first face-to-face conversation in months. She looked drawn and exhausted.

"Ben," she began, "I want you to know that I'm moving out of necessity. It promises more growth for me. I hope you're not taking this as some kind of retaliation."

That surprised me. "Thanks for that, Ida. I appreciate it. I have accepted the move. I'll miss the kids more than I can possibly say, but I don't have any ill will toward you."

The loud grind of an eighteen-wheeler's engine passed on the highway just yards from us. While we waited for it to be quiet enough to talk again, I saw that she had started to choke up. "The kids deeply need you as their father, Ben. I will do whatever I can to make it easier for you to fly up to see them. I'll pay part of the airfare if I can."

That touched me, because financially, she was even worse off than I was.

~

What I did not say was that in the past few months, I had bound myself to the children more deeply than before. The est Training woke me up to how precious they were to me, and our twice-weekly visits were things I looked forward to as if each time were Christmas. Ida's impending move with the children was so ominous that I felt acute sadness.

A few weeks after they left, I plunged into deep grief. True to form, the only advice my recipe provided was to change the subject by telling me to throw myself into the sales funnel process at work. I tried that, but soon found it to be useless.

When the anguish became intolerable, I resolved to do something about it. During the est Training, we had done an exercise designed to help us get complete with someone who was alive or dead. It was brutal, but I knew if I could get through it, the grief would not run me anymore.

One night I sat in a chair in my room, unplugged the phone, and turned out all the lights. I put a box of Kleenex nearby.

I then visualized bringing my children to me. I imagined little Conor stepping out of an elevator in front of me, running to me, and jumping in my arms. I held him and wept, knowing this was the last time I would ever see him. Then the elevator doors opened again, and Hannah came out, scampering to me and sitting on one knee while I held Conor on the other one. They were so beautiful, so smart, so very dear. I cried and cried, rocking back and forth with them in my lap until I thought I had no more tears left.

When I knew it was time for them to go, I gently set them on the floor. They stood in front of me, each one reaching out to touch my face and give me a kiss, then throw their arms around my neck to tell me they would always love me. I set them down again, and they slowly started to back away from me, blowing kisses and waving. The elevator doors opened, they stepped inside, blew another kiss to me, and disappeared forever.

I sobbed for an hour, lost in loneliness and despair. Exhausted, I turned on the lights and gulped down a glass of water to replenish the fluid I had cast off as tears.

I was numb. I went into the bathroom. It smelled faintly of the Ajax I had used to clean the sink that morning. Standing there, I recalled a time in the first rental house when the children were so small I could bathe both in the tub at the same time. Once, when I was washing them, I had the thought that even though the house Ida and I tried to build had been taken away, I would never have to give up the two toddlers in front of me. Back then they had looked up at me with wet and smiling faces, comforting me more than they could know.

Now they were gone. Ida would likely remarry, and another man would raise them. When that thought hit me, I had to steady myself against the sink.

Days passed. The ache inside slowly unwound itself, and I was able to concentrate on my selling. My mind returned often to Hannah and Conor, but after a week, I noticed that the charge was far less; I missed them terribly but no longer felt incapacitated by uncontrollable depression.

One day, it did return. That night, I did a repeat of the elevator exercise and from then on, my longing to be with them hardened into a tiny marble within my chest, one I could massage and placate by recalling happy times. Doing that transformed my experience of the loss, taking the charge out of it and allowing me to include the children in my thoughts with love instead of desperate sorrow.

Psychologists say that grief occurs in stages, starting with denial and ending in acceptance. Accepting death does not mean liking what happened, but coming to terms with the reality of it. The experience I put myself through in the elevator exercise sped all of that up so much that I got to acceptance swiftly, in just an hour of intense pain rather than weeks or months of gradually decreasing agony.

That was a severe solution. But it worked in an area of life where my winning recipe had been useless.

~

My room was such a sad place.

In there, my severe depression over Memorial Day weekend had been close to dangerous. After a happy Fourth of July, I went back inside those four walls and slipped into loneliness. And now I had sat in the room twice and consciously imagined saying good-bye to my two little children forever, knowing that was the best way to get over my grief even though I would visit them in New Jersey as soon as I could.

WHAT I COULD HAVE DONE DIFFERENTLY

I probably could have guessed that given Ida's attachment to her family up north, she could well take away our little girl and boy. Had I seen that, I might have been able to steel myself against the loss. But acutely painful as it was when it happened, letting go of my children was training for letting go of my recipe thirty years later.

Takeaways from Chapter 16

1. Your winning recipe cannot help you with loneliness, loss, or grief. You designed it to focus on achievement, not on relationships.

2. Accepting the loss of a loved one is not disloyalty, because you are only accepting that you cannot change what happened in life and in death. Seeing that brings a great relief.

3. You can accelerate the process of acceptance by mentally bringing the person to you and cherishing them one last time, then watching them disappear.

Reflective Questions

1. In what way have you tried to use your recipe to deal with grief? How effective or ineffective was that? I tried it by being methodical in the search for the body of our cat Babassu, whom we presumed to be dead. The activity did distract me from my grief, but otherwise did nothing to lessen the pain.

2. Do you believe that it is disloyal to accept that your loved one is gone? How do you think that belief might have prolonged your grief?

3. What dear person still pains you the most when you think of their passing or other type of exit from your life?

Practical Exercises

1. Write down what your recipe is telling you to do about accepting the loss of a dear person. Then write down why that advice has not produced results.

2. For the loss in Question 3, write down that you do not have to like it, but you do have to accept that you cannot change the fact of their loss.

3. For that same loss, do the "elevator" process. Notice whether this reduces the charge on the loss. If not, do the process again a few days later, and reassess.

~

What I did not know was that soon the single rented room where I lived, with its rainy windows, empty Kleenex boxes, and lone chair overlooking forlorn St. Augustine grass would be the setting for some of the happiest moments I would ever have.

17

Nonresistance:
The Girl from
Saga Bay

OCTOBER 1981. CORAL GABLES, FLORIDA. At the ICS store in Coral Gables, I worked with intelligent people in their twenties who loved to have fun. Just being around them helped me to pull my attention away from myself and onto other people.

John Travolta's *Urban Cowboy* continued to be ragingly popular, spawning several new country and western bars in South Florida that some of the other salespeople went to regularly. One time, they invited me to go with them. Unlike at Harvard, where I shunned all after-hours contact with peers, here in my post-training mindset I thought the idea was great. I bought a pair of boots, a western shirt, and a cowboy hat, and went with two young women and two young men to a place called Club Dallas in Fort Lauderdale.

I had a blast. I didn't know the Texas two-step or any line dances such as the "Cotton-Eyed Joe," but I watched the others and more or less caught on. I ended up dancing with a gorgeous Colombian girl who had only been in the country for a few months and loved the whole cowboy scene. When the DJ played Conway Twitty's "Tight Fittin' Jeans," I figured he must have been looking at her. She drifted off and danced with half a dozen other guys, but I was happy just to be out there doing something new and strange and fun.

It also helped that I was still doing weekly post–est Training seminars. I was enrolled in one called "The Experience of Integrity," where we explored insights such as this: Integrity is more than just telling the truth; it is also about keeping your agreements, even the tiniest ones, and cleaning up the mess if you fail to do what you promise.

At one point, a young woman stood up in front of over a hundred people and took the microphone from a runner. As her eyes scanned the audience, she looked like she was scared to death.

"My husband, Nathan, and I own a small business," she said. "I hired a woman named Vicki to be our new receptionist, and Nathan and she are now openly having an affair."

A murmur spread across the room.

"I have two small children and no other source of income. Nathan wants both of us, and until tonight, I believed it was *his* integrity that was out."

She paused to collect herself.

"But what I have to say is that sitting here in my chair, I just got that it is *my* integrity that is out for allowing this shit to continue!"

The room exploded in applause.

"I am done!" she yelled over the applause. "I am finished with him!"

~

One evening a few weeks later, during a break in the integrity seminar, I looked across three rows of chairs to the front of the room and noticed a woman standing there. She turned around and looked at me. It was the one who had spoken to the group so powerfully about integrity a few weeks before.

"Didn't I see you at Club Dallas?" she said, smiling.

The night she had spoken to the group, I was so impressed with her words that I had not really looked at her, and now I was stunned at how graceful and pretty she was.

Before I could answer her, the seminar leader called everyone back to their seats. I stuffed my introversion down and rushed around the end of my row to sit in an empty chair right next to her. I was improvising and felt excited to be doing it.

I noticed how put together she was. She was wearing a satin turquoise blouse, tan slacks, and four-inch tan heels, complemented by beautiful nails, a professional hairdo, and subdued makeup.

Women never approached me, ever. Now this lovely young woman was smiling to the point where her eyes glistened and invited me to talk to her.

"You sure did see me there," I said. "I went for the first time with some friends. How about you?"

"I went with a girlfriend. It was my first time too." She looked right at me and gave me a gentle smile.

Before we could say anything more, the group went back into session. It was just before the evening was scheduled to end, and as it did, the seminar leader asked everyone to turn to the person next to them and exchange phone numbers. We were to be phone buddies for the coming week to discuss the homework he had given us.

I was thrilled. Est homework was deep. It asked the participants to share openly about their insights, foibles, and triumphs. It was common for people who did not know each other but were est graduates to share the most intimate details of their lives with the hundred strangers in the group. These were things they might not tell their own families. In that environment, I knew this woman with the glistening eyes and I would get to know each other with lightning speed.

And we did, talking the next night for four straight hours. Amid an evening downpour that drove noisy raindrops against my sliding glass door, I learned her name was Sandy Lewis. She was thirty-three and recently separated. She lived in a development called Saga Bay just north of Cutler Ridge in southern Dade County. She had a six-year-old named

Rachel, a four-year-old named Rosie, and two Siamese cats: Charlie and Chou (pronounced "Joe").

The homework must have had something to do with sex because the topic came up quickly. Sandy pointed out that people needed communication in sex—to start it and during it. She then asked if a woman had ever asked *me* to have sex.

I almost fell off my chair. Not only had no woman ever asked me that, but also no such idea had ever even occurred to me. Nor had I ever thought to ask a woman to have sex. That idea was so unfamiliar as to be scary. The rejection could be brutal. But in that moment, I saw that any future rejection would likely be no worse than my present frustration at having no sex at all.

The more we talked, the more I had an incredible desire to hold Sandy and make love to her. I heard how gentle and sensitive she was, and how horny she was. She said that as a result of our talk, she realized that she wanted a lover, a divorce, and a job.

After we hung up, my mind worked tirelessly. Any concerns I had earlier about her flew out the window. She smoked, which I disliked, and she had small children, who I worried might not accept me if we ever got together.

But I no longer cared. All my defenses were down. The communication was two-way, with each of us listening intently and speaking from the heart. I experienced a gentle flowing, a parallel movement that was devoid of threats. I felt safe and warm.

Yet, what we talked about was painful for both of us. She spoke of her dead brother whom she loved so dearly. She asked how long it had been since I had had sex, and when I told her eighteen months, she could not believe it. It had been only six months since my divorce, but Ida and I had stopped having sex over a year earlier than that. For her, it had been only six weeks, and she was having a hard time with it.

~

Two days later at the next seminar meeting, I asked her if she would like to go to the beach the following Saturday, and she accepted.

To avoid the crowds, we went in the afternoon as the sun was dropping low behind us; a cool November breeze blew over us, but the sun kept us warm. Sandy took off her beach robe, revealing the two-piece bathing suit below, and all I could think of was how remarkable she looked and how happy I was to be there with her.

We waded into the warm surf and watched the horizon to see a ship pass slowly by; we did not swim but went back to our towels. After revealing so much of ourselves that night on the phone, we were curiously quiet, as if the words might destroy the pleasure of just being near each other.

I wanted to touch her but did not know how to start, so I asked if I could give her a foot rub. She grinned and reclined on the towel, extending her gorgeous legs for me. I looked down and noticed that the trim and polish on her toenails were immaculate.

I cupped one hand on the top of her left foot and pressed on the ball of the foot with my other hand. I worked my fingers along the underside of each toe pad and along the seam that ran across the base of them.

I had no idea that the seam could produce such emotion. She closed her eyes, dropping her mouth slowly open as if she could hardly drink in so much pleasure. I later learned she had never been touched like that in her entire life and felt like she wanted more of it to make up for what she had missed.

I switched to the other foot, and she started to moan. I saw how powerful a simple foot rub could be for a woman who longed for touch.

Soon, the wind became too chilly to stay on the beach, so we gathered up our towels. She put the robe back on her beautiful body, and I drove her home.

During our seminar session two days later, I asked if she would go dancing with me at Club Dallas on Friday night. She loved the idea and dressed up as the cutest cowgirl I'd ever seen: a western hat, country blouse, jeans, and soft boots with tassels hanging down the sides. I showed her the two-step; since I was such a novice myself, I got it wrong, but it didn't matter. We danced for two hours and just loved holding each other tight, especially during the slow songs.

Since she lived so far south, and the house where I lived in Miami Shores was on the way north to Fort Lauderdale where the club was, she drove her 1972 Mercedes 240D to my place and parked it there. We went on to Club Dallas in my beat-up Hornet, feeling safer parking that piece of junk at the bar instead of her spotless Mercedes. Afterward, we drove back to the 240D and stood in the driveway to say good-night.

This lovely woman utterly captivated me. She only wanted the gentleness that she had never known. I could not help but start planting light kisses on her forehead, her cheeks, and finally her lips; she embraced me, and we kissed for a long time. I told her I wanted to make love to her, then continued putting my lips very lightly all over her face with small little kisses. She asked where, and I said in my room in the house.

I was thirty-eight years old and had never asked a woman to accept me in that way. I was prepared for her to say no because this was only our second date, but we knew more about each other than if we had been dating for months. She hesitated for so long that I was sure she was going to decline; I was fine if she did because I loved just holding her and kissing her.

"Let's go," she said, with a nod toward the house.

~

Sandy told me later that if my room had been a mess, she would have walked out. But it was tidy, and the bathroom was sparkling clean. I had not expected to bring her back that night; it was just the way I liked to keep things.

Before our first time, she told me I did not need to use a condom because she'd had her tubes tied after her second daughter was born. This was well before the AIDS epidemic became widespread—the first cases had appeared only a few months earlier in June—and she figured I was safe because I had been celibate for so long. At that point, I was aware of other sexually transmitted diseases, but not of AIDS.

Neither of us had had much experience beyond our exes, so we both were nervous. But we enjoyed each other so intensely that over the next few months we returned to that room again and again, transforming it from a place of sadness into a site of joy.

Fig. 8. Sandy. Miami Shores, FL, 1981.

She craved a slow and gentle touch; I craved a woman as passion-ate as she was and soon fell in love with her. Her twelve-year marriage had been hard on her, so she was cautious, but I was patient. Within six weeks, we both realized we had something special that went beyond sex and declared our love for one another.

The more I came to know Sandy, the more I adored her. She was impeccable in keeping her time and other agreements. She communi-cated fully and easily. She was highly organized, as much of a planner as I was. She said things that were funny as hell. She was fully present when we were together. She was gentle and could go long periods without saying anything but was no introvert. And she was a grown-up, taking responsi-bility for her life and children with no excuses. She lived the distinctions of est as a normal and natural part of her life—as I was coming to do as well—so we had a solid relationship based on trust and safety. After the est Training, I was just as clear about personal responsibility in life as she was and consequently had absolutely none of the desire to be taken care of that I'd had with Ida.

The ICS computer sales showroom was across the street from the Southern Bell building on Ponce de Leon Boulevard. They had a bank of free phones at a sit-down counter for the public to use. So, in an age long before smartphones, I crossed the busy traffic on Ponce every day to call her. She spoke often about how anguished she was over her marriage.

One day, I could tell she was shaking when I called her. "Ben," she said, "I've decided to stop seeing you."

I let that sink in. I could not speak.

Nathan had called her a few hours earlier to say he wanted to get back together. He had hurt her so badly. But he was her husband, and she knew how much their little girls needed him.

Relieved that the nightmare was over, she had gone to the Publix supermarket on Allapattah to pick up the makings for lasagna, his favorite dinner. She had just gotten back.

"I want to be with the father of my children," she said, "regardless of how hard it might be on me."

"You were so sure about leaving him . . ."

"I have to give it another try," she said, almost in tears.

My heart broke. I assumed that was what I got for fooling around with a married woman.

I went to the vacant lot next to ICS and lay on the grass in the shade of the building. It felt cool and comforting on my back, but there was nothing I could do. She was the dearest treasure I had ever found, and now she was gone. It was late in the day, so I finished up in the showroom and went to my car.

The trip home on I-95 was the saddest, most morose drive I'd ever made. I had come so close to happiness. This loss was searing, grievous, and I knew it would take months or even years to heal.

When I walked into my room, the phone was ringing. It was Sandy.

"Ben," she said, "Nathan called again. He is not coming. He said he just cannot leave Vicki. I feel so foolish . . . I am so terribly sorry for putting you through all of this." She choked up and took a few moments to collect herself.

Then she said, "Would you be willing to see me again?"

I almost crawled up the phone wire. Of course I would! I loved her more than anything in the world, and I could not wait to hold her again. We set another date, and after we hung up, I wept.

He never again tried to come back.

In est, they suggested that men either *married* women like their mothers or did *not* marry women like their mothers. With Ida, I had definitely not married my mother, whose drinking and consequent loud behavior I hated. My mother was extremely talkative, and I ran away from that when I sought Ida. In Sandy, I had someone much closer to my mother—minus the drinking and excessive chatter—happy, willing to speak her mind, and hilarious to listen to at times. Getting complete with my mother in est, meaning acknowledging and accepting her, had allowed me to be open to a woman like Sandy and to be massively attentive to her.

Years later, I asked her what she saw in a geeky guy who lived in a single room and drove a piece-of-crap car.

"You were so *into* me," she said. "It was all the foot rubs and back scratching when we snuggled in bed. You were always so good to me and allowed me to be who I was and who I was not."

"But I was so broke," I replied.

"Well, when I peeked into the closet in your room one day, I saw your Harvard MBA diploma on the wall. I figured there might be some potential there."

After her breakthrough sharing in "The Experience of Integrity" that evening in the est group, Sandy had sought a divorce, and in the spring of 1982, it became final.

~

In the seminar I was taking with Sandy, I had learned that whatever people resisted in life tended to persist. As counterintuitive as it seemed, the best approach to something you could do nothing about was to surrender to it. I had imbibed that insight deeply. Even though I was devastated when she said she'd decided to stop seeing me, I had not argued with her, nor had I resisted what was happening. I did not know how I would ever find another woman I could love with such passion. But I still drove home in a mood of complete capitulation to the event.

Years later, Sandy told me that if I had resisted her terrible news, I could well have made the situation worse. It would have pissed her off. After her ex backed out, she might have then decided she did not want to be with a man who had opposed her over something as important as her decision to take Nathan back. I had not tried to stop her, and that made it easier for her to return to me.

I had not been able to control what she and her ex would or would not do. But I had been able to control myself by surrendering to the news that had brought me such grief.

~

Things had not worked out for Ida up north. To my immense joy and relief, she moved back to Miami with the kids in the early summer of 1982.

When she found out I was seeing someone, she insisted on meeting the woman before she would allow Hannah and Conor to be around her. So, Sandy invited Ida down to her modest house in Saga Bay for tea and pastries. She was only a recent smoker and had stopped months earlier, so the house smelled fresh. The visit could potentially be awkward, and I was nervous.

When Ida and the children appeared at the door, Sandy was there with her two adorable girls. Rachel had dark hair and appeared in a frilly white dress and patent leather shoes. She had a perpetually mischievous look on her face. Rosie was blond, an innocent cutie pie who was not old enough yet to care about how she looked, although her simple dress was pretty.

Sandy was utterly taken with Hannah and Conor, allowing Ida to see right away that this lady was a caring mother just like she was. As everyone walked into the living room, I felt relieved to see both women smiling. During a delightful visit, the four kids sized each other up and played together. Sandy's warmth and loving nature made Hannah and Conor feel accepted. From that moment on, I never detected that they had any concerns about me dating someone new. And Ida never again had a doubt about the quality and kindness of the woman I was with.

In July 1982, I traveled to upstate New York for the intensive est Six-Day Course. It was a rigorous eighteen-hour-a-day program designed to dig even deeper into all the "stuff" people still carried around after the training. The one hundred men and women slept separately in bungalows that housed groups of four people. Each day we were loudly awakened at 6:00 a.m. to run uphill for fifteen minutes, wolf down breakfast, and pack ourselves into a training room for lectures, sharing, and "processes" that lasted until midnight.

The course challenged people to face their fears in an elemental way. Inside the seminar, people often fell asleep when confronting things that made them anxious. To counteract that, the seminar leader had dozens of two-foot-long rough-hewn logs placed on the floor around the edges of the room. When people started to doze off—"go unconscious" in est parlance—they were required to get up out of their chairs, go to the back or sides of the room, pick up a log, and hold it over their heads until they were awake enough to be present. Like many others, I spent a lot of time stiff-arming heavy logs above my head.

~

When I got back from the course, I realized even more what a treasure Sandy was and knew I wanted to spend the rest of my life with her. I also realized my future in selling computers had limits. There was now more competition, the work had become so repetitive that its novelty had worn off, and I had to be "up" emotionally all the time at a level of extroversion that was not natural to me. I went to work each day amid increasing anxiety.

I knew I had to create something more secure. I observed from talking to my customers that automobile service stations were a market opportunity; there was no specific program for that industry. So, I decided to design one: a software accounting package for gas stations. I met a talented young programmer named Gerome Davies and formed a fifty-fifty partnership with him called Southeast Technology. He wrote the program based on my specifications, and soon I started selling systems around Miami. Meanwhile, I kept my day job at ICS.

A benefit of shifting into the software business, which I did not realize at the time, was that it freed me from being so obsessed with the sales funnel. This still applied to selling software, but not to design or customer support. As my attention fell from the funnel, I filled the void with a focus on Sandy. My reduced attention to a process was allowing me to appreciate that the love of my life was right in front of me.

In early 1983, I quit ICS and went full-time into designing enhancements for our gas station software, selling systems, and supplying customer support while Gerome oversaw the technical end. Meanwhile it had become too taxing for both Sandy and me to be located thirty miles apart, so I answered a "roommate wanted" ad and moved into another guy's apartment in Cutler Ridge, just minutes from her house. This allowed us to spend time together each weekend when our four kids were with our exes. When I told her my roommate was a slob and I was looking for another apartment, Sandy invited me to move in with her. And I did.

In July 1983, Sandy did the Six-Day Course herself, and I went with her to assist as a volunteer in the kitchen with a dozen other graduates. The work was hot, messy, exhausting, and frustrating to no end, because as we prepared the food, we had an agreement not to nibble on any of it. Most of the other kitchen staff were women; they complained about their feet hurting, so on breaks I started giving regular foot rubs to anybody who wanted one. I received many marriage proposals but had to tell them I was already taken.

One day on a break, Sandy and I met in the outdoor pavilion for brown-bag sandwiches of cheddar cheese, cucumbers, and mustard on whole grain bread. Between bites she told me that in the previous hour she had just realized her integrity was out.

"Because of the girls, I don't want to be living together without being married."

A lightning flash of insight pierced through me. I saw it would never, ever be better than this, that I would never be able to find a more perfect life partner than Sandy.

"Well, let's get married, then!" I said, before I even had time to think.

She had not tried to provoke that reaction from me, nor even expected it. When she realized what I was saying, she got a big grin on her face and leaned over the table to kiss me. We were engaged!

Part of my volunteer assisting duties were in the course room—running microphones to people who wanted to share and doing errands for the seminar leader. So nobody thought anything of it when I snuck into the back of Sandy's next course hour.

As he often did, the seminar leader asked if anybody had something to share, since breaks were fertile times for people to realize things about their lives. Sandy raised her hand and said she had something to say from the front of the room. Once there she pointed to me and asked me to come up and stand next to her. I put my arm around her, and as soon as she said we were engaged to be married, the room erupted with cheers and applause. We kissed and got even more applause.

~

Sandy's sister, Leah, and her husband, Adam, kindly made their beautiful home in Hollywood, Florida, available for the wedding. It took place in their living room on October 9, 1983. We had a big crowd, mostly Sandy's parents and relatives.

Our four children were there, and at ages six through eleven, they thought the whole thing was hilarious, laughing and stifling giggles even as we said our vows. Sandy dressed the three girls in color-coordinated outfits, and I put a white shirt and bow tie on Conor. All four looked adorable.

It heartened me that Hannah and Conor had accepted Sandy so quickly and wholeheartedly. She was always sweet to them, and they could see how happy I was to be with her. Sandy's younger daughter, Rosie, readily accepted me, but Rachel, the older girl, held back a bit and in later years would much prefer to spend time with her father and Vicki, who was now his wife.

My marriage to Sandy turned out to be magnificent for my relationship with the kids. It provided a loving space, stability, and a partner in dealing with life.

Sandy was thirty-five, and I was forty. We were in love more deeply than either of us had ever been in our lives. Rather than dwell on our past histories of one failed marriage apiece, we chose to reinvent marriage as a possibility and face the future together. That gave me the greatest peace of mind I had ever known.

~

As with the fear and danger I had experienced over the years, my winning recipe had been a complete bust in dealing with vulnerability. But in suffering through those shortcomings, I had learned the Four Breakthrough Tools for Detaching from the recipe:

- **Living Life Forward.** In Chapter 14, I related that my anguish over the loss of Ida and my partner Bruce got resolved after the est Training when I went outside the recipe and took responsibility for both situations. In est I also learned the powerful Be-Do-Have sequence for living life forward, but did not make transformational use of it until almost forty years later.

- **Intention.** In Chapter 15, during the depths of my Memorial Day depression, it was not a step-by-step process, but the discovery of intention that brought me back from the brink.

- **Accepting Acute Loss.** Chapter 16 pointed out that when the grief over the loss of my children was at its nadir, I did engage in a methodical approach, the "elevator" process for accepting acute loss. But that was far more powerful than the sales funnel my recipe reflexively wanted me to run as a distraction.

- **Nonresistance.** In Chapter 17, the nonresistance I adopted when Sandy said she was taking Nathan back was the opposite of the "let's talk this through" process that my recipe likely would have urged.

All these experiences were escapes from my step-by-step approach to life. But they were one-offs, individual wins that did not by themselves yet undermine the staying power of my obsession with my methodical approach to almost everything.

WHAT I COULD HAVE DONE DIFFERENTLY

I might have seen that getting involved with a married woman was bound to produce heartbreak at some point, but I did not. The loss of Sandy for the few hours that it occurred was searing, but it gave me a venue for not resisting—and for thereby creating the possibility for her to come back to me.

Takeaways from Chapter 17

1. What you resist in life tends to persist. Paradoxically, when you stop resisting it you can help it to disappear.

2. Your recipe promotes the antithesis of nonresistance. It is a fixed solution for everything, and therefore can become the very embodiment of resistance.

3. The things you resist provide a wide range of triggers for your recipe. Give up resistance and you take away much of the work the recipe has you perform.

Reflective Questions

1. What are you resisting Being, Doing, or Having right now? What are you afraid would happen if you stopped resisting it?

2. Your recipe lives in resistance to the extroverted world. You don't have to like that world, but you also don't have to resist it. Can you see yourself doing that?

3. What three patterns in the extroverted society activate your recipe the most often, and most predictably?

Practical Exercises

1. Pick something small that you are resisting. Start letting go, and notice how in your perception, and possibly in your reality, the thing slowly starts to disappear.

2. Pick an aspect of the extroverted world that you particularly resist, such as being expected to engage in small talk, be on a team at the office, or suffer extroverts taking over meetings with loud but shallow contributions. For one minute, imagine yourself still not liking it, but just allowing it to be. How did you feel at the end of that minute?

3. Name one thing in our extroverted society that regularly triggers you into running your recipe. Close your eyes and accept that thing for one minute. Notice whether it still activates your recipe.

~

Now that I had Sandy in my life, my winning recipe stayed away from the domain of relationships. It never again would call me to look for security and satisfaction in that area, because I already had more of it than I could ever want.

But the domain of business was different. My search for financial security would endure for more than another quarter century, a long period during which the recipe would be tireless in producing successive calamities, or inserting itself into those it did not create. Safety would stay well out of reach.

Part 5

Four Transformational Tools for Detaching

18

Completion and Possibility: The End of the Line

Over the next twenty-three years, I would launch several ventures. Each one would face its own obstacles and eventually peter out in failure. I would also get a steady job, but in time would be so unsatisfied with it, and later so unable to succeed at it, that I got let go.

1983-1992: RUIN

For three years after the wedding, I sold computers to gas stations. By 1986, however, the business had fizzled out due to increased competition. So, I launched two new projects and worked them simultaneously, counting on at least one of them to come through.

The first was MicroSomnia, a sleep reduction program for busy businesspeople. Using health principles known as *sleep hygiene*, I convinced over a hundred entrepreneurs and professionals that they could gain valuable work time by safely cutting back on sleep for up to three hours a night.

Despite successfully using the method myself and working the sales funnel for years, I eventually had to give it up. My relentless focus on the sleep and sales processes themselves prevented me from seeing the small size of the market.

Good thing, because if I had succeeded, I would probably be in jail right now. Researchers discovered in the 2010s that the body pumped spinal fluid through the brain during sleep. This meant that getting less than seven hours a night was a recipe for contracting Alzheimer's and other forms of dementia. Sustained sleep reduction was madness.

The other project was Documentation by Mail, a manual-writing service for small software developers. I used a three-draft process to produce bite-sized modules that explained the customers' programs using step-by-step instructions, something my winning recipe uniquely qualified me to produce. At the beginning, I had a lot of business. But again, my obsession with a process—this time the one for creating the small modules—kept me from seeing how small and poorly funded *that* market was.

Our cash flow was so uncertain from these businesses that it caused both of us, especially Sandy, a great deal of distress. Each year, we had the choice of saving for taxes or buying groceries, and eventually it caught up with us. To prevent the IRS from seizing our house, we had to file for bankruptcy in May 1992. Some twenty-three years after graduating from the Harvard Business School, I was now forty-nine and broke.

Just as Sandy and I were beginning to cope with the aftermath of declaring bankruptcy, on August 24, 1992, Hurricane Andrew barreled into Miami. We were ordered to evacuate, so we fled forty miles north with a few possessions in our tiny Dodge Colt to Hollywood, Florida, where Sandy's sister and brother-in-law took us in. We and our four children were all safe in different locations.

During the storm eighteen inches of stinking bilge from Biscayne Bay flowed into our Miami house. Large chunks of the roof got ripped off and now sat in the backyard, allowing torrential rain to fall on furnishings throughout the home.

A few days later we managed to salvage more than we expected but otherwise lost almost everything. The devastation and the uprooting of our lives were so appalling that for a time we were confused about what to do first.

I in particular was numb because my winning recipe always called me to be process-oriented. It was now insisting that I prioritize things before acting, advice that in such a situation was paralyzing. But with Sandy's help I abandoned that approach. She said it did not matter what we did first. There was so much to do that whatever we did would help. That got us both in action immediately.

Even more importantly, it helped us to discover a key secret to recovering from a disaster: to get small, frequent completions. Accomplishing even the tiniest task, such as hosing off a bicycle, or putting a pile of wet clothes in a van, or retrieving a treasured old photo from a pile of muck, gave us enormous pleasure. The solution to the hurricane had not been to listen to my recipe, but simply to aim for completions. Doing that released positive feelings within us, allowing us to walk away from the mess feeling relieved and even a little content.

Removing the astonishing amount of clutter from our lives also opened up the mental and emotional space for us to recall something we had learned over twelve years earlier in the est Training, the personal development course we had taken.

We remembered that it is too easy to see yourself as the product of your past based on your education, family environment, job experience, and so on. My winning recipe endorsed that view, or at least did not dispute it.

Another interpretation, however, is that your past choices, including those you made based on your winning recipe, are what generated where you are now. If you accept that as accurate, then it suggests the possibility of using the future as a place you can consciously move into by making different choices now. If you can identify what inspires you about that future, it can motivate you to act now to achieve it.

That is what Sandy and I did.

We began by adopting a new view of our *past*. We accepted that we were much less of a product of our upbringing, experience, ethnicity, and other demographics than we were a product of our former choices. This was crucial, because once we saw that we were the results of our own decision-based process, it freed us to use new decisions today to overcome the disaster we were in.

This led us to adopt a new view of our *future*. We saw it as a place of possibility, one where something that excited us drove us to think outside of my winning recipe and Sandy's history. Left to itself, the recipe would have created a default future for us, and it was likely to look much like a combination of our two pasts. We realized that if we stepped up with passion, however, and saw the future as a place we were keenly enthusiastic about, the future we got would be entirely different.

We then adopted a new view of our *present*. We used our newly discovered ardor for the future to rearrange our present. In other words, we let the future as possibility determine what we did now. We knew that we might need to get new training. Or move to another city. Or take on a task we never thought we could face. The possibilities were endless— so we picked the best one and chose to have it define our present.

The dream? To leave Miami and start new lives three hundred miles to the north in Gainesville, Florida. There had been no storm there, and it beckoned to us with a cooler climate, job opportunities, and none of the disaster-prone thinking that had so infested South Florida.

1992–2001: NUMBNESS

Days after the storm, we drove north to Gainesville to look for work. In time, we both found jobs there at a small medical software company.

Throughout the 1990s the firm prospered, as did we. Sandy served as the executive assistant to the CEO, while I built and ran a twenty-writer documentation department. These roles gave us a decade-long run of security, during which we repaired our finances. The firm went public in 1997, and three years later was acquired by WebMD.

In those years, I refined the company's documentation process into a high art, overlaying a standard format across more than ten thousand pages of manuals covering every company software product from managed care to prescriptions. My winning recipe loved it, because for the first time it could operate inside of a solid company.

But after a few years, I became numb, which illustrates what usually happens with every recipe: It gave me a job I knew how to do and was good at, but it did not produce satisfaction. I was finally safe, but I was uninspired. Year after year, even as it produced stability and good income, it left me feeling anesthetized and wanting more out of life.

2001-2006: THE BOOT

In 2001, I finally tired of the monotony of the documentation process. So, I requested a transfer to a team within the company called Network Services. I knew nothing about it, but they had a serious process problem I thought I could solve—namely, how to increase the glacial speed with which we enrolled doctors in submitting their claims electronically. I struggled for two years but made no progress in streamlining enrollments.

On September 3, 2003, the FBI and the IRS mounted massive raids on our Gainesville and Tampa sites, and on WebMD headquarters in New Jersey. A former employee had alleged that some of the executives had engaged in stock fraud, but it took until 2010 for a court to declare there was absolutely no evidence to support the claim. Due to stress, Sandy left the company in 2003. I did so at the end of 2004, knowing that for my non-performance in Network Services I was about to be fired.

Now age sixty-one, I was on the street. I could not trade on my Harvard MBA because in the past decade, I had done nothing to indicate I was top management material. Convinced I had failed at WebMD because I had tried to execute a process without being an expert in it, I got certified in a statistical discipline that was in high demand, called Six Sigma.

Blue Cross and Blue Shield of Minnesota promptly hired me as their Six Sigma deployment manager. Sandy and I moved to Minneapolis in early 2006, but I lasted only eight weeks before getting fired. I had paid so much attention to the statistical process itself and so little to promoting my team and Six Sigma across the company that my manager lost all confidence in me. It was July 2006, and this time I was out of work at age sixty-three.

2006: DESPERATION

My recipe obsession had led me to declare bankruptcy, suffer near paralysis during the Hurricane Andrew cleanup, attempt to reinvent a process at WebMD in an area where I had no expertise, and prioritize a statistical process instead of the people I was hired to manage at Blue Cross.

Yet, incredibly, I was no closer to seeing that the recipe itself was the root cause of why I had failed to find safety in these four cases.

By the summer of 2006, all this had again put Sandy and me in a bind. I was well past the age when many employers considered someone to be too old to hire. Worse, my strategy of running a process where I was an expert—Six Sigma—had failed miserably. It was clear that I did not have the people skills to be a deployment leader. That made my costly investment in the discipline close to worthless.

This was a terrifying realization. In the past, my process work had always helped me to compensate for my lack of extroversion. But now, even though I had a new type of expertise, it had not been enough for me to be successful.

My lifelong approach using formulas and systems had finally reached its limit. In my forties, it had led me into bankruptcy, in my fifties into numbness in a safe but boring job, and now in my sixties into two job losses in a row. My recipe had run its course, and now—at last—I was clear about the ineffectiveness of it.

WHAT I COULD HAVE DONE DIFFERENTLY

I probably could have foreseen that each of the many ventures I launched was doomed to failure, because I was not enough of an authentic entrepreneur to sense a sustainable market opportunity. Instead I just focused on recipe-driven processes. In contrast, the hurricane brought lessons in completion and possibility that helped Sandy and me to recover and become whole again.

Takeaways from Chapter 18

1. To reduce the chaos around you, avoid listening to your recipe and instead make small completions. That will lessen the sense of being overwhelmed and gradually restore order.

2. Living in possibility is the opposite of living from your past, so your recipe probably will not like it. It has only one fixed solution for everything and sees possibility as a threat.

3. Using a possible intended future to create your present may bring you more inspiration than you have ever felt. Don't let your recipe shut it down.

Reflective Questions

1. What small actions could you take—such as cleaning off your desk or cleaning out a closet—that would give you a sense of completion?

2. What possible future inspires you? How would you go about attaining it?

3. What small steps could you take today that would help to bring that future into your present?

Practical Exercises

1. Pick the messiest part of your house or office and organize just a small part of it. How did you feel afterward?

2. For the possible future that inspires you (from Question 2), notice that your default method of attaining it probably involves your recipe. Imagine achieving it some way that is free of the recipe, and write down three steps that would help you to do that.

3. Implement the three non-recipe steps in Exercise 2. How did that feel?

~

Our financial situation was desperate. We had nowhere near enough savings for me to retire, and because of my age and spotty employment history, I had no prospects for ever getting us to that point.

But I had survived a hurricane. And a bankruptcy. And a divorce. And a war. Now I just had to find a job.

I picked myself up and got to work.

19

The Peak Recipe:
The King of
All Processes

JUNE 2006. MINNEAPOLIS, MINNESOTA. Just three and a half weeks after Blue Cross threw me out, I landed on my feet. I was now working across town at UnitedHealthcare, looking around like a cat that had just jumped off a wall.

~

The Six Sigma outlay in time and money had not been a waste after all. On June 10, I found a director of process improvement opening at United that did require leading a Six Sigma team, but not from a promotional perspective—a competent deployment leader was already in place. United simply wanted someone who could get results.

I applied and on June 28 got a call from Julia Kowalski, the hiring manager herself, a senior vice president. From that one phone call, I could tell how different the culture in a for-profit enterprise like United was from Blue Cross. If Julia stood for the quality of the people there, it would be like going back to Harvard or Stanford, a place where the people around me were brilliant and stimulating. The thought scared me. But if they asked me to join them, I thought, it could be one of the most rewarding experiences of my life.

At the end of the call, she invited me in for an interview. The next day, I drove to United on a dazzlingly sunny day that reminded me of Florida, except that at forty-five degrees north latitude, the June air in Minneapolis was crisp and dry.

I was wary. This time, I would listen extremely carefully during the interview process to make sure this was not a promotional job in disguise, the way it had been at Blue Cross. And this team had Six Sigma Black Belts, professionals who had advanced training in the methods, tools, and leadership of the Six Sigma approach. They specialized in improving processes in order to eliminate defects, reduce variation, and improve efficiency. If these Black Belts were competent, I knew I could be an introvert and still do the job.

When I walked into United's building in Edina, I saw it was old and chopped up, an extensive facility that seemed to wander over acres on various levels built at different times. Yet it was clean and had character. It felt as lived in as an old shoe, quite a contrast from the sterile modernity of Blue Cross. United was a place of vibrancy and life; I expected that here people would not condemn me for walking too fast, something my team had said about me at Blue Cross.

~

My first meeting was with Julia. Tall, thin, and fortyish, she not only had a master of health care administration degree but was also a registered nurse and a Six Sigma Black Belt. She was highly professional, spoke to the point, and had a great sense of humor. I liked her instantly.

We met one-on-one for fifteen minutes. She did most of the talking and then brought in Ralph Jenner, a twenty-something director-level recent hire from a major consulting company. Don Little also came in; he was a five-year Black Belt with thinning hair and appeared to be in his late thirties. During the ensuing twenty minutes, Don was silent, and Ralph asked most of the questions. I could tell by his reaction, and Julia's, that they were happy with my answers.

When the two of them left, Don and I went to the cafeteria. The hallway was half a story higher than the floor of the restaurant, giving us a view of scores of people in eager conversation, or working on laptops, or just eating and staring into space. We walked down, passed up the food, and got a table.

Don began by describing United's culture and the team of Black Belts. During a pause I said, "I just came from Blue Cross, where seven Black Belts have been working for over a year. They have not produced a dime in savings. How many Black Belts are on our team?"

"Four."

"What kind of savings have they produced?"

"Over $14 million in only six months. And every month we generate more."

That was astonishing. I could tell Don was several cuts above any of the Black Belts at Blue Cross, and I guessed that to produce those kinds of numbers, the others had to be as well.

I then met with Orin Williams, the chief medical officer of United. A tall, gaunt, bearded, prematurely gray, and lawyer-like guy in his late forties, Orin conducted one of the most intense and unusual interviews I had ever been in. He wanted me to trace my entire background starting at Stanford and took notes as I went. He interrupted to ask pointed questions, such as why I chose a particular path and what I learned from it.

At the end, he asked, "What question did I *not* ask that I should have to really find out what makes you tick?"

I thought for a moment and said, "Why aren't you further along in life? You're a Harvard MBA who has had many years of experience. Why aren't you the CEO of a company somewhere?"

I could tell the bluntness and honesty of the question took him aback. He himself had an MBA from Stanford in addition to being an MD, so perhaps he was thinking the same thing. He asked me to tell him what the answer was.

"I never did any career planning," I replied. "I spent years in the wilderness of being an entrepreneur. I always jumped into what was in front of me, executing it with passion."

Entrepreneurship was the most visible reason why I had not gotten very far. It had provided an arena where I could freely design processes to my heart's content. But the root cause for my slow career was my obsession with the underlying processes. I planned to get into that if he continued probing, but he did not.

Instead, he asked, "Do you have any regrets?"

"At one level I do," I said. "I have not been able to give my children everything I might have if I had been a CEO. But my kids are wonderful. My daughter, Hannah, is a speech pathologist, and my son, Conor, is an MIT- and Harvard-educated architect. My stepdaughter Rachel is a successful communications executive in New York, and my other stepdaughter Rosie is a rising star in a property insurance company in Tampa. So, on balance, no, I have no regrets. I've had a wonderful, exciting life, and I would not change it."

The answer seemed to hit home with him.

During each interview, I listened with acute interest. I concluded that this job did not require me to be extroverted—all I had to do was help my team to stay focused on getting results.

The next day, Julia called to say they wanted me to join the company. HR would be making me an offer within the next day and a half. It turned out to be almost 20 percent more than I had earned at Blue Cross.

I had walked into this opportunity with two strikes against me, being let go at WebMD and again at Blue Cross. I intended to make sure there would not be a third.

~

I got the new job partly because I was a Six Sigma Black Belt. But that formula had just failed me, and I did not want to tie myself to it again too strongly. I would do the work, of course. But my passion for the method, and my ability in it, were only a veneer.

As I got the lay of the land at United, a spark went off inside me about a completely different process I had tried back in Gainesville. Called the balanced scorecard, it consisted of a powerful graphic that drew a picture of a company's strategy on a single piece of paper. A list of measurements supplemented the map by clearly telling the company how it was doing in meeting its strategic goals.

In January 2004, I had taken a two-day balanced scorecard seminar and returned as an evangelist, but nobody at WebMD was interested. At United, the situation was different: My new boss, Orin Williams, was curious. In September 2006, I built a strategy map for his department, and he not only valued it but also publicly acknowledged me for the work.

Encouraged, I started making the rounds. The chief human capital officer wanted a map for his department. So did the chief financial officer. Because these were C-suite executives in a $35 billion company, they really got my blood pumping. I saw that the balanced scorecard was the biggest, most effective, most salable process I had ever found in my life. I dove in deep.

Orin, ever the supporter, suggested that I approach the chief operating officer of UnitedHealthcare, Kevin Ruth. When I sent Kevin a PowerPoint presentation on how the thing worked, I thought he was going to lose his mind. In a phone meeting, he said this went so far beyond what he had been trying to do on the back of an envelope that he wanted to meet with me right away. A blizzard raged outside our building, but in my chest, I felt an expanding warmth.

Kevin was a muscular man who stood over six feet tall. Forty-seven years old, he had a receding hairline, sleepy eyes, and a compassionate face that hid the determination that had driven him up the hard way from a boyhood in rural Pennsylvania. He put himself through Temple University in Philadelphia, became a CPA, and from a start at the bottom in health care moving laundry in a hospital, he had become the CEO of a whole region of health plans at UnitedHealthcare. And now he was the chief operating officer of the entire company. Plainspoken, articulate, and gentle, he was afraid of nothing. Just by being himself, Kevin elicited enthusiastic loyalty from the people around him.

"You know what I like the most about this?" he asked. "We can use it to kill useless projects by comparing them against the strategy map."

"That's right," I agreed. "If there is no fit, we now have a good reason to stop the work in its tracks."

He grinned. "And nobody can argue with it."

By February 2007, six major departments had told me they wanted to pursue the balanced scorecard. In addition to Human Capital, Finance, Operations, and Orin Williams in Clinical Advancement, I was also talking with UnitedHealth Networks and ACME, our back-office processing department.

As I met with each executive, I never tired of looking out their corner office windows to see the snowplows and salt trucks hard at work outside. I also noticed that all the leaders carried a BlackBerry phone. Its tiny keyboard seemed so hard to use. A few weeks earlier, Steve Jobs had launched something called the "iPhone," and I wondered if it would get any traction among these leaders.

~

Kevin's mind became infected with the balanced scorecard, particularly with a strategy map I had prepared for United at the corporate level. I guessed I might be working for him soon.

He got into gear. He invited me to a meeting of the six regional CEOs in the impressive United boardroom to make a presentation. I sat in a chair at the back of the room next to a fragrant tray of coffee pots and pastries. But he stood up and asked me to take his seat at the huge table, an unbelievably strong endorsement for someone as new to the company as I was.

He lobbied to put me on his team and soon succeeded. He spoke to the CEO of United, Miles Bramovich, who stopped me in the hall one day and asked me to be sure to collaborate with his whole team. I was already talking to six of them and could not believe this was happening.

I forgot I was an introvert. Unlike with the est Training and its successor, the Forum, which required weekly attendance at seminars to keep me stoked, the balanced scorecard elicited a passion from within me that was so strong I just threw myself into situations I normally would have recoiled from. This was a sea change, the first process that I genuinely cared about. It was no longer about the mechanics of driving a formula; it was about discharging the strange fervor that welled up from inside me. Caring was something that had been missing from my processes all along.

Why was I so taken with this? For one thing, it drew on every ounce of my analytical ability. For another, it allowed me to dig beneath the surface like a detective to produce "aha" moments in leader after leader. In addition, it addressed the single biggest problem any company faced, especially ours: how to turn the pages of high-sounding rhetoric in our planning documents into a strategy that people from customer support reps to top executives could execute. But most importantly, it was the first process since college that truly made me feel secure. It allowed me to hide my introversion and still produce guaranteed results.

Off-site, I attended two more Kaplan and Norton seminars on the balanced scorecard and learned that building a strategy map for a department or a company took twenty hours. Four were for a preparation session with the senior leader and all his direct reports, and sixteen hours over two days were to coach the group to hammer out the map itself.

I soon found myself in the front of rooms leading most of those meetings, driven by the excitement of seeing—as I looked from face to face—that I was making a huge difference for each group. I led the finance sessions in June 2007 and supported a friend in leading the ones for Marketing in June and July. I also facilitated Dental and Vision, Product, and Human Capital. The United Leadership Academy approached me to do a two-and-a-half-hour training on strategy maps, and when I emailed David Norton, cofounder of the concept, he said he was open to speaking at it. There seemed to be no end to where United would go with this.

~

But there was an end, and it came overnight. In May 2008, Miles Bramovich, the United CEO who so strongly supported Kevin and me, was out.

Laura Schmidt replaced him. She had an influencing (promoting) behavioral style, tending to focus on the big picture and not get into details. Without support from the top, the balanced scorecard could not advance. By February 2009, United had announced at least three different nonintegrated strategies; the following month the senior team was back to doing business as usual.

Ironically, around that time, I completed all my Kaplan and Norton studies, passed the certification exam, and became one of only nine hundred balanced scorecard practitioners in the United States.

Consequently, I was despondent. With Kevin's relentless support, I had come so close to getting the balanced scorecard implemented that I could taste it. I was planning to set up and run an Office of Strategy Management, and now the opportunity was gone. Laura assigned Kevin to head the internal alignment of our clinical organization, and it looked like I would follow him there. We would build a map and compare initiatives to it, but that would be it—there would be no company-wide implementation.

I sat in my office and looked at the light sparkling on the small crystal alligator I had brought with me from Florida, reflecting on how different things were from my expectations. Except for the modest wins and respect I now enjoyed at UnitedHealthcare, since the day I got my MBA, I had never achieved significant business success. Now at age sixty-six, I still had only a small nest egg and no ability for Sandy and me to retire.

At the same time, I saw that, with Sandy, I had the most fabulous relationship a man could ever ask for. I had a twenty-seven-year history with a woman I adored who was a partner in every aspect of life. She was sexy, funny, enlightened, organized, committed, and strong—someone who had made the past three decades a joy despite all we had gone through and who promised to make the next three the best of our lives. Who knew what kind of person I would have been by now without her; how Hannah and Conor, Rachel and Rosie would have turned out; and whether I would be anywhere near as healthy and happy as I was now. At United, I saw up close in others that financial success in business often came at a terrible personal price. I never had had to pay it, and my life was much the better for it.

Early one morning while swishing a spearmint mouthwash, I looked in the mirror and had an insight. I saw that while we could say nature's purpose for humanity was reproduction, my purpose as a post-reproductive human being was longevity. It meant I needed to do things that supported and prolonged my mental, emotional, and physical health. And in turn, *that* meant I needed to give up the stress of trying to be more outgoing than I actually was. I had to start living openly as an introvert.

Seen through that filter, setting up and running an Office of Strategy Management could well have been a bad idea. Much as I loved the work, it would have required me to engage in a great deal of long-term, highly extroverted behavior that over the years might have worn thin. But staying where I was at United might under-challenge me, so the goal was to find a middle ground—a way to be a valuable contributor without killing myself in the process.

I had been chastising myself for not progressing further in my career. I still did not have the financial security that for decades I had been pursuing through my winning recipe. But at this point, it was not about progression. It was about contribution. And I now saw that at United I could do that best as a straight-up introvert, offering the back-of-the-room research and writing skills that came most naturally to me.

For me, this was a new context. For the first time ever, I made the choice to go through life with no outer shell of a recipe around me. This would mean analyzing the many problems in the health-care industry and providing innovative solutions through white papers and PowerPoint presentations. I felt safe in letting go of the recipe because I'd learned years ago, after grieving the acute loss of my children through the "elevator" process, that I could be successful in the face of such loss. Knowing I could cope with a devastating forfeiture such as letting go of the recipe had been a tool in my pocket ever since.

Rather than stressing me out, letting go of the recipe made me feel safer than I had in a long time. Being able to just be myself avoided the anxiety involved in trying to use a recipe to cover up who I really was.

Over several days, I reestablished my equilibrium and gradually let go of the balanced scorecard. It was the most powerful process I had ever found. But I quietly detached myself from it and stayed at United doing research and writing.

WHAT I COULD HAVE DONE DIFFERENTLY

I might have foreseen that in pursuing the balanced scorecard, I was allowing myself to be seduced by a glittering future that might not be optimal. But I did not, and it allowed my recipe to expand into a massive caricature of itself. That triggered me to realize that extreme achievement and ambition at my age were goals likely to shorten my life.

Takeaways from Chapter 19

1. One of the best ways to expose the bankruptcy of your recipe is to allow it to blossom into an extreme form. That will help to make clear to you that it is probably taking you in the wrong direction.

2. Use the extreme flowering of the recipe to contrast its overall direction with the outcome that would best support your growth and health. Doing so will probably cause the recipe to shrink back to size.

3. If you detach from the recipe prematurely, it will almost assuredly come roaring back. To prevent that you first must expose its false foundation—the notion that you as an introvert are defective.

Reflective Questions

1. What would the most extreme incarnation of your recipe look like, something so large that it would push aside everything else to become your top priority?

2. Does that priority align with your best long-term interests for achieving happiness and longevity?

3. Do you still believe that because you are an introvert you are defective in some way? Or have you let go of that by now? Probably not, if your recipe is still driving your behavior.

Practical Exercises

1. Imagine that you are 100 percent committed to the extreme form of your recipe in Question 1. Write down what it would have you Be, Do, and Have as a result.

2. Write down the ways in which your extreme-form recipe does not align with what you want to Be, Do, and Have in life. For example, in my case leading the balanced scorecard would not have allowed me to Be relaxed and stress-free, thereby limiting my longevity. It would not have allowed me to Do the research and writing full-time that I so enjoyed. And it would not have allowed me to Have the long life that in my sixties I so wanted to attain.

3. Imagine that you wholeheartedly reject the recipe now that you have seen it in monsterlike dimensions. Sit quietly with that. Notice that the recipe is already calling to you.

~

For two full weeks I lived in peace.

Then on July 2, 2009, a company called Cancer Therapy Professionals posted a job description online. It came into my home inbox via an automatic feed I had not yet turned off.

I saw it and gasped.

20

Choosing a Relationship: The Recipe Strikes Back

JULY 2009. MINNEAPOLIS, MINNESOTA. Cancer Therapy Professionals (CTP) was looking for a strategy management director. The job involved building a strategy map and balanced scorecard for the corporation, then setting up and running an Office of Strategy Management.

This was the epitome of the balanced scorecard—the ability to start from nothing in a company with top-down CEO support and engage the entire management team. After my acute disappointment at UnitedHealthcare, I was salivating.

CTP was a growing chain of specialty hospitals that focused on treating cancer. Based in the Pittsburgh area, they were a private company and had a highly unusual business model for health care. They competed based on excellence at the medical condition level, instead of by specialty like everybody else. They used multidisciplinary teams to treat patients while most other clinics did not bother to coordinate care. And they had already started reporting outcomes, something few health systems in the industry were doing yet.

This was next-generation stuff. Such a model, plus the company's spectacularly all-embracing focus on the balanced scorecard, quickly seduced me into abandoning my detachment from the method. I once again fell under its spell, and, with it, that of my winning recipe.

I could not get CTP out of my mind, so in late August I decided to apply. My mindset was different from when I first saw the ad. Passion no longer blurred my vision. Instead, I was taking a sober look at the possibility that a future at CTP might or might not be more satisfying than one at United.

Within a week, I had a phone interview with CTP's chief strategy officer, Evan Patel. He was a serious, thoughtful guy who reported directly to the CEO, and was in lockstep with him about the need to implement the balanced scorecard in the company. The CEO and leadership team had already met with Robert Kaplan, one of the scorecard's founders, over the phone for ninety minutes. The whole team was convinced they needed to do this.

On the call with Evan, I was so enthusiastic that I found myself standing up and gesturing as I spoke. He likely was not prepared for such depth of feeling. We talked for over an hour, and at the end, he invited me back East to meet the CEO and the executive team. When I hung up the phone, I said, "Yes!!" I looked out the glass panel of my United office to the sea of cubicles outside it and imagined myself flying above all of them and out the window on the far side of the building all the way to Pittsburgh.

Before going, I did some checking. The company was extremely successful, enjoying its ninth straight year of growth. It seemed to have plenty of cash, but not so much as to make it a lucrative takeover target. This was a live opportunity. But my eyes were still open to any sign of risk that might emerge.

~

On September 5, I went to Pittsburgh and nailed the interviews. Any lingering doubts I had about the company and its people all but vanished.

The firm sent a driver and white stretch limousine to pick me up. A brilliant late summer sun shone down on the freeway, reflecting sunlight off the chrome on the cars around us. As I looked through the tinted glass of the salon where I sat, those bright spots appeared blue. I extended my legs and lowered the window a crack to breathe in the fresh summer air, finding it hard to believe that any of this was happening.

Compared to United, CTP was a tiny company, and its Pittsburgh facility reflected it, making even the old Edina building at United seem more dignified. Fake wood paneling, pleather chairs, and inexpensive rugs gave the CTP headquarters the feel of a lawyer's office in a strip mall.

As soon as I walked in, I recalled what one doctor at United had told me about CTP, which I had promptly repressed: They were on the fringes of the medical establishment.

"Look at their consumer advertising," he had said. "Rather than a reputation for medical excellence, they rely on ads to gain patients."

"Interesting," I replied. "They also include acupuncture, meditation, and chiropractic in their treatments."

He nodded. "Valuable in some settings, but unproven for cancer. And the patients they attract tend to have few comorbidities. Their success ratios are skewed in favor of those who are most likely to survive."

At the time, I discounted all that as sour grapes. CTP was succeeding in a market where United was struggling, so leaders at United might have a bias against the company. Since I was not there to evaluate the furnishings, I chose to ignore the kitsch, and the doubts, and get on with the interviews.

The first was with Evan Patel, the fortyish, pensive chief strategy officer I had spoken with on the phone. He was an academic, a PhD candidate in epidemiology and biostatistics. Every time I pulled out some of the generic strategy map examples I had brought, he was amazed at the simplicity and clarity of the method.

Next, Evan and I met with Kirby Stone, the CEO. Kirby was a silver-haired, dapper, and kindly gentleman in his late sixties with a sharp analytical mind, a way with words about the company, and an appetite for detail. He had a strong commitment to managing strategy in the way described by Kaplan and Norton.

During the last hour of our ninety-minute meeting, I went over half a dozen sheets of examples with him. I showed him sanitized strategy maps, balanced scorecards, and grids detailing how to end non-strategic initiatives, those in operations, innovation, customer satisfaction, or regulatory compliance that had no relationship whatsoever to any of the goals on the corporate strategy map. He had the same reaction as Evan: incredulity at the simplicity, concreteness, and plain good sense of it all. Once again, the innate power of this methodology had brought me out of myself.

I met with three other leaders and after the visit was over called Sandy on the way to the airport to report all of this with breathless enthusiasm. Yet after we hung up, I sipped from a cold bottle of Nestlé water and noticed that something was starting to bother me. As the CTP limo wound its way through freeway traffic, I recalled that the CEO wanted me to report to Evan. Yet he was quite junior to me in strategy execution, maturity, and experience. He seemed to have far more passion for research than for strategy.

It was time for me to talk to Kevin. We had shared our mutual unhappiness with the direction that strategy was going at United, so it was no surprise when I called him on my return to let him know I might be leaving. I shared that this opportunity had all the ingredients of success: enthusiastic support by the CEO, a management team that knew they needed a system for managing their strategy, and a business model that was truly distinctive that drove 20 percent annual growth.

"Ben, I support you one million percent," he said. "You are at the time in life where you need to be doing what you want, and I would never do anything to hold you back."

He continued, "At the same time, I don't want you to take my calm demeanor as a sign that I want you to leave. I very much do not. I hope the deal falls through, and, if it does, I have a thousand things for you to do. I will miss talking to you and will continue interacting with you normally until you tell me you are definitely leaving."

He went on. "I will be waiting for you to call me any day to break my heart. If so, it will not be good-bye; we will remain friends, and I will be calling you after you leave." He laughed. "At that point, I won't be writing your reviews, so I'll be able to speak more openly than I can now!"

An outpouring of emotion washed over me.

"Kevin, you mean more to me than I could ever express. After having such an unstable career, I had come to doubt my own competence. But in just two years you have helped me to heal." For years I had shared myself in est and Forum seminars with that kind of heartfelt wording, and it expressed exactly how I felt.

~

I faced a stark choice. On one hand, I had stumbled on the process of a lifetime—the balanced scorecard—and a company that was ready to hire me to drive it across their entire business.

On the other hand, at United I had built a close relationship with an inspiring boss, one whom I trusted and who made me feel better about myself every time I interacted with him. He actively drew on my strengths as a quiet person by assigning me a steady flow of research and writing projects, thereby providing me with secure work as an introvert. Around him, I felt peace, satisfaction, and relief.

Ever since I was ten years old, I had been running stepwise processes to get predictable results without having to engage other people all that much. Was I now going to abandon that approach just for a professional relationship with Kevin? Give up what could not only be the pinnacle of my career, but also let go of a system so sophisticated and powerful that it could propel me to more success and security than I had ever known? It would allow me to help the company turn its theoretical strategic plan into an executable map of interrelated objectives, and actually measure their achievement in real time. My gut reaction was that to give up this opportunity was unthinkable.

At United, I had seen that my highest loyalty was to a magnificent process I cared about deeply. But during my weeks of disengagement from it, I discovered something I cared about even more: my own longevity. It would come from having less stress, specifically by living and contributing openly as an introvert. And now I was unearthing something I had come to care about even more than that, because it made being a straight-up introvert possible: working with Kevin Ruth.

Formulas had attracted me for a lifetime, and now something was happening I never would have expected. A relationship—the very thing I had sought to minimize my whole life—was now more important to me than the best process I had ever found.

Prioritizing Kevin added a valued individual to my very small circle of close people. However, doing that did not tempt me to expand that circle any further. And I was totally fine with that, because, well, I am an introvert.

WHAT I COULD HAVE DONE DIFFERENTLY

A little voice within told me it was madness to leave my current supervisor. But because I ignored it and instead listened to my recipe, I was forced into a choice between a cherished relationship and the recipe. That allowed me to do the unthinkable, and not execute on the very purpose for which I had designed the recipe in the first place—namely, to distance myself from other people.

Takeaways from Chapter 20

1. The last thing your recipe wants is for you to abandon it for a relationship. It will be deeply threatened by that and urge you not to take such action.

2. Choosing a person over the recipe is the single most devastating blow you can deliver to your recipe, because its very existence depends on keeping people at bay.

3. It's important that the person you choose be someone who supports you to live openly as an introvert, and can help you to do so.

Reflective Questions

1. If you had to choose between your recipe and a trusted relationship, as I did, which would you choose?

2. If you settled on a relationship, can the person you chose be of help in allowing you to live openly as an introvert? If not, who else would you choose who could do that?

3. As an authentic introvert, what can you provide to the person you chose in Question 2 that they want and need?

Practical Exercises

1. Choose a person who can be of help in allowing you to live openly as an introvert.

2. Find something the person you chose wants and needs, and that you can provide as an authentic introvert—that is, in opposition to the way you normally operate due to your recipe. In my case, I saw that as chief operating officer, Kevin wanted a simple yet comprehensive way to execute the strategy that he was responsible for implementing. For me this was not executing my normal step-by-step procedures. Instead, it was deep research and inspirational writing that elevated me out of myself and allowed me to contribute something extremely valuable to him.

3. On your own initiative, start providing what that person wants and needs. How does that feel?

~

Giving up the balanced scorecard was something my recipe did not like. It had already struck back once, and I could feel it gearing up to do so again. During the wee hours of the morning, I had thoughts about reconsidering my decision to stay at United, and instead to pursue this wonderful opportunity in Pittsburgh. In my early-morning stupor, I found it difficult to counter that idea.

21

You Have
No Defect to Fix:
Baronial Splendor

SEPTEMBER 2009. MINNEAPOLIS, MINNESOTA. After due consideration, I told my recipe to stuff it. On September 18, I formally withdrew my application from CTP.

A few days later, Kevin wrote me a note saying he was so glad to have me back in the game. What an incredible guy—most bosses would have been upset that I even looked at another company. Kevin was not only happy I stayed but also willing to say so openly.

I got to work improving the strategy map for his new Enterprise Clinical (EC) group. This was my fourth attempt. A few slides into the presentation I asked him how he was doing, and he laughed. He said, "You had me at hello. This is very cool and very timely. People have been asking me to explain the EC strategy, and they will love this."

I still valued the balanced scorecard and would continue to promote it at United as much as I could. But I had gotten some distance from it. I was not willing to upend my career and personal life to pursue it.

~

That was the best business decision I ever made.

Over the next decade, CTP opened no new hospitals, laid off hundreds of employees, and took flak for its heavy consumer advertising and questionable use of alternative medicine in cancer care. In contrast, United had ten straight years of growth and provided me with fascinating work and steadily increasing income.

For the first time ever, I intentionally started working without a guiding process. I became a pinch hitter for Kevin, doing detailed research and building PowerPoint presentations for him to circulate among senior management. He considered himself to be a rabble-rouser and often took positions contrary to the conventional wisdom in the company. We did not always get agreement with what we proposed, but we got enough wins to make the effort worthwhile.

My recipe had struck back in the form of the email from CTP looking for an executive to implement their balanced scorecard. But I stopped it in its tracks by choosing to stay with Kevin instead of going elsewhere. Doing so was not a larger move into relationships, however. I still honored my childhood choice to avoid overstimulation by minimizing contact with others.

Staying with Kevin brought me closer to the one person who could permit me to contribute at work by using my full range of quiet-person capabilities. That made it much easier for me to back away from my winning recipe; I simply didn't need it anymore. I had built it to use processes to get results and, in turn, seem more outgoing. But now that I was directly getting results as an introvert, my recipe no longer had a job to do.

In 2013, Susan Cain's *Quiet: The Power of Introverts in a World That Can't Stop Talking* appeared and had an immediate effect on me. Not being okay with who I was had led to my first step-by-step approach—my initial recipe—in the 1950s and had been behind my serial creation of other processes for decades. Cain's book removed the last vestiges of any desire to live by processes because it convinced me that being an introvert was okay: *I had no defect to compensate for.* My level of sociability was just fine.

Now that the flaw was gone, I was not only reconciled to my introversion, but proud of it as well. Good thing, because soon after I read the book, for the first time in my four years of working backstage, Kevin asked me to take on a more public role.

He was leading an all-day conference called Reversing Trend, during which we planned to highlight the ways in which United could overturn the inexorable increase in American medical costs each year. In front of a team of leaders he had assembled, he asked if I would facilitate one of the sessions for thirty to forty people.

I declined with a smile, politely and confidently, and he instantly got it. He never again asked me to get in front of a room. From then on, he consistently played to my strengths as a back-of-the-room guy.

~

To my great surprise, doing that year after year brought me even more satisfaction than working with the balanced scorecard had. I dealt with few people and was free of any concerns about trying to be more extroverted.

For more than a decade, Kevin and I met every Friday morning at 8:00 a.m. He overflowed with ideas about how to streamline operations, improve customer service, make our insurance more affordable, and otherwise better serve our customers. Frequently, however, his ideas were half-baked, and he knew it. So often, after sharing one of his new notions, he would say, "Could you Ben Plumb this for me?"

What he meant was for me to research his concept down to the bare metal, then deliver the results to him verbally at our next meeting via a PowerPoint presentation. I loved doing that work more than anything I had ever engaged in before. It was pure-play research and writing, something far more rewarding to me than any of the processes I had implemented.

The reason was simple: I was *not* doing the work to cover up some supposed defect. All my previous processes, even the balanced score-card, had been efforts to appear to be more extroverted than I really was. In contrast, Ben Plumbing things allowed me to lean straight into my strengths as an introvert: deep thought, unusual focus, and joy in detecting patterns. Expressing those qualities allowed me to be my full, authentic self.

Moreover, I was now a totally out introvert who had no requirement ever to speak in public, or to interact with more than the small team around Kevin. If the Harvard Business School had been introvert hell, this was introvert paradise.

~

Unfortunately, when Stephen Hemsley stepped down as the longtime CEO of United Health Group in 2017, Kevin lost his main champion. Within two years, his entire team, including me, was on the street. Kevin's departure followed in early 2020.

We had no regrets. We had given our all every year and felt good about what we had done, even though the new regime was undoing some of it. Kevin and I remain personal friends and still talk on the phone every two weeks.

He is a good man. His coaching of me and his receptivity to my coaching of him—as seventeen years his senior—has always made for a productive two-way relationship that enriches us both.

The most unexpected outcome was that when I was laid off, I discovered Sandy and I could retire right then, when I was seventy-six, rather than having to wait as planned until I was eighty. We had more assets than we realized.

My former partner Bruce Fraser had coined the phrase "baronial splendor" back in the 1970s when he and I, along with Max, our Chilean partner, were eking out a living building houses in Latin America. I never formed a mental picture of what such splendor would look like beyond physical prosperity. But now I knew, almost fifty years later, that whatever it might be, the most important part of it was not material wealth. I shared this realization with Bruce in 2022, and he was happy to hear it before he passed away two years later.

In each other, Sandy and I have the love of our lives. Even during the long lockdowns of the COVID-19 pandemic, we kept busy, had fun, and enjoyed hanging out with the one person who had meant the most to us for almost forty years. Our love seemed to get deeper every week. We adored each other, acknowledging and holding one another close every day. We were happy beyond words just to share the same space. And except for minor aches and pains, our health was good. If all of this was not baronial splendor, then we did not know what was.

Best of all, I was no longer tethered to my winning recipe. I was massively content as an introvert, able to be open about it with the people around me, and therefore able to live the quiet, secure life that the recipe had always denied to me. Instead of pretending to be out-going and happy to engage in social interactions, I declined them with grace and good humor, finding that, more often than not, other people respected my authenticity.

~

We rejoice in the success of our children.

Hannah, fifty-three, earned a master's degree in speech-language pathology at Florida State University and for years was a senior speech pathologist working with children at a nationally acclaimed health system in Tampa. Her husband is a partner in his own law firm.

Conor, fifty, received a bachelor's degree in architecture from MIT, then completed his master's at Harvard. He and his wife live in the Boston area, where he works for a major architectural firm.

Rachel, fifty, earned an English degree from Syracuse University and is a highly successful communications executive in the pharmaceutical industry in the New York metropolitan area. Her husband is a talented advertising director in Manhattan.

Rosie, forty-eight, graduated from the University of Florida in political science and is a respected manager in one of the largest property insurance firms in Florida. Her partner is an attorney engaged in drafting judicial decisions for judges across Hillsborough County.

Between the four children we have ten grandchildren—five in the north and five locally.

All parents doubt their child-rearing abilities, and Sandy and I were no exception. But how our four children turned out made us realize that despite everything, we had provided the emotional support and guidance they needed. All four were now raising their own families using the compassion and good sense we had always hoped to provide as parents ourselves. Since nobody was in jail, or on drugs, or living with us—and neither were their kids!—we figured that we, along with Ida, and Sandy's ex-husband, Nathan, must all have done our jobs.

Sandy bought me a cup that said "Introvert: Social Distancing Expert" as a joke, but it accurately reflected where I was in my relationships, other than a few close friends and family members. Because of the pandemic and serious concern over the impact the COVID-19 virus could have on us at our ages, we stayed in touch with family almost exclusively via FaceTime for over a year and a half. That was harder on Sandy than it was on me—hence the cup!

~

Ida never remarried. Some years after the divorce, she earned a master's degree in art therapy and began consulting regularly in elementary schools. Unfortunately, she had to give that up when she suffered a series of falls in 2018, after which she was diagnosed with Parkinson's disease. She moved into an assisted living facility not far from Hannah, and died in 2023 at age seventy-eight from an unexpected brain hemorrhage. Ida's mother, Kate, had died ten years earlier, and her father, Leo, in 2020.

My mother passed away in 1995 and my father in 2000. I had never repaired my relationship with him over the money I had borrowed in the

1970s. I was not able to finish paying it off until just before he died, and he was not lucid enough at the end to understand I had finally squared the debt. To this day, I regard borrowing those funds as one of the greatest mistakes I ever made.

I flew to Los Angeles for my father's memorial and afterward visited the cemetery where my parents' ashes lay. I had not grieved for either one of them until that moment. At the graveside, I silently thanked them for always making my sisters and me feel good about ourselves. They used words as a salve to reward us for behavior they knew would build character. They never once belittled us.

When it was time to go, I knelt and kissed the grass. I stayed there for a long moment with the flat of my hand on the graves, thanking them again for the magnificent humanity they had shown to me and my sisters and for the wondrous love they shared between themselves and with us. It was a gift to the whole world, and through their great-grandchildren, that love would endure.

WHAT I COULD HAVE DONE DIFFERENTLY

I would have preferred to come on my own to the conclusion that just because I was an introvert I was not flawed. But I could not, and had to be told by a credible source, Susan Cain, before I could internalize that knowledge. Once I did, I was able to live openly as an introvert, with no recipe to shield me from the world. To recap some insights from Susan Cain that made a deep impression on me, please see the upcoming Practical Exercise 3.

Takeaways from Chapter 21

1. Your recipe rests on a totally false foundation—that because you are an introvert you are flawed. That childhood decision may well have been running your life ever since you made it.

2. Hearing that you have no defect is only the start. You need to internalize that at such a deep level that you can just laugh at your recipe whenever it tries to come back, which it will.

3. As an introvert, you have a unique set of skills to contribute to our extroverted world. Focus on using them to make a difference for others, and the recipe will no longer run you.

Reflective Questions

1. After everything you have read so far in this book, are you still convinced that because you are an introvert you are somehow flawed?

2. Do you believe me when I tell you that you do not have a defect just because you are an introvert? And in fact that you have much to contribute to the people around you, especially the extroverts?

3. What introvert skills are you the most adept at? Which ones are you most passionate about sharing with the world? Profound concentration? Writing? Deep conversations? You can prompt yourself by referring to the list of traits in the following Practical Exercise 3.

Practical Exercises

1. Go back to your first recollection of being "defective" because you were not outgoing enough. Write down how young you were, and why at that age you were unequipped to make such a huge, permanent decision about yourself.

2. Please read Susan Cain's landmark book *Quiet*. After I lived my bankrupt recipe for sixty years, she finally convinced me that as an introvert I had nothing that needed to be fixed. My guess is you might find the same.

3. Cain points out that introverts are often identified as having these
traits: preferring to listen more than talk, thinking before speaking, expressing themselves better in writing than in discussions,
avoiding conflict, shunning small talk and preferring deep conversations, concentrating on one thing at a time, working slowly and
being able to focus deeply on the task at hand. Considering these
traits, list three skills that you are committed to emphasizing as an
"out" introvert. Now start emphasizing them!

~

I had believed a process of some kind would get me to this place in
life—the gentle acceptance that I am not like most people but am an
introvert—but it did not. Such devices did insulate me from people for
decades and did create some predictable outcomes based on formulas.
But I always felt dependent, and they often produced disastrous results.

When it came down to it, I realized that as an introvert, I had no
flaw to compensate for and could best gain the security and satisfaction
I sought by proudly and openly emphasizing my quiet-person strengths.

I still admired powerful processes. But for the last ten years of my
career, none of that ran me any longer. I was free to be me.

Fig 9. Sandy and myself. Odessa, FL.

Conclusion

The Satisfied Introvert

As introverts, we attempt—as children—to cope with an extroverted world by adopting some kind of winning recipe. We try to be inclusive, or precise, or driven, or dependable, or any other way we think will make us feel safe in the world.

In this story, I offer the warning that while such mechanisms may produce good results every once in a while, they almost always generate unintended consequences, put distance between us and other people, and ultimately do not provide security or satisfaction. My own winning recipe, an obsession with processes, had those results in ways I shared throughout my story.

The worst problem with this approach was that in using it, I was attempting to offset who I was. I could not embrace being an introvert, so instead I embraced one external process after another in a fruitless search for security. Eventually that turned out to be a ruinous way to live.

The root cause was the paradox that emerged when I tried to use my recipe as a general approach to life: It promised safety, but most often was the very thing that prevented me from attaining it. For decades, this kept me stuck in recurring anxiety and dissatisfaction.

Only at the very end was I able to distance myself from the need to compensate for being an introvert. In so doing, I barely escaped making yet one more mistake by changing companies. Yet by giving up on the pursuit of what I believed was one of the world's greatest processes (something my recipe would have loved), and instead choosing to embrace a close personal and professional friendship I had developed at UnitedHealthcare, I gave up on my process-loving recipe and ended up experiencing ten of the best years of my career.

The ray of hope in this story is that as introverts, we are all okay. We can be proud of our ability to listen closer and think more deeply than many of the people around us. We can take satisfaction in our skill at expressing things well in writing, better than we can in conversation. We can celebrate our avoidance of conflict and small talk. And we can rejoice in our capacity for deep concentration, a slow work pace, and a laser-like focus on whatever we are doing.

~

It took me over six decades to learn all this. In the end, I detached from my recipe by bringing the Four Transformational Tools of Detachment to bear:

THE PEAK RECIPE

In Chapter 19, I showed that in 2009, when my recipe ballooned into an extreme form as the balanced scorecard, I stepped inside a new framework: that henceforth my life would be about longevity, instead of the stress of trying to be more outgoing through a winning recipe. It was the first thing that ever put some daylight between me and my recipe. It made me feel safe, perhaps because it was the recipe itself that had been causing problems all along. However, on its own, the context was not enough. It only lasted for two weeks before the recipe struck back. That threw me off-balance, and I almost left the great job and boss that I had. But I soon mounted a counterattack from an unexpected direction.

CHOOSING A RELATIONSHIP

In Chapter 20, I chose my manager—my most valued business relationship—over my recipe. That did not reverse the choice I had made as a child to distance myself from other people to cut down on noise. But it did draw me closer to the one individual at work who could most actively help me live openly as an introvert. He allowed me to feel secure about contributing as a quiet person, and that kept my recipe at bay for another four years.

YOU HAVE NO DEFECT TO FIX

In Chapter 21, I related that by 2013, my manager was moving toward having me take a more active public role. That year, after reading the book *Quiet*, I saw that as an introvert, I was okay exactly the way I was. I could best contribute by *leaning into my strengths as an introvert*: deep focus, single-minded concentration, and thoughtful analysis. Based on that realization, when he asked me to facilitate a large meeting, I felt safe enough to decline. From then on, he accepted my role as being exclusively in the back room. What resulted were the financial security I had always sought and more emotional satisfaction from just being a straight-up introvert than I ever thought possible.

LIVING LIFE FORWARD

As mentioned in Chapter 14, I learned this powerful tool in 1980 but did not use it. When I retired in 2019, and began to prepare for writing this book by reviewing my many years of journal entries, I saw that my recipe was a paradox. On one hand, I had unwittingly created it in childhood in the form of Be-Do-Have so I could succeed in an extroverted world.

But on the other hand, the Being part of the recipe was itself hopelessly inauthentic. I believed that being methodical would allow me to Be an introvert amid all the extroversion around me, Do introvert things such as decline social invitations and retreat into quiet places, and as a result Have satisfaction and security. But as shown throughout this book, what resulted were distant relationships, career missteps, and a posture of often presenting myself inauthentically to others.

Once retired, I made the quiet internal decision to Be an *authentic* introvert once and for all, not the false one in my recipe, and implement it by writing a story that would allow other introverts to Be authentic themselves. I came "out" as an introvert to the people around me, being unapologetic about taking alone time, avoiding loud groups, and seeking out deep, thoughtful conversations. By Doing these things I ended up Having more ease, more energy, and more clarity about the direction of my life. I was able to Be my authentic introvert self simply by choosing it and becoming massively committed to it. I did not need to fix myself. I simply promised myself to Be authentic as an introvert, and the rest followed.

~

I am still drawn to using processes to improve my diet, exercise, and sleep routines. They help me to stay healthy by rotating the foods I eat, by alternating between cardio and weight-bearing exercise, and by supplementing seven hours of nighttime sleep with occasional short naps. But my winning recipe no longer runs me. I am free to be the introvert I had always tried to hide.

Hopefully, my story will inspire you to learn all of this more quickly than I did.

As an introvert you are at your best when you accept and enjoy who you are. You need make no apologies for being quieter than others. Your introvert traits make you an asset to everyone you know.

For a recap of how to identify and detach from your winning recipe, please see the Appendix, and visit https://thesatisfiedintrovert.com/.

Fig. 10. Image from Post #1 on TheSatisfiedIntrovert.com. 2022.

You can follow Ben on https://www.facebook.com/thesatisfiedintrovert

To the Reader

If this book has touched you, you may wish to pass it quietly to someone who walks a similar path.

We introverts speak softly, but the resonance endures.

Appendix

The Road to Freedom: A Guide to the Twelve Tools of Detachment

These tools are interconnected, but are not necessarily linear in order. Please learn and apply them in the way that best fits your own situation.

TOOL #1: OBSERVING THE MIND (CHAPTER 7)

The first step in detaching from your recipe is to learn to watch your mind in operation from the outside. When you do this, you likely will notice that any meaning you hold in your head is merely an interpretation, one you are free to change. This realization helps you see that the formula you created in childhood is based on a false interpretation—that as an introvert you are somehow defective, and need a recipe to cope with the world.

TOOL #2: UNIFIED AWARENESS (CHAPTER 8)

You live in your mind a lot. Once you are able to observe your own thinking processes, you will see how skewed away from the external world your whole awareness tends to be. Unifying that awareness with the observation of everything going on around you will increase your safety and peace of mind, reducing the frequency of surprises from the outside that trigger your recipe into action.

TOOL #3: EMOTIONAL CONTEXT (CHAPTER 9)

The external world is full of events that cause you to have an emotional reaction. Sometimes the impact is extreme, such as when you are in a highly fearful situation. When that occurs, it can overwhelm you to the point where it seems like the fear is your very identity.

Just as Tool #1 helped you see that you are not your mind, but rather the space in which it occurs, Tool #3 allows you to see that you are not your emotions either. You are the context in which they show up. This realization puts some distance between you and them, reducing the frequency and intensity with which they overstimulate you and drive you to act out your recipe.

TOOL #4: THE LITTLE VOICE (CHAPTER 10)

You likely have a quiet little interior voice that often shares inconvenient truths—your conscience, or whatever you want to call it. It can show up at what seems like precisely the wrong time, but actually may be exactly the right time. It cautions you to do the opposite of what you are contemplating, or not do anything at all. If you ignore this voice at the insistence of your recipe, it can produce negative long-term consequences. Trust the voice, and you can possibly avoid many years of unhappiness, thus depriving the recipe of much of the raw material that triggers it into action.

TOOL #5: LIVING LIFE FORWARD (CHAPTER 14)

Three everyday experiences are especially prone to trigger your recipe into action: a sense of futility, regular complaining, and frequent drama. Reducing the incidence of these experiences will go a long way to stop activating your recipe.

Futility usually results from living backward against the flow of reality, from Having, to Doing, to Being. By living forward, from Being to Doing to Having, much of the futility in life disappears.[7]

A complaint is the result of not taking responsibility for something. Instead of complaining, figure out what is wanted and needed, and then provide it, even if you don't think you know how. Just being in action will begin to help the complaint to start going away.

Drama is the result of not maintaining your integrity. Keep all your agreements, or remake them, and the drama in your life will be much reduced.

TOOL #6: INTENTION (CHAPTER 15)

In life you tend to achieve what you intend, not necessarily what you want. Establishing a strong intention to detach from your recipe is many times more powerful than simply wanting to do so. When you repeatedly declare what you intend, you bring drive and momentum to any goal, and that includes uncoupling yourself from your recipe.

TOOL #7: ACCEPTING ACUTE LOSS (CHAPTER 16)

Your recipe has been such a part of you for so long that contemplating its demise can feel like someone you treasure is going to die. Gaining experience in embracing a painful loss through something like the "elevator"

---

7 Your recipe has used a forward progression since the day you created it. But because its way of Being is inauthentic, it creates more problems than it solves. In contrast, authentic Being leads to authentic Doing, making it possible to Have what you intend.

process (where I imagined my children coming to me from an elevator, and then going back inside it to disappear forever) can greatly help you to let go of the recipe whenever you are ready.

TOOL #8: NONRESISTANCE (CHAPTER 17)

Anything unwanted in your life that persists is likely held in place by your own resistance to it. You may not be resisting your recipe, because you may not have even been aware that it existed or was a problem. But planning to give up your recipe by resisting it is only going to make it stick around longer. Being willing to let it be is an important precondition for helping it to go away.

TOOL #9: COMPLETION AND POSSIBILITY (CHAPTER 18)

Making small completions helps to remove clutter from your life, clearing the way for you to glimpse new possibilities. One is the possibility of detaching from your recipe, something you may not be able to foresee convincingly if you are surrounded by a mess. Clean it up via one completion at a time, and it will be much easier to visualize a possible future without your recipe.

TOOL #10: THE PEAK RECIPE (CHAPTER 19)

Much of the power of your recipe lies in its hidden nature. But if you bring it out of the shadows, and blow it up to bigger-than-life proportions, its flaws and costs are likely to become far more obvious. Find a way to incite your recipe to expand into a huge caricature of itself, and you will take a giant step toward detaching from it.

TOOL #11: CHOOSING A RELATIONSHIP
(CHAPTER 20)

Relationships are the very things that you designed your recipe to minimize. As a child you likely noticed that other people were the source of much of the overstimulation you felt, so you concocted a persona or mask that let you get results without relying on others too directly.

If you now do the exact opposite, and prioritize a trusted relationship over acting out the urges of your recipe, you gravely damage it. If you select a person to focus on who can be of material value in helping you live openly as an introvert, that will bring you a double advantage: striking a blow at the recipe where it most hurts, and making your new life a reality as an openly introvert individual.

TOOL #12: YOU HAVE NO DEFECT TO FIX
(CHAPTER 21)

The fallacy that underpins your whole recipe is a wrong conclusion you reached as a young child: that you could never "win" in life by being yourself in an extroverted world. If you now expose that error by actively confirming that you are free of any such defect, it will remove the very foundation on which the recipe exists.

Find a source that you believe on this point—author Susan Cain, myself, or anyone else you trust—and declare often that far from containing a flaw, being an introvert allows you to make wonderful contributions to a society that has gone overboard in prioritizing extroversion.

Acknowledgments

I would like to thank the following people, all of whom provided vital help during the creation of this book:

LIVED EXPERIENCE AND PERSONAL ENCOURAGEMENT

Sandy Plumb, my wife and life partner, who not only shared with me many of the adventures described in these pages, but also read the manuscript countless times—helping me shape it from raw journal entries into a work that faithfully reflected my life, my voice, and my journey.

Kevin Ruth, my manager at UnitedHealthcare, who made it possible for me to live and work openly as an introvert for the first time in my life—a gift that deeply influenced the personal growth I attained in this book.

EDITORIAL DEVELOPMENT

Elizabeth Brown, my editor at River Grove, whose thoughtful, incisive comments consistently elevated the manuscript and made the editorial process not only productive, but also deeply engaging.

Maxine Marshall, my lead editor at River Grove, who provided invaluable guidance on the subtitle and brought the manuscript to its final form by overseeing a discerning and meticulous line edit.

PUBLISHING STRATEGY AND PRODUCTION

Haj Chenzira-Pinnock, my River Grove book strategist, who graciously and patiently answered every question I had about the publishing process, and guided me through each step of the contract and planning phases.

Brian Welch, my River Grove project manager, who kept the team aligned and on schedule, and whose consistent updates and attention to detail made the production phase smooth and reassuring.

Joel Richards, whose thoughtful narration brought clarity and life to every page of the audiobook

DESIGN, MARKETING, AND DISTRIBUTION

Chase Quarterman, my River Grove designer, who translated my vision for the cover into four distinctive and compelling concepts, enhancing each one with expert guidance rooted in his deep understanding of the self-help genre.

Jamie White, the Director of Marketing who helped me build a professional platform that aligned with my introverted nature and respected the boundaries of how I preferred to show up in the world.

Brittany Jones-Pugh, my distribution strategist at River Grove, who provided critical insights into how to position the book for maximum reach in retail and digital marketplaces.

Kyle Peterson, my contact for marketing and digital media outreach, who helped craft the message of this book so it could resonate with the right audiences and attract attention across multiple platforms.

To each of you: thank you for helping me bring this project to completion with clarity, heart, and integrity. I am profoundly grateful.

—Benjamin Plumb

About the Author

Benjamin Plumb was born and raised in Los Angeles as the only introvert in a family of five.

Like almost all introvert children, he sought to feel safe in an extroverted world by adopting a "winning recipe." At age ten, he decided he would be methodical in everything he did—one of the thousands of possible recipes that quiet people choose.

This formula brought him honors at Stanford and an MBA from Harvard, but it enticed him into unsatisfying careers as an entrepreneur and an executive. Those roles led ultimately to a divorce in his thirties, a bankruptcy in his forties, and two job losses in a row in his sixties.

At last he saw that what all these failures had in common was the recipe. He taught himself to detach from it, openly embraced his introversion, and thereafter worked quietly as a writer and researcher. In so doing, he finally attained the success and safety that he was never able to achieve through a winning recipe.

Ben and Sandy, his wife of more than forty years, live in the Tampa Bay area. They have four children and ten grandchildren.

www.ingramcontent.com/pod-product-compliance
Lightning Source LLC
Chambersburg PA
CBHW021212130626
46554CB00004B/1190